HAVE YOU GOT BALLS

Mark le Foncé

First edition. 2020.

Typeset using LaTeX.

This book is dedicated to my children whom I so
dearly love
to the moon and back a million times—and more.
And to my family.
Without you I would have surely succumbed
under the onslaught.

Prologue

To my children,

I hope one day you will see the suffering we had to go through during the divorce process that you were dragged into as innocent parties. I had to fight bitterly in order to protect you from a lot of elements.

Thankfully, for most part, you were too young to realize and understand the battles we endured together, but the potential psychological scars were very real. At the time, and still today, you were, and will always be my light and shining inspiration on a daily basis, to continue the onslaught of the legal, criminal, psychological and financial dramas that were imposed into our lives. Simply put, without your smiles, love and innocent support, we would not be where we are now!

Please always forgive people for their wrongdoings. As you may well have gathered by now, most of those that do wrong, do so out of insecurity and fear. And they dont even realize what they are doing to others. Rise and stand above that, we need more strong souls, forgiving people and unconditional love to make this world go round.

In life there are no problems, just challenges, which can certainly be overcome depending on your own attitude. Your attitude determines your altitude.

Keep shining my angels!

To the reader,

Firstly, a massive thank you for your support.

What started out as 'vomit on paper' to keep my own mind sane in a totally insane situation, has now become a printed version of my journey.

It's a journey that I had to endure, not because I like dramas in my life, but because I got sucked into my partners psychotic vortex—a world of malignant narcissism.

It was abuse so psychotic, that I lost myself for a while in the process. I was subjected to domestic violence on an emotional and mental level. I was subjected to abuse from a grossly biased legal system and society as a whole. The only things that kept me sane in this battle were:

- My natural parental urge to protect my kids at any cost.

- Expressing myself through this book, making music and other hobbies.

- Unconditional love and support from not only family and friends, but also my legal representatives and professionals in the industry. The committed and ethical ones that is.

- My sense of humour and always trying to look at things on the bright side of life.

I must warn you in advance though. This is not your usual book. I was advised by my lawyer, Johan, to start writing my experiences down as the court cases started to become more and more bizarre. Even if it was only for myself. Im not really a literally person, and Im not an author, but I talk from my heart about my experiences and thought processes.

I am aware and apologize for some things are repeated at various points in the book. This is because I wrote most of it down as it happened, or shortly thereafter. The repetitiveness of these points highlights my mindset and also my concerns at the time. Being stuck with a malignant narcissist is comparable to being stuck in a washing machine on spin cycle. A dizzying experience, hard to get out of.

This book is a memoir. I suppose it's also a self help guide for quite a number of people. It's a psycho-drama, a legal drama and a journey into my mind as a normal run of the mill person that went through emotional, psychological, physical and legal hell and back.

In my journey I've learned that there are a lot of acrimonious divorces out there where men, and also women, due to their lack of commitment to the divorce process, end up being persecuted and thrown to the dogs. I also believe that narcissistic traits (in either sex) are quite common and becoming more common in our global society. Psychological and emotional abuse happens quite a lot in both sexes, but its a hidden, unspoken reality. People are afraid to talk. Especially men. A lot of it is so unnecessary and viscous in its own right.

Men, however, and Im talking generally of course, dont easily talk about these kinds of topics at all, fearing possible ridicule or being blamed for being pathetic or a sissy. Who, after all gets beaten or abused by their wife? Often depression sets in, and the state doesnt have many resources available in the form of support for the male gender. Suicide rates go up and lives are destroyed. Not only that of the fathers, but of their children too.

Our stories are real and need to be heard.

If you do happen to be in an acrimonious divorce (or are about to go into one), in an abusive relationship or maybe you have no access to your kids, this book will appeal to you and will hopefully give you strength and inspiration to continue your fight. Remember you have rights too. And so do your kids. Stand up for yourself and grow a pair, there is nothing sissy or feminine about admitting you are in an abusive situation. Abuse doesn't always mean a black eye or a broken arm either. Psychological abuse is just as, if not more hurtful and can leave much longer lasting scars in the long run. Especially if the legal system and unscrupulous lawyers are fueling the onslaught.

Sorry ladies, this book is not here to slag you off at all. This book is here to portray and share my experiences. My experiences from a man's perspective dealing with a biased society raising kids on my own and fighting emotional battles. I'm sure that some feminists out there will take a serious dig at me, but haters will be haters.

This book is actually about love, forgiveness and peace and I believe that all women who love their men, (husbands, brothers, uncles, sons, mentors, bosses) should read it too. It may be the inspiration you need to protect your man. Read it together, discuss it and have your say. We as men, after all, do feature in approximately fifty percent of your lives. We do love you and we need you.

However, for the real abusers out there, both male as well as female, I hope you will face your consequences! Karma is certainly coming.

So guys, stand up for yourself and open up. And proudly ask yourself: Have you got balls? A quick peek down there should hopefully confirm.

Legal Disclaimer

The conversations in this book all come from the author's recollections, though they are not written to represent word for word transcripts. Rather, the author has retold them in a way that evokes the feeling and meaning what was said and in all instances, the essence of the dialogue is accurate, mostly based on true events, it is depicted as a real life struggle many men and women deal with on a daily basis.

As this is a memoir, I have tried to recreate events, locales and conversations from my memories of them, which may in some cases be failing me In order to protect certain individuals, myself and my family, and in order to protect their anonymity, I have changed the names of all individuals and some places. All efforts have been made to change some identifying characteristics and details such as physical properties, occupations and places of residence, not to cause intentional harm to any individual or institution.

This book was written with the intent to provide information and motivation to the reader, with some humour in between. The writer is by no means any type of psychologist, legal representative and does not offer any type of the abovementioned advice. Neither the writer nor the publisher shall be held liable for any physical, psychological, emotional, financial or commercial damages, including but not limited to special, incidental consequential or other damage, since no willful derogatory remarks are made, unless implied by the readers themselves.

Contents

CONTENTS

One

You have the right to remain silent

The coffee tasted good. It was a lovely spring morning. I was sitting at my kitchen table sipping away at the bitter brew that I love so much. The soft cool morning breeze blew fresh air with the faint scent of jasmine flowers into the house. My daily routine was about to start, but first I needed my caffeine to kick start my day. I fired up my laptop to browse through the emails that had come in overnight. I wasn't dressed yet. Showering I'd do only later after Sophie arrived.

It was already hot that morning so I was sitting in my boxer shorts at the kitchen table going through and responding to some work emails. It's one of those quirks I have. Sending emails to powerful CEO's and company owners whilst sitting half naked in the kitchen. It had something empowering about it. If they only knew! I often giggled at the thought.

I loved working from home and the kids were with their mom today, so I didn't have to rush them off to crèche. Today, I could take it a bit easier. Today, dropping them off would be mom's task. Jane and I had separated almost a year earlier and, as she moved just a few hundred metres up the road, we agreed to a fifty-fifty parenting split while our divorce was being finalised. One night the kids would be with me, the next the kids would be with her. It was a strenuous arrangement, but, under the acrimonious

1

situation and circumstance, probably the best for the kids at that time. I never wanted any acrimony during the divorce, but Jane seemed to take it very hard and lashed out a lot.

Working from home has its obvious advantages. No rush hour traffic, artificial work environments, time constraints, office gossip, politics and so on. And of course, I could wake up much later than all the other rat-raced city dwellers. I was comfortable in my four bedroom home set in a leafy suburb in the North of Johannesburg. I had been living there for ten years. It was a typical family home, ideal for the kids as well. It was close to down town Sandton with all the amenities I needed. I also enjoyed the open patio doors that lead to the garden with a large pool. I had no air-conditioning at home, but the swimming pool in my yard provided for ample cooling off as and when I needed it. I was content and happy there and I felt good in my own skin. Today in particularly I acknowledged the fact that I was a lucky man having so much freedom in my life.

I heard keys fumbling and the front door opened.

"Morning Sophie."

I greeted my housekeeper in my usual fashion from the kitchen table. She's part of the family and has seen me a million times in my underwear before, so I wasn't particularly worried about covering up. No point in being a prude. She's had her own set of keys to get in and out as she needed. Besides ensuring that the house was clean and the washing done, she also helped me to look after my babies on the days they were with me.

She knew everything about my life, the divorce and even the intimate goings on. Probably even more so than my own parents and family.

From where I was sitting, I could not see the front door and she didn't respond to my greeting. Mhhh...odd, I thought to myself. Maybe she didn't hear me.

"Morning Sophie!" I repeated a little louder.

I looked up from my laptop. Did I hear a male voice?

Sophie appeared around the corner from the entrance hall passage. She was as white as a sheet. Considering she's of dark complexion, I immediately knew something was up. Was she ill?

"What is wrong Sophie?"

Before she had the chance to answer, I saw them. Right behind her there were three guys. They stormed into the passage towards the bedroom section of the house. My heart skipped a beat. I jumped up to intercept the intruders. Sprinting through the lounge, I was ready to attack these guys with all my might, adamant to protect myself and my property. Adrenalin fueled frenzy took its hold over me.

Within seconds, however my frazzled mind recognized the uniforms.

Cops? Police? What the heck?

I stopped in mid stride like a fly splattering on the windshield at a hundred and twenty km per hour.

"I'm captain Mandell." said the head honcho.

"We're here to do a drug search of your property. We received an anonymous tip off. You have the right to remain silent. Everything you say or do may and will be held against you in a court of law."

My adrenaline fueled body immediately went into flight or fight mode with my mind spinning and racing in confusion. I was completely dazed and it felt like, I had just had a car accident. I had never had a run in with the law in my life before, beside the odd speeding fine here and there but now, out of the blue I had cops raiding my house?

It didn't take long before modesty got the better of me. My nerves still on edge, all of a sudden I felt rather exposed in my jocks, surrounded by big these macho police brutes wearing bullet proof vests.

I wasn't sure what was more important, getting some pants on me or telling these guys to get out of my house.

With some difficulty I managed to compose myself. I took a deep breath and with a brave attitude I told them:

"Go right ahead. I don't do drugs and never have. I do need to phone my lawyer though if you don't mind. And I'd like to get some clothes on!"

Captain Mandell nodded his approval while his assistants started going through my cupboards. In hindsight I never actually knew anything about warrants, but no warrant was presented to me. I never dealt with situations like this. Words like warrants didn't feature in my life!

Meanwhile, I must have looked rather pathetic, half naked with my middle aged body and I'm sure they actually wanted me to get dressed. Unable to prioritize between pants and phone I wasn't sure what was more urgent at this point. Multitasking and fumbling my way to the bedroom, cops right on my heels, watching my every move, I looked for some tracksuit pants while frantically dialing my lawyer at the same time.

How the tracksuit and T-shirt managed to get on me I still don't remember, but I succeeded somehow.

With trembling hands I held the phone to my ear.

Ring Ring...

"Answer your phone Johan" I kept on thinking.

Ring Ring...

Ring Ring...

"Answer your phone Johan..." I thought. "Answer your flipping phone."

Ring Ring.

The three times it rang felt like ages to me. Johan answered. I didn't give him the chance to greet:

"Johan, I've got the cops here doing a drug search. What's going on?" I told him in a trembling voice.

"What? Hold on a second.... OK wait don't panic," he said, while I heard the panic in his voice. "Who's the person in charge there?"

"Captain Mandell" I responded.

"OK put him on the line. I want to speak to him. I'm worried about drug planting."

"Drug planting?" I replied. "But I don't grow anything funny in my garden! I never have."

"No man! It means when someone puts drugs on your property to frame you."

I saw a slight quirky smile on Captain Mandell's face. My naïve conversation and the way my house was all organized gave him a good idea that I was likely to be innocent. It certainly didn't look like a dingy drug user or dealer's den. I handed him the phone and Johan exchanged some words with the captain before hanging up.

The cops continued to search the house. They were actually surprisingly respectful with my stuff and after a good thirty minutes or so the house was cleared. No drugs! Captain Mandell, slightly friendlier now, said:

"Well so far it's looking good."

Relieved and with my personality and bravado returning I told him straight:

"I didn't expect anything else. I don't do drugs. My soon to be ex-wife is probably causing shit again."

He asked me if I could show him my car and all of a sudden a queasy unnerving feeling in my stomach set in. Something in my subconscious mind triggered. I remembered the previous Thursday, during handover of the kids.

My estranged wife Jane was behaving weirdly around my car five days prior when I picked up our two and three year old kids, Julia and Sean from her house. With pumping heart, and adrenalin coursing through my veins I looked for my misplaced car keys, and once found, we went outside and I opened the car doors for them. They started their search.

My unease was not for nothing and it didn't take long before Capt. Mandell called me closer.

"Come and have a look here" he remarked standing by the back passenger door.

Planted in the base under the baby car seat, without an inkling of concealment and in plain sight, they found two packets of powdery stuff in a cling film parcel. They walked over to the other side of the car to my daughter, Julia's car seat. More parcels! Another package with some capsules that looked like vitamin pills to me. Although flabbergasted, I wasn't totally surprised. It was clear that my soon to be ex-wife had set me up! My heart sank instantaneously and an apathetic feeling washed over me.

"Don't touch the parcels!" I shouted at him. "You need to get fingerprints off of them."

Captain Mandell shook his head and smiled.

"We can't lift prints off these. Believe me, I've been dealing with drug cases for decades."

Two of Mandell's assistants were flanking me on either side of me in case I bailed.

They searched the car some more, but that was all there was.

The captain returned.

"I don't want you to worry too much. I'm not actually allowed to say anything, but this looks highly...... Actually, never mind.... I better keep quiet and not say anything now.

"Unfortunately I have to place you under arrest for possession of suspected narcotics."

I couldn't believe it. From there on everything became a blur again.

I understood, as they found the drugs in my car, that they needed to arrest me, even though it looked suspect to them. It was procedure. But more worrisome was, that the state now had a case of drug possession against me. It was in my car after all!

"Can I at least put on some decent clothes?"

They agreed and we went back into the house.

I shouted some orders to Sophie to keep the doors locked and the house safe whilst putting on some jeans and a clean T shirt. Sophie was in a state, stammering, shaking, and still white as a sheet. I got changed and ready to leave, all under the watchful eyes of the police. They would not let me out of their sight. Thank God I'm not a prude. Capt. Mandell, told me to take a jacket as the cells get cold.

"You mean you're gonna lock me up?"

"Oh yes mister. Sorry to be the bearer of bad news, but that's standard procedure."

I didn't know what to think anymore. I was loaded in the back of the police van like a criminal. Some rather excited sniffer dogs kept a watchful yet playful eye on me in the same compartment, and I was carted to the Randburg Police station. On arrival there, and out of precaution they put handcuffs on me. They brought me to the office of Station commander, Captain van Tonder.

I knew this guy van Tonder and he remembered me from a previous drama that ex-wife Jane arranged a year prior, while we were separating. Jane had attempted to get a protection order on me and the police were told by her that I owned guns. I was called into the station already then, to make a statement that I didn't own any firearms and never had previously. In her false statements, she claimed that I was a danger to myself, a suicide risk and a 'violent' man! Having had a long meeting with him at the time he remembered me well. He was also well aware what we were dealing with here, and had summonsed Mandell to bring me into his office when he heard my name and address come up on the police radio.

I waited for five minutes in the corridors, before I was called in. His office was a hive of activity and crowded with colleagues and other uniformed people. When I walked in he looked up at me gravely and shook his head.

"Same woman again Mr le Foncé?"

I nodded.

"Evil cow," he muttered.

"I'll get you out in no time. Don't stress. We just have to process the documents. Oh and tell your lawyer you're here."

I already had. I called and updated Johan from the back of the van. He knew of the arrest and he was on the way to the cop shop already. Capt van Tonder ordered a couple of subordinates to open dockets and the necessary files without delay. Most cops were pretty friendly to me, and understanding but I got transferred to the holding cells regardless.

I couldn't believe it. I was actually getting locked up in a jail cell just like a real criminal!

I had to hand over my phone, all the personal belongings on me. Shoe laces, keys, the works. After that I was patted down and had to sign for my belongings. An officer escorted me through the next metal door. Clang clang, keys twisting and noises coming from within the gated courtyard. I was nervous. This was a new experience for me. I was also under the false impression that I'd end up in a cell on my own. But no. No private 'suite' for me!

As I entered through the cell door, eleven other detainees glared at me and checked me out thoroughly from top to toe. I didn't like the looks they gave me initially. It sent shivers down my spine. But, as I found out later, they were all just as frazzled and scared as me.

I cleared my throat.

"'Sup brothas?" I said to them flicking my chin up doing my best gangster impersonation I could muster. I tried to use my coolest and most collective tone of voice, with a swagger to match pretending that this was regular occurrence for me.

My act clearly impressed no-one, as I got no answers. Just approving nods, mumbles and some groans. It was eerily quiet in there and a stench of old piss, and sweaty armpits mingled with the unmistakably musky sour smell of a freshly smoked joint.

Should I fear? Should I talk to them? Are they stoned and calm now? Will they get violent later? What's the protocol in here? Are these real murderers and robbers? Or innocent guys like me? Thoughts penetrated my head fast and furious with this new experience, but after a while I realised that these guys were just as nervous as I was. In actual fact they turned out to be very friendly, supportive and not aggressive at all. But at that stage, without a doubt I was shitting myself.

After a couple of minutes pondering, idle chit chat here and there with the other detainees, I started accepting my fate and sat down to try and relax a bit.

I followed the other inmates' example and I claimed a spot in the corner of the eight by four meter prison cell. It was the perfect spot to check out and scan my new environment. Gymnastic type mattresses, covered in plastic were scattered all over the floor. A bunch of dirt cheap grey blankets made of felt were thrown into the mix with the compliments and hospitality of the South African Police Service. A distinctive pungent ammonia like smell of stale piss was emanating from the encrusted stainless steel toilet placed strategically in the corner—for everyone to witness in all its glory, and with all the senses. The smell got worse and worse as the day got hotter. It was one of those smells you cannot ignore, no matter how hard you tried. I had no choice but to give into my situation.

Well...

Here I was.

No phone, no email, fellow inmates snoring away or stoned and I had nothing else to do.

It was time to reflect...

Little did I know at that point I'd be spending a lot more time in that very same cell a week and a half later.

Two

The 'Fairy Tale' starts

ONCE UPON A TIME...A long long time ago, a handsome prince met a princess. Online!

Well actually no. It wasn't such a long time ago.

One very, very lonely night, late 2009, I went online and opened my then 'favourite' site called 'Dating Buzz' in search for my perfect beauty, the sex goddess and future mother of my children. I suppose I was a little lonely in the bedroom department and at a ripe old age of 39, I needed something more stable and serious in my life and not the fly by nights, one night stands and the clingers that you pick up for an evening that never leave. I wasn't really sure what to expect from internet dating, so I gave it a shot and I figured that internet dating, was indeed the 'buzz'. (This was way before Tinder.)

From the comfort of your own home you get to meet people and chat to them. And even though you see all these online articles warning you of the "dangers of internet dating" (sounds scary no?) you still opt for the easy way out from time to time. Plus it's cheaper than a night out at the pub, or dinner dates.

You can chat instantly to those online and their profiles give you immediate information about the person you are chatting to! Well, provided they're not lying of course!

I suppose for our microwave/instant gratification driven society, it works for most people. I logged on.

That night, I started chatting to a lady by the nick name

of "Playtime2349" who was apparently in search of an eligible bachelor. Mhhhh something aroused my interest. She was open minded, interesting, had some rather amazing stories to impress me with, and knew how to turn the topic to a rather sexy kinda talk as well. Her 'nickname' also indicated that she was rather open minded by the looks of it. Playtime sounded good to me! She stirred my interest.

I'm an open book, so I tell things like they are and don't lie. I say it as it is, which sometimes get me in trouble, but honesty first. I hate liars actually and naturally I assume that other people don't lie either. I don't believe in pretending to be better than you are if you're sitting behind a computer screen. I found a lot of people do that, but they get caught out quickly. So, if you ask me about my interests, I'll give you a detailed, un-edited account of my likes, dislikes and experiences in life.

At the time I was running a tour operator business: Short day trips to hidden and tucked away areas around the city and I went to game parks with my guests, where I played with elephants and lions on an almost daily basis. I was outdoorsy. I did river rafting, mountaineering, biking, quad biking, horse riding in the wild and all sorts of wicked and wonderful things with my clientele who wanting to go into the bush for the day. I had a blast with my groups, but it also turned out to be long hours. From early morning till late at night sometimes, depending on what they'd want to do. It was an interesting job, I made decent cash, and earned money whilst having a good party. Overall I was happy, tanned, fit from the bush and making a decent living.

All I needed now was a love in my life, some good sex and possibly a family. In other words I needed a complete myself with a strong partner and settle myself for the future.

Well there she was. She was open-minded, she liked everything I liked and was particularly interested in my life and what I did. I suppose I was successful in my own maverick way and she admired that. I had a "fan" and after a couple of chats we swapped numbers and decided to meet for coffee the next day.

We met up at a place with a playground as she had a five year old son who had to come with her. Okay...a date with a difference! I hadn't really dated anyone with kids before, but it wasn't a real problem for me as I love kids. I always wanted kids of my own.

The place was abuzz with screeching toddles and their chasing mommies. It was definitely not the kind of place to meet for a quiet coffee.

Steven was a very vocal five year old child just at that point between toddler stage and young boy. Heaps and bounds of excitement and energy were part of his daily routine. Although curious about who mom was meeting he wasn't too phased by me. I just got a quick glance over while we were seated at a table.

"Hello" I said. 'What's your name?' "

"Steven."

"OK, how old are you Steven?" I asked.

"Five and three quarter."

"Wow, you're big already! What do you like doing?"

"Playing on the jungle gym."

He dashed off to the nearby jungle gym in mid-sentence to join the maddening shrieks and general pandemonium in the pile of children already occupying an overcrowded brightly coloured structure that looked like a giant clown. I wasn't used to seeing so many kids together. As a long term bachelor, I didn't even know that such restaurants and places existed. Let alone so many kids together. Definite change of scenery for me!

I managed to chat to Jane and got some form of conversation going in between the numerous interruptions and major mayhem in the children's coffee shop. As you can imagine, openly flirting in such a place was out of the question. Adults were outnumbered by kids all over and, I have to add, I did spot some other good looking yummy mommies in gym leotards.

The coffee went well but there were too many interruptions. We decided to have dinner the next day at her house, in order to be in a quieter environment and talk better without all the distractions. She was going to cook dinner for me. How nice! I would bring the wine and salad, and she'd do the rest.

Dinner the next day was rather quick and simple with some idle chit chat. Kiddo was in his bed shortly after dinner. We carried on chatting in the garden and drank some more wine. Once that was finished, the kissing started and it didn't take long before we overcame our nerves and we were naked in the bed doing business.

The body, mind spirit connection wasn't entirely there yet, but it definitely wasn't bad for a first time!

Sexually I still don't know who was the lead and initiator—her or me, but it didn't matter, it was good, satisfying, sexy and we both got a good adult 'playdate' out of it.

And so it all started. The prince found his princess and they lived happily ever after.

Oh no... wait.

The story has a twist.

Three

Picket Fences and Dirty Dogs

In the beginning, all was fine and well. Like I said, she was open-minded, adventurous, sex was fun, I got spoiled, she tuned in nicely to me and overall, we were on the way to getting serious. OK, admittedly she was a bit quick on the serious part. She wanted to move in with me. Was I going to finally settle down? Was she the one?

That was a bit of a problem, because yes, I had a four bedroom house, but I rented three of the four bedrooms out to housemates. That, plus the income of the cottage more than covered my costs. I ran it like an up market commune. It was like a business for me.

Having discussed some options and scenarios, we decided that with her contributing towards the household, we should manage. Ideal situation no? Warm bed at night, less people in the house, instant family, no more irritating housemates and voila, a recipe for success! It seemed like my life was finally complete!

Four months after I had met Jane, the housemates had received their notice, were out of the house and Jane and Steven moved into my place. The only problem was that we had way too much furniture due to the double household. We had to get rid of some furniture (mostly mine of course —you know how women are— their stuff is "always better") but I reluctantly agreed as we were in it for the long haul in any case! I don't really make a fuss over things like that too much. It's just furniture after all.

So Jane, her son Steven and I settled down as a family. She

also had two (rather stinky) old dogs, Margaret Thatcher and Brandy Crawford. They appeared to be a big part of her life and had free reign in the household. They were not too bad and quite cute actually, but I preferred to keep dogs outside rather than having hairs and slobber all over the couch and bed.

My apparent strict ruling was 'vetoed' by the rest of the family and now female presence in the house. It was irritating, but hey, being the nice guy, I adapted accordingly. Jane was adamant about her pets, yet I found her ways of dealing with them strange. I was told stories that she re-homed dogs and did work for pet adoption agencies, all for the 'love' of animals. I had absolutely no problem with that, but a year later on, and on the flip side of the coin, I saw how she put the two dogs down, just because they were old. No not sick! Just old! Mhhh. Red flag right there.

Shortly after the move, other irritations started creeping in. Her son was taking over the TV constantly blaring out cartoons, her dogs were dirty and still irritated me, making a mess on the couch and digging up the garden. I had to live with furniture that I did not particularly like, but also that, I accepted as part of the package. I had a family after all, so I gave in a little. There was no point in arguing over something so trivial and wasn't important in the greater scheme of things.

In hindsight, however, these were actually serious red flags I should have taken more notice of, but I gave in. I knew it was a major adjustment period for me having a full family with a kid and after being a bachelor for so long.

The reality was that my boundaries were slowly but surely being eroded and my opinion was not important. I had let a controlling person and personality take over into my life, but I was living in ignorant bliss and full denial of that.

Every time I would raise an issue, she'd sweet talk her way out of it. I'd be spoiled with something or I'd be redirected onto other topics.

Jane was a kitchen and architectural draftsman by trade and quite a pro at what she did. By the time she'd moved in she had no fixed job, but was freelancing for a company and doing lots of designs from home. I didn't think much of it as she appeared to have it quite together and was (according to her) making some major cash with commissions and orders. Our dinner time discussions, were about work, clients, business deals, projects she was working on and she mentioned some hefty commissions due on the jobs she was working on. I liked the designs she was making and she impressed me with her creativity.

After a month, when the bills had to be paid, she contributed according to plan and budgets, and in spite of the stinky dogs and cartoons on the TV, we had a good arrangement. The second month though, she was waiting for some commissions to come in and she'd pay me half now and the other half when her client paid. No problem, I was making decent money too so I'd fit the bill for now. We would surely work things out at a later stage.

By the third month it was a similar story. Although my pocket was now being affected, I still didn't think much of it. Cash flow problems happen and you do what you can together and things will pull right. (Operative word being together.) I blindly believed she'd pay me back when her cash would come in. We were a happy family after all and we had plans. I was convinced things would work out and overall, I was content, working hard and making cash.

But then the bomb dropped...

Four

'Babe, I'm pregnant!'

I nearly fell over backwards.

"Sorry? Excuse me? No ways! How? What? Well actually I know how, but hell, this is not possible! You've just moved in!"

Two weeks prior we had a discussion after sex:

"Mark I know you love kids. I see how you and young Steven get along so well. You are a brilliant father figure and I think we should start thinking about kids. Should I go off the pill?"

I always wanted to be a father, but didn't want to rush it. Especially with someone you have just met. I had to think about that a little, but then I wasn't too concerned, because apart from a scare or two, I had never conceived a child (to my knowledge at least) in my adult life. It just didn't feature any more. I was too old for that. I had missed that boat.

Besides, two couples I knew, had been spending fortunes on fertility clinics and trying to fall pregnant for years. I didn't think having kids was an option any more for me at this stage of the game. I was nearly forty years old, and seeing first-hand the battles in my immediate surroundings of people in the same age group as me, I didn't have much hope.

At every dinner party we went to with these friends the topics of conversation were often around vitamin pills, powders, fertility drugs, artificial inseminations, doctors, specialists, false hopes, miscarriages and the expenses they endured to try and conceive.

I even joked with my best friend Darryl to try turning his

wife around and try the other hole, because he was clearly doing it wrong! I had a lot of compassion for them and did feel sorry. They'd been trying so hard and they really wanted kids. I was, over the years, emotionally living with them in their hopes, aspirations and downfalls.

Having them as a close example didn't provide me with much hope of ever being a daddy. After seeing all this, the possibility of having my own kids was just not in my mind at all.

So, when Jane asked me, should I go off the pill, it was a no brainer.

"Pfff... why are you even on the pill in the first place? It'll take years for us to conceive. It's not that easy to just pop out kids any more." I'd remark.

Well obviously it was.

She was pregnant within a month after that little talk.

Holy cow! That was not part of the plan... well..., it was exciting, but very unexpected. In my mind it would take years for that! Wow, my brain went into overload while I stared in disbelief at the two blue lines on the midstream pregnancy test kit.

I'm gonna be a daddy!

Shit I'm gonna be a DADDY!

A REAL DADDY!

A real real daddy of a real baby.

Sweeeet!

Shit. How are we going to tell our friends? They've been battling for years and we're impregnating on round one. Sensitive issue! Let's not tell anyone just yet. First trimesters are risky. Lots can go wrong. We shouldn't tell anyone yet.

We decided to wait for the first trimester to complete to ensure everything is hanging in and staying in there. In spite of it all, my brain was overjoyed and in full gear daddy mode. I always wanted to have kids and now it was really happening.

A real daddy! I was gonna be a REAL daddy! YAY!

I wanted to shout it from the rooftops, but with difficulty I managed to keep my mouth shut for a bit. Nevertheless, I was, and stayed on cloud nine. I was glowing from the inside outwards, and already planning changes to the house and what colour the baby room had to be.

"Shhhh...Keep quiet Mark, no one must know yet!" I had to keep reminding myself.

Our first gynaecologist appointment was scheduled in week four. Yep, this was getting for real.

And true as Bob, there it was. On the scanner at the doctor's office. It wasn't much of a baby yet though. It looked more like a coffee bean stuck on the side of a round bucket. A cluster of cells formed by one tiny sperm meeting one tiny egg. At this point the growth was probably really the size of a small coffee bean, but that first picture looked so cool.

I went all 'gaga, googo and coochy' over a cluster of cells the size of a pimple that's growing inside your woman! And I mad that happen! Yes, yes, yes. I think for any male that must be a proud moment, to know that your virility, swimmers and fishing tackle is working as it should and that you're capable creating life. And just like that, at that instant, you feel like a stud. A virile bull that can sire children. Blessed by the God's of procreation themselves! It's an amazing feeling which I think every father can proudly relate to. And so, for the next month, I was walking with my head up high and with a bounce in my step.

The cloud nine feeling didn't last though. A month later, on the second check-up there was bad news:

"I'm sorry to tell you guys this, but we're going to have to terminate this pregnancy" the doctor told us. "It's not a viable pregnancy".

My heart sank and a nervous, gut wrenching feeling over-whelmed me. After that first sentence, I didn't take in much what the doctor said, but he explained something along the lines of having a chicken egg without a yolk growing in there, but the body is still fooled into believing it is pregnant. I was disappointed to say the least and Jane was devastated. She didn't handle the news well at all.

I suppose as a guy you deal with it differently as you don't have things and babies growing inside you. To console myself, as well as Jane, I started rationalizing and looking for excuses.

"You see babe, it's not that easy at our age. Look at everyone else around us. They've been trying for years. It just wasn't meant to be."

I had a business trip scheduled to Germany a few days after the second gynaecologist appointment. We were also doing renovations to the house with the help of my dad who was an experienced building contractor and helping us with the renovations. While in Germany, I had Jane on the phone and Skype every night. She had some serious issues with the loss of the baby and pretty much started attacking me for that loss in a bizarre and indirect way. My father started having fall outs with her while doing the renovations and complained to me that nothing was good enough for her and that she was being a bitch.

I, in turn protected her by telling him that she was going through a rough emotional time having lost the baby but at the same time I agreed with him that her behavior was a bit irrational and over the top.

"It'll pass." I told him.

"She'll get over it. Just give her time."

Two weeks later I returned from Germany. The drama wasn't over yet and she kept wallowing deeply into 'her big loss', making out as if it was only her loss. As a guy I thought to myself—'I don't know what women feel or go through the minute they fall pregnant so I better keep quiet'. Of course it was a loss, yes, but hell, she kept on going on and on and on about it and blaming me for not understanding how she felt. I still had an enormous amount of empathy for her, while trying to deal with the loss myself as well! It was a bit much for me, but being the good boyfriend (and let's face it, us guys battle to understand women's emotions) I consoled her where I could. This, sadly, was still not good enough for her most of the time and she wallowed a bit too deeply in a drama that, in my opinion, she was making worse herself.

But, the universe had different plans for us though and yes...a baby was indeed meant to be.

Two months after the miscarriage, Jane was pregnant again! What? Again? No ways! We weren't over the shock and grief yet of our previous loss less than two months earlier and now she was pregnant again!

Well that was definitely a miracle and totally meant to be! The universe or God works in mysterious ways. I wondered and pondered and treaded cautiously into the future with apprehension.

Was it going to stick in there? Was it viable? Should I get my hopes up again or rather stay cautious until we knew more?

It was quite a stressful time, considering we just lost one. Knowing what I learned then, I had a much better understanding what Darryl and his wife had been going through over the years. Overjoyed we were of course, but at the same time cautious on the anticipation. However, in the weeks that followed, that pregnancy started to take shape and it was for real. With apprehension we went through the first trimester and all looked good and well.

Although the relationship between us wasn't ideal at that stage, my focus was on the new arrival and I was over the moon. However we weren't even married! What was I to do? Was it legally better for the child for us to be married? We were going to be parents now, so we would have to stick it out in the long run! Did I love her enough to get married? I didn't even know her for a year yet! Internal turmoil resulted, but I didn't have much time to decide, I had to make a plan.

Thankfully I am the 'make a plan' type of guy, so I made a plan very quickly. Was it well thought out? Maybe, maybe not, but I also wanted to make the best out of any situation and I wanted to be a happy family! We would make a plan!

Five

Elephants and orgaSMS

I kept on running my tour operator business and I worked with a particular game lodge almost daily, bringing them people for game drives. I asked my game ranger mates and the manager of the lodge if they could organize me something. At this particular game lodge, Jane was organizing my fortieth birthday party. She wanted all the friends and family together and we were going to celebrate in style. The lodge was only a forty-five minute drive from Johannesburg. It was a beautiful place and she asked the owners if we could book out the restaurant and deck for the occasion. This was the perfect opportunity for me, I thought to myself.

No one knew what my wicked plan was, but I was going to propose to her. In a huge way. And yes, it was in a huge way. With the help of my game ranger colleagues and friends at the same lodge, I was going to use three elephants for the occasion. At the lodge there were some semi tame African elephants you could interact with. The elephants knew me well from my almost daily game drives I did with clientele. I already had a strong bond with these animals. They'd come up to me and greet me every time I brought people and the baby elephants would wrestle and play with me. I got their approval and the game rangers and I got to work. We painted the biggest mommy elephant and wrote on her left flank 'Will you marry me'. This was like a scene straight out of the Steven Sellers movie—'The Party'.

The plan was that I would walk into the lodge, underneath the deck where everyone was sitting, with this elephant and her two babies, right flank (blank side) showing and then turn her around to expose the painted left side. It worked like a bomb and exactly as planned.

How could she say no to that? I was in full tuxedo, on my birthday, on my knees in the bush with an audience of around a hundred people, proposing with an elephant! (I should be in showbiz—actually I am, but more about that later.)

The proposal was accepted of course, much to the delight of all the guests (except for my direct family) and, in December we got married. It wasn't a big wedding. It was just a get together in a restaurant with a small gathering of around twenty family and friends. Much smaller than my birthday party and proposal actually.

The build up to the wedding was tense though. Family started fighting. Jane had issues with my mom and dad and there was quite a bit of bickering and bitching going on all round. Jane didn't want my family involved in the preparations and managed to cause deeper rifts. Anything my mom or sisters proposed was rejected outright. My family, for the sake of peace started pulling away more and more which hurt me as we were always a close family.

Even though it irked me, I focused on the future and kept a positive outlook whilst ignoring the red flags and sticking my head in the sand. I asked Jane not to be so resistant to everyone in my family and we also had words from time to time. When it flared up she'd say,

"Sorry, it's the hormones from the pregnancy that cause me to be bitchy from time to time."

I chose to keep myself in ignorant bliss. I mean, what did I know about pregnancy and hormones and moods? I'm a guy. All I know from a guy's perspective is that it takes nine months to get out of a vagina and the rest of your life to try and get back in! I knew nothing about moods, hormones and 'women issues', so I accepted her stories blindly. And maybe it was better that way at that time and under the circumstances.

Our bedroom antics had its ups and down. Excuse the pun. I remember one night particularly well. We had a good day for a change and she looked very sexy with her six month pregnant and growing belly. Knowing that I was responsible for that was quite a turn on in its own right. The mood was obviously there, she was there, I was there and that's all that we needed.

The night wasn't planned and no words were exchanged. From a simple after dinner coffee to kissing, one thing led to the next and our clothes quickly came off. God it was sexy. Our bodies were rubbing against each other. Skin on skin, I could feel her hard nipples and bloated belly sliding over my abdomen whilst our tongues were exploring and flicking away at the sensitive bits. Every hair on my body was on high alert. My groin was throbbing and leaking in anticipation of her welcoming gestures.

And welcoming it was! She parted her legs and my impatient throbbing member pushed against her willing vulva enveloping it with a perfect fit. The combination of our combined juices were an electrifying mix and in one thrust I got sucked in, literally balls deep.

"Oh my God..."

We both gasped as my member hit her deep on the cervix. I could feel her tighten up all along my shaft. Her muscles quivered around me and it felt so good. I slowly slid out again and thrust in deep.

Oh my ......

Our lovemaking intensified ever so slowly. Groins connected and muscles started moving, trembling and thrusting in waves. This was lovemaking on another level, just enjoying the journey without focusing on the destination. We lost our minds and the pleasure intensified with every quiver and thrust. I had trouble keeping myself under control and had to stop myself from going over the edge a couple of times. She, however, came a few times and we swapped positions. She sat on top of me impaling herself deeply on me. The squishy wet noises combined with our own low groans and moans turned me on even more. She got wetter and wetter with every stroke. Being on top and totally in control now, she took her pleasure from me and I let her have it. I lay back and watched the show of which I was very much a part of. She came again. This time so hard that I could feel her juices flowing all over my groin area.

Oh shit, this was so hot. I was so close and needed to explode soon. Her orgasm intensified, her body spasmed, and she clamped down on me with quivering muscles choking my manhood and pulling me in. I could feel my own juices rising and a wave after wave welling up from deep within.

Oh babe... I'm cuuuummming... Ohh... My.... G...... We both came hard and at the same time. She literally milked me dry and we were one sticky and slippery mess. Still heaving and firmly stuck inside her we just lay there hugging, saying nothing in the afterglow. Mr Happy slowly shrunk back to normal. The sensitive tip on my deflating organ made me quiver one more time as it popped out.

"Wow." I whispered in her ear. "That was something else."

She got up and put on a robe.

"I'm going outside to have a ciggie." Her words came out rather flatly.

"Okay, I'll see you outside just now. I just want to jump in the shower quickly."

She left the room and I put on the shower taps. I was still in post orgasmic bliss whilst the water and soap washed away the love juices. I stood there for at least five minutes, letting the warm steamy water massage my body and back. Once clean, I dried up and walked through to the lounge, but Jane wasn't there. The back door was ajar, but the outside light wasn't on. I walked out and found Jane outside on the grass in the dark.

"Do you want some coffee?" I asked but I got no response.

My eyes adjusted to the dark and saw her sitting in a hunched up bundle.

With her head in her hands she was sitting there weeping quietly.

"Hey babe, what's wrong?" I asked her, thinking that she got a phone call or a bad message.

"You just don't care do you?"

"What do you mean? What's going on? What happened?" She looked up at me with piercing steely eyes. Her eyelids contracted as if to say, don't mess with me. Then out of the blue in a very aggressive manner, she attacked me from a dizzying height. She screamed so loud, that the neighbours could hear.

"You are just a selfish bastard and you don't care about anything except yourself! You didn't even notice that I wasn't enjoying myself now in the bed."

"What?"

My jaw dropped on the floor.

"You, I mean we just had... the most mind blowing orgasm? What, what are you talking about?"

"YOU had the most mind blowing orgasm, but you didn't even notice that I didn't come." She retaliated.

I was gob smacked. I know us men, can be naïve sometimes when it comes to women's bits, but I wasn't buying this crap. Just ten minutes earlier she was riding me like Dolly Parton on a mechanical rodeo bull. Not only that, but I could feel her enjoyment be her own orgasmic contractions when she came. It was those exact contractions and her flowing juices that sent me right over the edge!

Now I was really confused. My head spun as if I had just had a beating by a professional boxer. Sheepishly and quietly I responded.

"Uhhmmm well... I'm sorry if you didn't come... I thought.... Well... Uhhmmm."

I really didn't know what to say. I was gob smacked. I tried to give her a hug, but that was met with a rather uncharming push and a shove away.

Dazzled and confused, I went to bed on my own pondering what the heck just happened. This was way beyond me.

All I really wished for now was for the baby to come into a happy and peaceful world full of love. The kind of love and togetherness I thought I felt in the bedroom.

Six

Instant love

Our marriage caused chaos in the family dynamic. I am close to my immediate and extended family. But I was starting to get torn between my family and my wife who was now heavily pregnant. I started seeing my folks less and less, as there was always something to fight about or argue about. And even though it had more to do with Jane vs my Parents/sisters, I was piggy in the middle. I grew tired.

Putting out fires on both fronts, wore me down and stated to take its emotional toll on me. I tried to keep the peace everywhere, but that proved to be a hard task. I tended to side with my wife, because after all, she was the person who was bearing my child and whom I had made a lifelong commitment with.

The following April, less than four months after the wedding, Julia, our daughter, was born. She was delivered via caesarean section in Fourways clinic at 07:20am. I witnessed the entire birth in the operating theatre and I was elated. Nothing can take away the surreal feeling of seeing your very own child for the first time. This was getting serious now. Fatherhood was all of sudden very real. For a brief moment, I couldn't care less about the world and its problems! I was in seventh heaven. Julia was gorgeous from the word go and a hundred percent healthy. Within hours, she was already checking out her surroundings and looked me straight in the eyes. She knew then already who was her daddy! She had a huge personality radiating from her big brown eyes and I knew I had met my match in character. From the moment our eyes met, she told me in no uncertain terms—"I've got you wrapped around my little finger". Of course, happy daddy fell in love all over again instantaneously.

At this point, my parents had some massive issues with Jane and Jane had some massive issues with them. She was keeping them at arm's length and it caused a damper on the festivities surrounding the birth. The dynamic was already difficult based on the previous months' happenings where Jane had successfully scared them off with her nonsense, verbal attacks and aggression. Tense moments! They visited once in hospital and quickly left again, scared that another argument/fight would erupt.

After a brief two day hospital stay Jane and Julia came back home to our growing family.

As a father you do as much as you can, and particularly me, I wanted to be involved in all areas. I was making bottles, changing nappies, feeding the family, cleaning up, doing shopping. Life got chaotic, but it was fun. I was busy and my mind was off worries for a while.

Jane stayed at home during the recovery period. I was still running the tour operating business, but had to make some more income. I secured a half day management consultancy in the 3PL industry, where I originally came from. The extra income was absolutely needed, as Jane was still not contributing much to the household at all. Even though she was now employed herself on a full time basis, her commissions were always coming, on the way or delayed. I was blind but I chose to believe her lies.

We had many arguments over money as well at that stage. I managed to continue bringing in cash, but we were barely keeping our heads above the water.

The costs were mounting, plus I took over the bulk of the cooking, cleaning, baby care, feeding, playing and night shifts. I also took over the main care of Steven who was very close to me. Things started to become very one sided and her excuse this time was Post Natal Depression. There was always some medical term or excuse for her shortcomings. Yes, I had a family now, but it was far from a happy one.

What struck me most at that time, was that her motherly instincts were very weird or almost non-existent. She was unable to quieten Julia when she had colic, was uncomfortable or crying for some reason. Whenever I took over and held her, Julia would be quiet within minutes. Over the next couple of months I had spent hours pacing up and down the passage in the middle of the night and pacifying her when needed. Whatever I did, somehow worked. Perhaps it was an energy thing.

Jane, on the other hand resigned herself to the fact that I was better at those kind of things, but it was met with anticipated jealousy. Did she have a different bond with her? Was she not able to care about babies and kids? I couldn't help but wonder if Jane lacked some form of emotional bond with her baby.

This jealousy was repeated by her older son Steven, because at seven years old, he, all of a sudden had to share me as a father, which he didn't like.

Not only that, but I had heard afterwards that he was told by his mom that since Julia was born, he was not 'his son' anymore and I loved Julia more than him! What a totally horrible thing to say to a boy that age and it was completely untrue and unfounded. At the time though I was unaware that his mom had put this poison in his head.

Life carried on and I got myself more busy wangling between chores and work. Jane, in my opinion, was the type that would take things too easy. She gave up breastfeeding, because it was a 'pain' and took up too much time and effort. She couldn't be bothered to warm up bottled milk because according to her babies get used to cold milk, as per some report/phony website she read somewhere. She started feeding Julia solids at three months and always mentioned stuff about the ninetieth percentile, as if the baby was some super wonder. What the fuck?

Granted, it was my first baby, but in consulting with nurses and looking up things on the internet myself, I could see that Jane was obviously totally misinformed and making some very dangerous and weird decisions under the pretense that she knew better.

When Jane was not at work, she'd be in bed depressed with her so called post-natal depression, mostly reading books. She would literally park the kids in front of the TV and generally didn't care. She relied on me and our part-time cleaner and nanny to take over the motherly roles. Was she really depressed? Was she

OK? I started questioning her again about all these things, but the excuses came in fast and furious.

"Do you know what it is like giving birth? My back is killing me, I need an operation. Have you never heard of post-natal depression? I have brought up a child already, I know what I'm doing."

During the pregnancy and for nearly nine months I'd heard about pre-natal hormones and the like, but I was really hoping things would get better with her. It was not to be, things got worse!

Our relationship deteriorated even more. I wasn't coping financially anymore and repeatedly insisted that this horse couldn't pull the cart on his own. Her contributions by now were almost non-existent. She put me under more and more pressure to keep the boat afloat as the 'man of the family'. It was my 'duty' to provide for everyone. Debt collectors started calling me and tensions on my side were high. The wolves were at the door! Clearly, I wasn't happy with this arrangement at all.

Out of desperation and pure need I looked for a full time job—despite the fact that I had been working on my own making good money for over ten years. I was lucky to find a good job at a large 3PL company which I accepted with both hands. It did, however mean that I could spend less time with the kids and managing the household, so, against my wishes, Julia went to a crèche/day care center on a full day basis from a very early age .

At least some decent and regular income was happening from my side and it alleviated some of the stress. I could pay the bond on time and we had proper medical aid and so on.

At home we carried on fighting a lot about her non-existent contributions to the household which were now virtually nothing, despite her being back at work full time. It almost seemed like she was hiding money from me, because I could not figure out where her money went. We argued a lot, not only about money, but also about her nonchalant attitude towards raising kids. She had a weird relationship with Steven and Julia, almost, non-emotional. Her older son Steven was closer to me then she was with him and he confided in me a lot.

This was not the family I had anticipated and the so called happy ever after, was not happening. She was a bad mother and a non-committed wife. She had a lot of secrets, blamed me for things which were not true and I didn't feel safe, secure or comfortable in any way with her. My needs were not being met at all.

I initiated a therapist to come and look at our situation. Reluctantly Jane agreed to go with me to couples therapy. I myself had been in therapy for a while already. Although I didn't know if it was working for me, it did help me see things from an outside perspective and I realised that things were very wrong in our relationship.

We saw the marriage counselor three times before she told us she couldn't help us. I think she realised and knew something I didn't know.

That December, we went on holiday to Jane's parents who were living at the coast. I looked forward to it and I was secretly hoping that it would relax us and improve our relationship somewhat. I hoped the break would do us good.

Her parents took over some of the responsibilities and helped with the kids during the holidays. I was at my wits end and went for daily walks on the beach for hours on end. I obviously needed to have that time on my own to and gather my thoughts and deal with my frustrations. It was my little escape to freedom and I felt a little bit relieved in those hours. No cellphone, no people, no nagging.

Things were not improving, even on holiday. We had 'make up' sex once that month—wow! We did it very quietly, so as not to wake up my mother-in-law in the room next door or the kids. It certainly wasn't fireworks, but better than nothing. I was at that stage suffering from a severe bout of SRS (sperm retention syndrome).

By the end of the holiday I just knew that this was not going to work out in the long run. Too much damage had been done. Too much water under the bridge. Too much confusion, lies and stress. Jane's parents also picked this up. We 'celebrated' our first wedding anniversary at a local family restaurant, but there was more bitterness than elation.

Seven

More swimmers

"Wake up, wake up!"

Jane viciously shook my shoulder. It was a rude awakening so early on a Sunday morning. From a deep sleep, I groaned, turned my head and tried to open my eyes.

"Look what you've done!" she said in an aggressive and stern voice. She repeatedly slapped something on my cheek which fell on the pillow next to my face. It was still very early in the morning. Way too early to wake up.

Dazed, confused and rubbing the sleep out of my eyes, I focused on the oblong object which I recognized instantly. It was an over the counter pregnancy test. The type you get any pharmacy. This wasn't just pregnancy test though. This was a pregnancy test that had just been urinated on and slapped in my face.

The two blue lines were undoubtedly indicating a positive result.

"Look what you've done" she repeated.

I nearly had an early morning heart attack.

"Oh my God but... but you were on the pill?" I said to her.

"Yes I was, but remember I took antibiotics in December?"

"Ehhmmm no."

I did not remember. I did not remember that at all in fact. Surely she would have told me about any antibiotics and I would have seen them around the house? I knew she loved her medical dramas and fake illnesses, but still to this day I do not remember

31

her telling me that she had gone to the doctor for something. I was flummoxed by this news of another pregnancy.

I needed coffee. Desperately and urgently.

In order to avoid an upcoming argument I got up, kept quiet and pretended that I somewhat remembered.

"Surely though, even with antibiotics cancelling out the pill, you don't fall pregnant just like that with one hit?"

"Well clearly you have good swimmers!"

Clearly I did.

Aren't you excited?" she asked me.

I cleared my throat, and nodded unenthusiastically.

I wasn't sure what to think but I wasn't impressed at this point. I mean babies are great, but there were responsibilities to think of too. I'd have a dozen babies if I could afford it, but not under these circumstances. It felt like she had set me up. This was also a far cry from the last two pregnancy announcements, for sure. I needed to clear my head. Where was that coffee?

I was also pretty pissed off with the way it was announced. Slapping a stick in my face that's just been urinated on is not really my style. Something was very wrong here and I needed to figure out what was going on. Internalizing and processing everything I could, I pulled back and avoided Jane for the rest of the day and didn't bring up the topic again.

The next day, Monday, at the office, we were chatting online on Skype. She had a bad habit of chatting via text on Skype, occupying me with useless conversations and she managed to keep me busy with trivial stuff that could take up half of my work day. Bling Bling... message... Bling bling... more messages. At times I just had to switch it off or pretend I was in a meeting because it became too much.

But that day, too much was at stake and I wanted to know more. The shocking news had settled in somewhat and I was a lot calmer.

"So how on earth did you fall pregnant Jane? Our relationship is on the rocks! I can count on my one hand the times we had sex in the last few months. Wind pollination? A miracle? God's intervention?" I asked.

"No, you remember that time when we did it in the garden just after we came back from holiday?"

I didn't. I remembered a garden session many moons ago, but certainly not in January. January was a dry spell all together.

"I only remember that quicky we had just after Christmas on Boxing Day at your parents' house. And believe me, that WAS the only time. I know full well when I got laid! There was certainly NO garden sex in January. You're mixing things up!"

She made out as if I was dumb and forgetting things. She kept adamantly defending herself with this fabrication of a story and that I need to go and seek help for forgetting sex in the garden. Hell no. Doggy style in the garden in January I would have definitely remembered. She was trying to gaslight me.

Much later on I learned about gaslighting, which is a term they use in psychology. It's a tactic used by narcissists where they want you to believe their stories and will hammer it into you so much, that you eventually start doubting your own mind and sanity and will then believe the narcissist's lies.

"So you don't believe me?" she said.

"Ehhm no."

"So are you saying I cheated?"

"Well I don't know what to think Jane! We shagged once in December while you were supposedly on the pill. Then you come up with antibiotic stories that I knew nothing about, and now the conception date is shifted from mid-December to early January after having wild sex in the garden—which never happened? I'm not stupid. We haven't had sex in the garden in ages, let alone in January."

She tried a few more vague attempts to blame me and convince me otherwise, but I wasn't being fooled this time. She was getting angry with me because I didn't believe her stories.

In my mind, I was going through the options. Did she cheat on me? Did she deliberately fall pregnant? Did she secretly have a stash of my sperm in the back of the freezer and inseminated herself? Did she really have antibiotics? Is this really a one hit wonder? And of course the next thing that was going through my mind was—she's going to be an absolute bitch again for the next nine months and blame it on pregnancy hormones.

I resigned myself to the fact that I was going to have another child—albeit unexpected. Of course I'd welcome it with open arms and circumstances aside, any pregnancy is one of life's wonderful miracles. Abortion is an absolute no go area for me. It's not a religious thing or anything, it's a moral issue. I don't believe in taking an innocent life away. A person is a person, no matter how small.

My life was now taken over with looking after kids, making an income, doing all the work mostly myself and focusing and getting ready for the next child. All the while not being happy in the relationship, but ignoring that fact for the time being. I was still secretly hoping for a miracle that things would change for the better.

The pregnancy went as "un-smoothly" as expected. Jane's moods ramped up. More fights with her and my family. Inflammatory emails were exchanged without my knowledge between Jane and my family. Everyone kept their secrets to themselves. I saw my folks less and less. At home I was brainwashed into believing my family and also my friends were bad people with issues and problems. Jane always had something to pick on. She always had something to criticize. She literally kept these conversations going for hours on end in an attempt to brainwash me. Ironically she'd always pick on someone's bad character trait which was partially true, but would blow that so out of proportion that you ended up believing she was talking about an axe murderer. Smoke and mirrors. . . Smoke and mirrors.

In April that year, we had a major fall out: Jane, my parents and I. We had visited my parent's farm for Easter. There were a lot of guests and Jane had created a huge drama over a petty little thing. This time she had an audience. Before I even knew what was happening in the chaos, she and the kids had stormed out and drove off in my car leaving me stranded at the farm. My mom was in tears, my sister was in tears, my dad cursing. And all over what? Jane's behavior!

Jane concocted another email to my mom being totally inflammatory blaming my mom for raising a monster (me!). Admittedly her command of the English language and her writing style was immaculate, but very convincing and very damaging. As usual, I wasn't aware of the mail at that time. It was also sent behind my back and my mom didn't want to discuss it with me.

I had reached my pivotal point. Pregnant or not, something snapped within me. Being stuck between loyalties proved to be too much of a burden.

When I eventually got a lift home that night after the bomb hit earlier that day, I found the kitchen table covered with print outs of rental properties all over town. She decided that she was now "moving out" as she couldn't "carry on like this". I hoped that she would stick to her words.

The following week's arguments were preoccupied with 'where do we as a couple go from here?'. Every suggestion I put on the table was taken in and spat out later in my face. There was no compromise. No winning. No resolution with her. To add another dose of confusion, she wanted to stay, make up, and regularly declared her undying love for me. She now loved me more than ever. I learned that that behavior is called Hoovering, but it didn't work on me.

Her parents got involved. I didn't know where to turn anymore and my support structure both from family and friends was severely strained. Upcoming baby again, family relations broken, financial issues. The list didn't end and it started to wear me down severely.

Where to from here? What now? Hang in for the birth? Leave? Stay? Give it an absolute final chance? Talk?

I had to weigh up all my options. With my therapist, I started seeing slowly but surely that I was in an abusive relationship. I was walking on eggshells. And I was in denial. I mean which strapping staunch 'man' ends up being abused by a woman!? Gosh really? Have some balls! Nevertheless, with Jane I stood my ground and got my strength back. I started believing in myself. Because of this, and after the Easter drama failed on her part, she came home with another fabrication.

"I have Addison's disease!" she remarked.

"Oh no...now what? What the heck is that?" I asked her.

Another medical drama she loved so well. Please God no!

"Well basically, because of the increased stress levels from the Easter Fall out caused by your parents, my cortisol levels went through the roof and my adrenal glands are damaged."

She rambled on a host of medical terms and conditions and told me that the doctor said she cannot get herself into any stressful situations during the remainder of the pregnancy, and thus she cannot see my parents or my family any more at all. She also needed lots and lots of bed rest and I wasn't to cause any further stress in the relationship.

"Doctors orders" she exclaimed.

"Why, didn't you tell me you went to the doctor? Again? Which doctor did you go to now?" I said.

"I went with my mom to doctor Jacobs and his medical team. He is a highly acclaimed endocrinologist, and if I don't listen to his advice, I'll lose the baby. Or he's going to come out deformed."

"Oh really?"

I was now helluva confused trying to let the bullshit sink in. It wasn't just a doctor, but a doctor and his entire 'medical team'!

"Did you get medication?"

"No they can't give me medicine, because I'm pregnant. I'll have to wait till the end of the pregnancy and then go on lifelong treatment. This is a chronic condition and is incurable."

"Holy shit!"

(Why I even entertained this crap from her at the time is still beyond me. She obviously still had me under her spell of sorts and I, again gave her the benefit of the doubt. She sounded convincing enough.)

She emailed my mother, behind my back of course, with the same diagnosis and re-enforced no contact with them.

The rest of the pregnancy went by without contact with my parents and friends. She had now effectively isolated me from the rest of the world. The months that followed were a nightmare. I was confused as to whether her diagnosis was real or not and in a zombie-like state, I carried on walking on eggshells which were, in fact, more like glass shards dipped in pool acid on a fiery bed of red hot coals.

Working in a strict corporate environment now, I lost all my independence, spent three hours a day commuting, eight hours a day at work, and the nights consisted of cooking and looking after Julia and Steven as Jane was too "sick" to get out of bed, and too "tired" from working and being pregnant. She "had to take it easy"!

I was a fraction of the happy go lucky Mark I once was.

I felt the downward spiral happening to me. Something so beautiful as having a child and going through pregnancy, now had such a big damper on it. This was definitely not what I had anticipated from family life when we met online! What happened to her as a person and maybe more importantly, what was happening to me? I kept on focusing on the only positive in my life at that point. The upcoming baby which was calculated to arrive end of September according to Jane. This made perfect sense with my own calculations of the conception date in December I had worked out, but baby Sean decided to have his birthday two weeks earlier than planned. That Saturday during breakfast, Jane went unexpectedly into labour. I was in total disbelief when she panicked and told me.

"We have to go to hospital now!"

"Why?" I asked her.

"I'm getting cramps." Her face flinched as she said it.

"Naaa don't worry. He's not due for another two weeks at least."

It really didn't feature in my mind that babies do arrive early and...you know, I had a lot of things to do that weekend. Fixing the baby room, painting it and making it nice were just a few of the things I had planned. I casually poured another coffee.

"I'm going to get dressed" she said. "Will you get the car ready?"

"Why?" I asked again, totally oblivious to the reality of what was happening.

"Because I'm going into labour!" she screamed at me and held her stomach at the same time.

It hit me like a ton of bricks. Oh my God, she really is having the baby! I grabbed her and helped her up the stairs to the bedroom. Got her dressed and packed the overnight bag, toothpaste, nighties and all the stuff Jane and a newborn might need. Within five minutes we were on the road.

Jane did all the paperwork at the reception and was checked into the maternity ward. The labour section at first before going into the recovery ward. Sean was born two hours later by caesarean section. I was over the moon again. A healthy beautiful little boy, grown full term. I was present in the operating theatre with classical music blaring over the speaker system. Dr Paul asked me if I wanted to cut the umbilical cord and I happily obliged. Both mom and son went into the post-op recovery area and I sat down in the coffee shop phoning friends and family with the unexpected news.

When I went back up to the general ward to see Jane and Sean an hour later, the first thing I noticed was the name tag on Jane's bed as well as on Sean's hospital cot. They were marked "Mrs de Jager" and "Baby de Jager" by the hospital staff. That's the surname of Jane's ex-husband?!?!

"Why is your and Sean's bed marked with your ex-husband's surname?" I asked Jane.

"Oh, oh…ehhm, it must have been an admin error when I checked in. Something to do with the medical aid still having me on there as de Jager."

The jubilation of the actual birth was now dampened again with something as silly as that. What was going on? Was it true? Did they really make a mistake or was this one of her tricks again? Was she having me on? And if so, for what? Needless to say it pissed my parents off to no end as well when they arrived later that afternoon.

However, the real blow came forty eight hours later. Still in hospital, the home affairs lady came to me and asked me to sign some paperwork so that they could issue the birth certificate and for me to be listed as the father. I had filled in and signed some papers already two days earlier, but she said that I had to acknowledge that the child was born out of wedlock?

"What? No!! Wait! But I AM married to Jane. There must be an error somewhere."

The home affairs lady looked through some papers.

"Well according to our system you are single and she's still married to, ehhm a guy by the name of Michael de Jager".

"Hold on a seccie……. JAAAAAAANE!"

I stormed back to the ward with the papers in hand.

"What the heck is going on here?" I was livid!

"Why are you still married to Michael? Are you now a bigamist too?"

She swore and claimed innocence and she did not know what was going on herself. She had no idea about that and she would look into it the minute she'd get home from hospital. It must have been some administrative error according to her.

For me to be actually listed as the father on the birth certificate, I had to sign the papers stating the child was born out of wedlock. Ironically, they never asked me to do that when Julia was born. Granted our internal administration services in South Africa are a complete balls up to say the least, but this was really getting on my nerves, and I demanded an unabridged birth certificate with my name and Sean's name clearly stated on it.

When Sean and Jane returned two days later, home life got more hectic. Although having a new bundle of joy at home, Jane was now seriously getting into my head and nerves. Like a worm digging holes into the grey matter of your brain, she was constantly on my mind.

The same month of the birth, I got a call from a company called BeeCee's debt collectors.

"Hi Mr Le Foncé, we are calling you to collect forty two thousand Rand in outstanding school fees for your son Steven."

"Huh? What?"

Another investigation! It appeared, despite reassurance from Jane that her father was paying for school fees for my stepson Steven, (and her ex Michael too) she had pocketed the money and made me the responsible party for the account. On visiting the accounts department of the school in question, and having a meeting with them, I was advised that she listed me as Steven's father and therefore I had a responsibility to pay for his accounts! I took two days, wasted on affidavits stamped by the police and making statements that I was not his father, nor his adoptive father. But eventually they cleared my name. I was, however, black listed for a long time and the call centre still kept phoning me for years after that incident.

Needless to say this was another confrontation with Jane. I heard all the excuses under the sun. She was of the opinion that the school made an admin error and this was all a mistake and she'd sort it out with her Dad and Michael and and and.... The damage was done...

And I had had enough!

Eight

Couple therapy and exes

Between the joyful celebration of another addition to the family and the news that I'd received about the home affairs saga, my mind went into overdrive and I was living in a fuzzed state of disbelief. I tried to keep things civil at home but I was done. Family and friends brought heaps of baby clothes, nappies, toys and other baby paraphernalia. It all washed over me in a hazed fog. I started running away from home over the weekends. Usually with three kids in tow. I just couldn't face Jane anymore.

When I was at home I took over the parenting role almost completely. I kept the kids entertained, fed, bathed, changed and happy. I took them to doctor's appointments, got medications for them and made sure their inoculations were up to date.

Jane's input was absolutely minimal and she was still complaining about her "Addison's disease" and now she also had to go for a spinal fusion soon, as her lower back was 'severely damaged'. This operation would be so high risk that she could end up being bedridden for the rest of her life! These were all bullshit stories of course. But 'because of her back', she couldn't pick up the kids. She hardly had physical interaction and cuddling time with them. With Sean she didn't even try to breastfeed and he went straight onto the 'cold' bottle (Yes cold...she couldn't even be bothered to warm it up). Steven, Julia and Sean grew emotionally so close to me and demanded and craved double attention due to the lack of attention from their mom. I had to supply all

40

the love and attention. Don't get me wrong, I loved doing it, but it got extremely tiring at times!

At work I was exhausted and not really motivated. The company was too corporate for my liking and the days were interrupted with a barrage of Skype messages from Jane trying to rectify the chaos she'd left in her psychopathic wake whilst trying to brainwash me into believing other things she made up. I actually wondered when she had the time to work and keep her job. Sometimes I'd answer politely just to avoid confrontation all together. Most of the times she attempted to gaslight and provoke arguments which the attempt to stuff up my day. I tried my hardest not to let it get to me. That unfortunately proved to be an impossible task! I couldn't focus on work anymore. She was on me like a witch hunt, controlling my every move and ensuring my emotions and thoughts were completely preoccupied by her.

I became totally distrusting of everything she said and wasn't believing her stories at all anymore. I wasn't giving her the benefit of the doubt like I did previously. I tried to get hold of her ex-husband Michael, in Yemen to find out what had transpired in their marriage. I had so little knowledge of any of her past and I wanted to know more. Things didn't gel at all. I also wanted to tell him that, according to the South African Home Affairs at least, he was still married to Jane and not me!

I looked up his number on my phone when I had a moment alone. I knew it was there somewhere at one point, but I couldn't find it.

Strange. I had never deleted it!

I checked on Skype. I had his address there for sure. It was on my laptop, because earlier that year, I facilitated for him and his son Steven to chat on Skype for a bit. Oddly, that too, abruptly stopped after a few weeks of activity and Jane had told me that was not surprising as Michael didn't really care about his son.

She said: "Even when you load him on Skype, he couldn't be bothered to build a relationship with his own child."

That was her version at least. According to her, Michael had also never paid maintenance so a lot of Steven's costs ended up on my head while we were together because she was the struggling single mom. Not that I could really afford it, but hey, you support each other as a family, right?

I went on my search for Michael and checking on the Skype system, his contact details there were also gone.

Very odd. It aroused my suspicions as Jane had the password for my laptop.

I certainly never deleted it. I proceeded to do a public search online and picked up his Skype address. I put the address in the connect box of Skype and an automated response popped up on the screen:

> You blocked this person from your contact list on February 08, 2012. Are you sure you want to re-connect?

Holy shit! I didn't know you could even block people on Skype! Jane's devious cracks and intentions were certainly starting to show.

Why? How? What? What for? What is she up to?

Why does she block Michael from contacting his son and pretends that Michael is such a bad father? What is going on here?

I requested Michael to reconnect on Skype by sending him a message. Within a day he accepted my invite and we got chatting. I told him about him being blocked on my Skype and that I didn't really know him as a person, but wanted to ask a few questions about their marriage. I told him about the home affairs saga, Sean's surname listing in the hospital, my intentions to break up this marriage now and, that according to the South African administration he was still married to Jane.

He was as flabbergasted as I was.

Michael advised me that he has been trying for years to build up a meaningful relationship with his son, but that he always got blocked and side stepped. He had tried desperately for years to have some contact with Steven.

His instructions from Jane was to phone at five thirty pm every Sunday night once a week as that was the only 'convenient' time for her and Steven in their extremely busy schedules. Every week he tried though he could never or hardly get through and always received an SMS message afterwards along the likes of:

> Sorry I didn't hear the phone

or

Sorry, it's an inopportune moment. Try again next week.

As it turned out she would mostly switch her phone off on Sunday late afternoon in order to block him.

Interesting! As worrisome as it sounded this was very interesting. The plot started thickening but I had no clue what I was dealing with and what was yet to come!

Clearly a divorce was now on the cards. Staying together was out of the question. There was no hope for us. I had no trust in her and I, from being an energetic, happy-go-lucky person, had become a miserably controlled, depressed, emasculated and manipulated person. I used all the tiny bits of positive energy that I had left on the kids. Without much hope and as a last minute feeble attempt, I arranged for one more couple therapist to see us. I was a futile exercise.

We lasted no more than three sessions. I did, however, continue to go to my own weekly shrink to try and keep some sort of emotional and mental form of sanity for myself. Jane's psychopathic vortex had me deeply entrenched in its clutches.

I contacted an organization called FAMSA, (a family counseling organization) who would be able to assist with family matters and divorces for cheap. They recommended we should still try and give it one more shot on the therapy front. It would be the best for the kids and we were reffered to their in-house psychologist, Diane.

So we went in April. I still could not get a grip on Jane and had no clue what she was secretly up to. I had received more information from her ex-husband, Michael, who told me their whole divorce saga ten years earlier in Canada. To cut a long story short, Michael came home one day from work to an empty house, save for a writing desk and a single mattress to sleep on. Jane and his then newborn son had vanished without an inkling of a clue or a hint in advance. Interestingly, this was literally within the month of Jane and Steven receiving Canadian passports. She had left Michael with a huge pile of debt (which sounded very familiar to me) and there was nothing he could do legally. He just couldn't afford international legal counsel at the time. The poor guy was left broke and devastated.

Armed with that knowledge, we went to into our third therapy session with Diane at FAMSA. The previous ones did not amount to much and I didn't have much hope for this one either. As expected, the session was totally uneventful besides a new story Jane had come up with. With tears in her eyes she announced that her father was diagnosed with cancer and he only had four months to live. I could see on her face that the emotions weren't real, but she did a pretty good job faking it and lying in therapy. Diane got caught up in it, hook, line and sinker.

Apparently her dad had not been to seen an oncologist yet as he didn't want to live anymore. He also didn't want to burden his family with a prolonged illness and I had to swear blind that I was not to talk about it to him or anyone else. This was his dying wish in his last few months of life. (At the time of print, seven years on, the father is still alive and not going anywhere soon.)

Right! Now I'd heard it all. Drama after drama, after drama. The lying pathology was as clear as daylight. Bloody liar! I was starting to read the drama queen quite well. Did Diane see through this all? It didn't appear so to me. Jane rambled on and on and I had difficulty not slipping into my own inner mental world and cocoon. I tried my best to participate and to focus on her ramblings.

I cleared my throat and interrupted Jane's theatrics and announced:

"Sorry Jane, but I want a divorce. I know we've spoken about it many times before, but this time I mean it. I'd rather be a divorced and happy and good father to my kids then try to resolve this bizarre and sinister situation to which I see no end. I also don't see a real commitment from your side to try and save us. I only hear lip service."

She instantly burst into more tears. Actually it was more of a complete hysteria. She curled up into a heaving ball in the corner of the office. Diane just sat there. I just sat there too! We looked at each other and in her best 'therapist' voice she said:

"Oh shame, well I know it's hard. And clearly it is hard for Jane too. Are you sure about your decision?"

I nodded an affirmative 'yes' with a facial expression that mirrored my sentiments.

Diane looked at me for another minute. We both remained in our seats. I just looked back with that 'face' that said it all. What else could I do? Jane continued howling hysterically in the corner of the room ensuring the whole neigbourhood could hear the wailing.

"Would you like to...eehhm...maybe console her?" Diane broke off our staring contest.

"No thanks. I'm good."

I wasn't at all fazed by the hysterical outbursts. I had no empathy left in me, especially knowing that the show wasn't real. It didn't do anything to me anymore. In fact I should be the one crying here, but I wasn't going to get hoovered in again.

Jane remained in the corner still heaving and crying. The staring contest between Diane and I resumed. Clearly she had no clue how to resolve this or what to say to us. We sat and glanced at each other for another five long minutes. Jane's hysteria came and went but didn't subside totally. With nothing happening I eventually got up and picked up my bag. I addressed Diane.

"I think I better go".

Diane nodded in approval. Our session wasn't finished yet, but there was no point in hanging in there any longer.

On my way out I politely greeted the receptionist behind the desk who looked at me wide eyed. I wonder what went through her mind having heard the howling going on behind the closed door. Probably something along the lines of—what a bastard!

The session was taxing on me and with my mind still fuzzy and on autopilot, I descended the steps of the building and walked to my car. I was oblivious of my surroundings and it felt like my brain was wrapped in cotton wool from all the turbulent emotions. I fumbled for my car keys and opened my car door. My mind was shocked back into reality with a jolt when a hand violently gripped my shoulder and yanked me backwards. It was Jane.

"You fucking bastard" she screamed at me.

"You NEVER believed in us. Look what you're putting me through. Now I have to go through a divorce again. I'll get you back for this you low life scum."

Her eyes were aglow with an evil glint I hadn't seen before. Her voice hissed from deep within her body. It was like she was possessed by some demon! I was seriously scared of her at that moment.

Wow, that was a change of mood from the pity party on display inside the therapy room two minutes earlier. I felt like calling Diane and showing her this side. But knowing that would be a pointless exercise, I got in the car and drove home. Jane was still hurling insults at me while I drove off.

Nine

The legals begin with a rock to match

Needless to say at home things were getting more tense, but I didn't want the kids to suffer under the circumstances. Already then, whilst we were still in the same house we 'swapped' weekends and days with the kids. I often took them out to my parents' farm over the weekend, just to get away from it all and receive their support. It did us all good to get away from that toxic environment and it was good to start reconnecting with the family, who themselves were helpless onlookers in my dilemma over the last two years. I took the kids to birthday parties, zoo visits and plenty of playground time to keep them entertained. Jane didn't do much with them at all and never took them anywhere. She was too pre-occupied with herself and the planning of the divorce. I was definitely taking on the role of single daddy now, going alone to places with three very young kids, actually, babies in tow without any help. I even conducted business meetings with Sean in his car seat and Julia in the stroller if the nanny wasn't around. I remarked to one of my clients once,

"Sorry, I am babysitting today, I hope you don't mind if I bring the kids with me."

He didn't, but when he saw six month old Sean at the meeting, he remarked:

"Wow, you sure weren't kidding about 'baby' sitting part.

That is a really young baby. Where is the mother?"

"Don't ask" I replied and smiled politely.

Strangers and by passers in coffee shops, farmyards and markets were always there to lend a helping hand though when things got too much. With baby vomit over my shoulder, or no place to change Sean or Julia's stinky nappies, a friendly stranger was always on standby to look after the other little ones while I could concentrate on the task at hand. That's when you realise there are still good people in the world and usually the conversation started with 'Where is the mother?' Again, 'Don't ask' or 'working', was my usual reply, not really wanting to go into detail. Jane was either working on a Saturday or lying in bed, busy with her 'disease, headache, sore back or other medical condition' all while I ensured the kids (and me) were having a good time socializing, experiencing life, and avoiding the toxic household as much as we could.

About two months prior to her moving out of the house, Jane all of a sudden got very busy on her laptop. Every night she was secretly 'working' on something while I ensured the kids were fed or reading books to them. She was obsessing about something. From the time I got home from work until late at night she was typing and typing and doing things. A briefcase full of paperwork sat next to her.

She would position herself on the couch in such a way that you could not see the screen and instead of focusing on her motherly duties, she was pre-occupied with whatever she was pre-occupied with. Something was shrouded in secrecy and she wanted to show it. I never asked what she was so busy doing, because I knew it was a childish attention seeking move from her side.

The 'work' and frantic typing continued, literally every night, for weeks on end. In the odd occasion, if for some reason I had to pass by on the other side of the couch or I'd walk by too close, she'd quickly close the laptop screen with a bang and curse me for being on that side of the couch. The situation was bizarrely pathetic. She was mentally losing it.

Occasionally I would remark:

"Don't you think you should rather spend some time with your children? Just a suggestion."

"Fuck off" was the usual response.

Two weeks after the last therapist at FAMSA in April, we decided to utilize their services for a divorce. They assist with divorce and legal matters as well. Uncontested divorce matters, that is.

We were married out of community of property and without accrual, so it was simply a case of drawing up a parenting plan, getting it stamped by a court, paying a couple of grand and move on. Well that is how it was supposed to be.

FAMSA's legal department asked us to come in for an interview the following Wednesday evening after work. We agreed, but Jane didn't pitch up that night. With some feeble excuse from her side, we rescheduled for a week later.

In the meeting a social worker and a lawyer were present documenting our discussion and helping out if there were any disagreements. It all appeared to go well in the meeting and I hoped that we could close this chapter amicably and soon. The week after, we had to submit some financials in order to work out maintenance for the kids, if at all applicable. We each had decent jobs with payslips, so it wouldn't really be too difficult to work out. That's, however where Jane started protesting and did not see the need why she had to 'expose' herself like that.

"Well that is standard procedure" the lawyer said.

The social worker also wanted to conduct an interview with Steven, to get a feel of his viewpoint and the family dynamic. A meeting was set up a week later, but Jane and Steven didn't pitch up at that meeting either.

To add insult to injury, my body had enough of the continuous stress and caved in that very same week. I woke up at four am on Thursday morning, feeling a huge cramp in my belly on the side. Oh well, I thought, some bug and probably a massive fart that needs to come out. Add in a dose of explosive diarrhea and it's all sorted out! I didn't think much of it.

But by seven am while dressing for work it got a lot worse and it didn't feel so much like diarrhea anymore. This was something else I had never felt before. I called the doctor to see if I could come in and get something for it before I went to work.

"Yea sure," he said, "I'm here early and no appointments yet. Come on over now if you can."

I was at his office at seven thirty. He stared probing my abdomen here and there.

"Does this hurt?"

"Yes."

"Does this hurt?"

"Yes."

"Does this......"

"WHOOOAAA...Shit! ...Oh my God...! Yes that HURT like crazy!"

"OK," he said calmly "Here's a bottle, pee in it if you can."

I got up from the examination table and moved to the sink on the other side of the room. I dropped my trousers, flopped out my ding dong whilst hanging over the sink. With the bottle in hand, I started urinating. A pathetic couple of drops came dribbling out. I pushed a bit harder to speed up the stream and all of a sudden it happened. My knees buckled, the blood in my face drained and the most intense pain I'd ever felt overwhelmed me. Instant nausea engulfed my entire being, whilst sweat formed on my brow. Trying not to faint, I held on to the sink. The bottle dropped on the floor and the doctor managed to catch me just in time.

"You're not going anywhere my man. I'm checking you into the ward right now and sending you in for X-rays.

"It looks like you've got a kidney stone."

Nice! Just what I needed at that moment—NOT! A kidney stone. I never had a kidney stone in my life! And well, a kidney stone and-a-half it was! The X-rays and CAT scan showed a monster at nearly one and half cm in diameter. It was wedged between the kidney itself and the pee tube that goes to your bladder. My plumbing was blocked good and well. I got dosed up with a huge amount of pain killers and they booked me in for the day and night for observation, and on the slim possibility the stone might pass. Yea right! That was like trying to fly a Jumbo jet through the hole of a doughnut! The kidney was under severe strain already from the build-up, and the stone was just too large to pass. They had me on standby for an operation the next day.

Although we weren't communicating much at all, I SMSed Jane:

Sorry Jane, I've been booked into hospital. I have a Kidney stone. They're keeping me here and I've got to stay overnight. I will likely have an operation tomorrow and will only come home Saturday morning.

Her response was less than empathetic:

Oh well that's too bad. Just make sure you make arrangements for the kids on Saturday morning. I'm not there in the morning and it's your day with the kids. Just get a baby sitter or something. This doesn't suit me at all! I have to go to work.

What on earth? Not an ounce of compassion, not an inkling of feeling sorry and just barking orders about baby sitters for Saturday morning, all while I'm about to be operated on! This woman was completely off her rocker!

The operation the next day went well and in fact the actual hospital stay and the drug induced painkillers were actually a welcome break from my chaotic world at the time. Despite my request, Jane didn't bring the kids through for a visit to my disappointment, but I knew her game by now.

Thankfully a lot of my friends and family came to visit and brought love and compassion.

Ten

Lawyering up

The real legal storm had started to brew by now.

FAMSA legal counseling meeting was cancelled by Jane after the second session. She didn't want to discover or expose her finances. She announced that she'll take this case to high court and will divorce there. What a waste of money again. She also advised them that she was going to take out a restraining order on me. What? A restraining order? What for? She had absolutely no basis for that, but it was now game on for her. What her reasoning for that was, God only knows. FAMSA's policy on this is that they don't get involved in acrimonious divorces or in matters outside of normal divorce proceedings, such as restraining orders. That restraining order never came, so I thought she was bluffing. It was a threat to try and control me and make me scared.

At home things stayed tense. I went through this phase in total 'ignore' mode while she kept threatening every night that the "sheriff is coming to deliver divorce papers" and "You'll be served by the sheriff, I am talking to my legal team daily".

"OK fine, I can't wait for the paperwork. Make my day. In the interim, please don't forget to make plans to move out as well at some point, as I'm not happy with you in my space anymore and it's affecting the kids negatively. You need to now seriously move out of my house."

Two weeks later, there was still no sheriff, still no paperwork and I asked her again:

"Jane, where is your paperwork for the divorce?"

"I am still working on it with my lawyer" was all that she could bark back at me.

"OK well tell him to hurry up."

It was the same scenario two weeks after that, and by week six, I had had enough of waiting. I was tired and needed to move on. I was under the impression that she was lying, and that she had not been to see a lawyer, nor was she busy 'doing paperwork'. She was stalling the process.

"OK, if you don't apply for the divorce, I will!" I announced.

It was met with a resistance and she responded that her lawyer was very busy with the paperwork. My God. How long does he need?

Not willing to wait on her any more, I called my lawyer Johan the next day and met up with him.

Johan had been my lawyer for a couple of smaller things he had handled for my business. He had a small general law firm, and was successful in what he did. He wasn't specialized in divorces per se or family law as such, but he had the knowledge, and I liked his honestly most of all. I also had a consultation with a specialist family lawyer, but I decided to stay with Johan instead.

In our meeting we quickly established what was what and how to proceed. We had an ante nuptial agreement and we were married out of community of property. We also didn't apply the accrual system and roughly, we were earning similar kinds of salaries.

"It's just a custody battle then," Johan said.

"If you get 50/50 parental rights, then neither one pays the other anything. You share costs and that's it! Easy divorce. I'll prepare the paperwork and I'll have it ready the day after tomorrow."

Two days after, Johan had my papers ready. A simple, two page divorce application stating the basics and I signed. This was going to be delivered by the sheriff at her work. I asked Johan if I should notify Jane in advance and he told me it'd probably be better and courteous at least. So I sent Jane a text message that read:

"With your failure to produce divorce papers as discussed, I had no choice but to launch the application from my side. The sheriff will come and deliver the paperwork to you shortly."

53

Her answers were nothing short of charming.

"I told you I am busy with the lawyers on this. I am not accepting your papers."

And she didn't. For a good three weeks she managed to duck and dive from the sheriff's service. The sheriff already reported to us with feedback that he'd seen and identified her at work but she pretended to be someone else. How did she manage that? He described her to the T and even told us what car she drove. Why he couldn't deliver, I still don't know, but she was very good at avoiding him.

Meanwhile, she then quickly appointed a lawyer from her side to get the paperwork done. She was adamant to be the applicant in this divorce.

Jane employed a law firm called Mike Vermont. I did a quick Google search and wow! Stunning website, beautiful images and a rolling text page of how many people he helped divorce and get money. Lots of soppy and dramatic testimonials were on display with happy endings. Women would get rich by divorcing their husbands. Wow. He made people go from rags to riches in no time! The firm obviously had a brilliant marketing campaign, that's for sure. They even had billboards all over town. It all sounded so good, that is was almost surreal. Was this an advertising agency or a law firm? To me it looked more like a washing powder commercial, promising to make bright colours brighter. Quite sick that firms advertise their wares like this and destroying lives in the process.

In order to keep their marketing campaign up to speed, their rates were apparently hefty as well. Approximately three times as much as the norm. It didn't scare me. Law is law, no matter how much your lawyer costs.

So Mike Vermont had drafted the High Court divorce application on instructions of his client, Jane. The sheriff came by to my place of work and delivered a hefty pack of documents. I went through it at my desk, shaking my head. A complete absurdity of a divorce application with all sorts of false allegations. She had now officially launched a total smear campaign against me.

It was a nice try, but I wasn't having this! She claimed for relocation fees, support payments and legal assistance to the tune of three hundred thousand Rand. She wanted maintenance for herself and the kids. She needed money for Steven who was not my responsibility, but for her convenience, included in the calculation. She wanted thirty five thousand Rand per month plus other expenses PER child! She came up with mega cost claims on supposed fictitious loans she lent me. What idiocy was this? Was this a bizarre attempt to extract money out of me after all these years of supporting her? This was a joke.

The joke had only just started though. One Thursday afternoon in July, two months after the FAMSA fiasco, I arrived home from work and I found most of my furniture outside on the lawn. A whole bunch of other furniture and stuff was now occupying the space in my very own house. The toddlers were crawling around in nothing but their nappies clambering unsupervised all over the furniture. Now what? I stormed in, looking for Jane demanding to know what was going on.

Her parents were moving to the coast and gave her a truckload of furniture. Couches, cupboards, stuff and more stuff everywhere! I had to squeeze past furniture and things to get into my house which looked like a bomb had hit it. I flipped my lid!

To make matter worse, my tenant in the cottage who had also just gotten home from work came out freaking at me. Apparently Jane had taken over half her cottage too. Jane needed the space for "storage" purposes.

I was absolutely floored! I had to calm the tenant down, had to calm myself down and approached Jane.

I really had a hard time to keep my composure and not losing my temper.

"Oh no, this is only temporary," Jane said as if this was the absolute norm. She was as cool as a cucumber but simultaneously was enjoying the freak show I was providing her with.

"I'll be moving out at the end of the month." She said. "I just found a place and signed the lease."

"Fantastic! It's about time you get the hell out of here."

Even though I was freaking about the furniture in the garden and house, those very words were coming out like music to my ears. It was like a weight had dropped off my shoulders and I basked in the knowledge and anticipation that she would finally be gone forever. Thank God. I had had enough of her shit and the chaotic life I had to endure for the last two years.

On Facebook she started announcing upcoming house warming parties and get-togethers. Those never happened as it was just for attention seeking purposes and a ploy to make me jealous and insecure. When she got the keys for the place, more Facebook updates in the form of poetic (and pathetic) descriptions of birds cheeping in her new garden and frogs in her lounge. It oozed attention seeking all around and she made it appear as if she was the happiest person alive!

Facebook was her tool for attention. She'd throw half-baked statements out there, such as:

"If only people knew." and "Why does this only happen to me".

These messages served as a conversation opener and an attention seeking tool so that people could ask:

"What happened" or

"Oh shame, Jane are you OK?"

It was all about the number of comments on her posts. Commentary and likes were most important to her. Pretense and the appearance of a picture perfect life were displayed without shame or holding back for the world to see. At that time particularly it started to escalate and she went so far that she'd put up naked pictures of the kids, full frontals and all. One day she uploaded another photoset of herself in a newly acquired corset! I reported it to the lawyers, because I didn't like the feel of this at all, and not only that, what if some sick pervert sits online and gets all horny over your kids pictures? It was too sickening to think that a mother was actually posting this kind of stuff.

Attention seeking and bizarre behavior started coming up more frequently from her side and I started reading up on the psychology behind this. I was about to learn a lot.

Eleven

Finally separated

On August the first, she finally moved. I was elated! I was at the end of my tether with her and the bizarre situation that unfolded and actually couldn't wait for her to be gone and move on with life. I know it sounds harsh, but I'd been walking on eggshells for over two years and dealing with everything, from single parenting to earning money and her continuous onslaught on my time, integrity and human rights. I was tired and needed to get rid of the stress.

Even though she packed up most of my stuff along with hers and stole lots of items from me, I couldn't care less. It was only stuff after all, and I knew I'd bounce back quickly. I had more important things to worry about than 'stuff'.

To me, her moving out was a massive relief. My house was now bare and almost empty, but spacious again and after a good scrubbing and therapeutic deep cleansing, it felt like I had my home back. To ensure the negative energy was gone properly, I smudged the inside and outside of the house thoroughly with sage. When the smoke cleared, the vibe instantly changed and there was a huge senses of energetic clearing. I bought some new curtains here and there and filled the gaps with the essential missing items fairly quickly. Now it was my very own place again, the way I wanted it. No stinky dogs, no more fights, no more walking on eggshells in my own space. It was home sweet home once more!

I am a rather house-proud person and like to have my home cozy and well kept. Granted it's not always tidy, but cleanliness and being able to call the place home where you can relax is important to me. Her moving out was a massive weight off my shoulders. I had breathing space again and I would not be told by her what was nice and what had to be thrown out. My family and friends commented on how much better the house looked. Time to start afresh!

We decided and agreed that the kids, (including Steven) would stay at my house on Tuesdays, Thursdays and alternate weekends, including sleepovers. Ideally I didn't think splitting the kids over two houses was appropriate and I would have wanted to fight for them to stay with me, but realistically speaking I also thought to myself that they need their mom in their lives. As nuts as I felt she was, the kids had a right to know her. I hoped that I could control any damage she did to them in the time they spent with me. There's no such thing as a perfect parent, and after all who was I to decide on the kids' wellbeing on my own! I had to resign myself to the fact that the courts were probably going to grant me fifty percent in any case, so we had made that agreement, albeit verbal, as the interim solution until the divorce was finalised.

The nanny that we had in our employ at my house was going to move with her to her place as she had accommodation for her, and she could stay on the premises to assist with the kids. On Tuesdays and Thursdays, the nanny would then come to my place to help me clean and look after the kids if and when necessary. This also ensured she kept her full time employment with us.

That worked well, for two weeks! I got an email from Jane that 'her' nanny was not to be abused by me and she was not to come to my house on Tuesdays and Thursdays any more. She had signed a new contract with the nanny behind my back and I was not to interfere or try to amend the new arrangement with her employee! A calculated move from her side to make things difficult for me.

The kids loved their nanny, *Gogo*, and I let it go on the basis of—they're better off with the nanny then with mom. They had a close bond with, probably deeper than with their own mom.

Jane used that tactic so that she could minimize my contact with the kids. She wouldn't let me have them during the day on Tuesday's and Thursdays either as the kids were under her 'care and control'—or rather, she'd leave them with *Gogo*.

Right, she was now in full control freak mode. As I wasn't home during the week and still working in a corporate office during the day, I let it go and generally picked up the kids after work as early as half past four or five o'clock to spend as much time with them as possible. Their mom was also working during the days, so in terms of actual time spent with the kids, it didn't really matter at which residence they'd be. They were taken care of by the nanny. It was still a fifty/fifty arrangement after all. All of a sudden towards the end of August, I started getting bombarded with stupid emails and requests from her lawyer, on her instructions of course. They were silly things and blatant lies like:

> Your house is not safe for the kids, you have no pool net.
>
> You have a dangerous staircase in the home.
>
> Your kitchen cupboards have sharp corner.

The house was perfectly secure of course, with a fence around the pool I had built myself eighteen months earlier and the staircase had a self-closing gate. It was more than baby proofed enough! Even the kitchen cupboards had selfclosing locks on and the medicine cupboard was high up, locked and out of reach. What was she on about? Her allegations were totally unfounded! She was just causing shit, but my lawyer had to answer each and every allegation. This drove up the billing of course and that was exactly her plan. Little did I realise then how much further she'd push this agenda to the extreme.

Twelve

The restraining order

A month after the separation in September, there was someone in a car hooting outside the driveway gate. I went outside and didn't recognize the car or the person.

"Hi, can I help you?" I said to the man behind the gate.

"I'm here to serve you papers. I am the sheriff of the court." he responded.

"What? What's this all about? I've already got my divorce documents."

"It's a restraining order."

He handed me the papers through the gate. I read a couple of paragraphs while the sheriff looked uneasily around him into the street.

"Do you mind if I come in?" his voice had an uneasy sense of urgency to it. "I need to tell you something."

"No, well maybe.... Actually...Never mind. Come in."

I opened the gate and I let him in. He turned out to be a very friendly guy and we started chatting. I sat him down at my kitchen table and offered him some coffee. I was rather perturbed, in fact freaked out, by this 'restraining order' and what it meant exactly.

He proceeded and said,

"I can see this is worrying you, and it's none of my business really, but I had a good look at these papers before I came here.

Believe me when I tell you that she has no substance in this application at all."

I looked at him with trepidation.

"In fact, she seems very odd to me. She's been phoning me all day as well and I just met up with her, down the road!"

Now I realised why he was nervously looking around when he stood outside in the driveway. She was probably still lurking in the shadows and stalking the sheriff behind some bush in the street. The sheriff continued,

"She's adamant, almost obsessed, to get these papers delivered to you, and she insisted to meet with me now so that she could show me the way to your house. She's very strange!"

No kidding about that statement! I however, was more concerned about restraining order at that point. I was well aware that she was doing strange things at the moment. That was not news to me.

"A restraining order was taken out for what though? I was never violent or abusive."

The Protection order application was nothing but a load of hogwash and fabrications. I had apparently

- abused her,

- threatened the kids,

- slammed her hand in the door.

If anyone were to believe the allegations contained therein, I was made out to be nothing short of a potential murderer out on the run. Her wording was cleverly twisting and concealing real truths on which she based her application. She was a sharp cookie. She was on a total smear campaign now. She was out to destroy me.

In reality, I am probably one of the most relaxed, laid back and totally non-violent personalities you'll ever come across and except for one occasion where I acted in selfdefense years and years earlier, I have never lifted a finger on anyone. It takes a helluva lot of provocation from someone to make me lose my temper. Personally, I rather walk away from a situation and cool off than lose my temper, with potentially dire consequences.

The sheriff consoled me.

"A lot of women in divorce situations try to pull these kinds of stunts, don't worry about it. They're just trying to get ahead of the game."

His kind words didn't convince me though! How can someone, that supposedly loved you, put you in a predicament like this? I was gob smacked. Knowing my innocence and the way she painted a picture of me in that affidavit, which was one huge lie under oath. I immediately scanned and sent the application off to Johan to review and respond on.

Now in South African Law, when a restraining order is granted, the applicant gets approval immediately for a warrant of arrest. In other words, if a person is really abused by another person, you are able to take out a restraining order and based on your word, the applicant gets granted an interim order by a magistrate instantaneously.

This interim order becomes effective the minute a law enforcement official such as a sheriff or a police officer has served the documents on the offending party. It is then considered an 'interim protection order' and stays in place until the court has heard the case on the date listed in the paperwork. On the court date itself, you will then have the chance to argue and defend your case whether this order gets made permanent or not.

Now based on her application and without any proof, evidence and physical violence present, I knew she was going to have a hard time getting this restraining order granted permanently. But you still worry and the anxiety and tension was very high for me. How could someone you had loved and cared for blatantly set you up like this? To me it was like being in a horror movie and it was totally surreal.

To ramp the bizarre situation up a notch, and to make matters more confusing, my cell phone bleeped that very same evening. An SMS from Jane:

> Hi, I know I've discussed this before, but I'd really like to start arranging our weekly dinner with the kids, so that they can see we're still a team as parents. Should we do dinner at my new house tomorrow?

WHAT THE ACTUAL FUCK? I had a wobbly all on my own. My return SMS was clear:

You have JUST taken out a restraining order on me and you invite me to dinner at your place? Are you out of your flipping mind?

The next morning another SMS arrived:

As you know Sean will be having his first birthday next week Sunday. I'll be having people over for a party. It would be really nice if you can come. Will you bring the cake?

Again it took me a while to pick up my jaw from the floor. This was delusionality at its utter best, but just like her request for me to go to a swingers club before, it was probably all part of a calculated set up to nail me.

Thirteen

Paedophile accusations

I had some serious questions that needed answering. With Jane being gone out of the house, I was somewhat more relaxed and not under her full flurry of demands and questions and orders. Although still on eggshells with her, I was starting to get clarity back in my head. The fog was lifting, so to speak. Being able to see my friends and family more frequently I started talking about my problems, which in turn made me realise what kind of relationship I had with Jane. Why did I fall into that hole, hook line and sinker? Granted, the kids (still babies actually) had me on my toes all the time as well, both during our relationship and after, but I was starting to see that Jane's 'oddities' were not just 'oddities', but rather a sign of some severe mental or emotional disease!

But what was she really suffering from and how could this be resolved? She was definitely mental, but what? Bipolar? Split personality? Psycho? Borderline? I wanted to know. I wanted clarity on this, because I couldn't understand her behaviour.

Of course it's easy to label people, especially when you are going through an acrimonious divorce. Your own emotions run so high after all. But emotions aside, it dawned on me that there was a serious flaw here with this woman. These red flags were something my friends and family had warned me about previously, but I chose to ignore them. Why did I do that? My standard usual answer to that at the time was:

"Come on, she's just being difficult and it'll pass". I protected her fully.

Apparently even for a psychologist with years and years of experience, to make a proper diagnosis on a person is hard, and I'm certainly not qualified to do that. I have a fascination for people's minds, their psychology and what makes humans tick, but I started intensifying my quest to find out what mental disease she had.

Googling for answers I found plenty of information online, but you have to be careful with what people say and what you read. There's a lot of hogwash and rubbish online. I generally found the psychology sites and medical sites most informative, but the peer-reviewed reports were difficult to read or comprehend.

Forums and blogs tend to have people blaming and venting about other 'mental cases' and 'psycho exes, partners and family"but that's not researched material; more like personal opinions and blaming. It's quite easy to label someone as a psycho when you're going through an emotional break up or divorce and that's what you read a lot. Emotional ventin However, armed with a bit more knowledge, my own research did start pointing to a 'diagnosis' on Jane. It really sounded like she was suffering from Borderline Personality Disorder, aka BPD or psychopathy. Within this group you have sub categories such as Narcissistic Personality Disorder, Histrionic Personality Disorder, Antisocial Personality Disorder and various others. These conditions can go hand in hand with Bipolar, Schizophrenia and a host of other possible combinations. This was all confusing to say the least. But it made some sense. She was confusing and she confused everything and everyone around her and if people didn't agree with her, she'll just eradicate them and 'smear' them out of her life. That explained why she had no real long term friendships.

My research continued over the next few months and I learned a lot about psychology in general. In the interim I was still seeing my own shrink on a weekly basis, but she'd never join in the discussion about Jane's diagnosis as I was in therapy for me and not for her! I must say, where my own therapy helped me is to keep a clear head, put up my own mirror and face myself and what I wanted in life. The fog of the relationship started clearing out of my head and I had a better overall picture of where I wanted to be and go in my life. There was so much to do in my own life still after this divorce, and I was rearing to go tackle life. I started to feel a bit like me again! But alas, Jane wouldn't have it.

Jane's onslaught, continued throughout September and August 2013. She launched a proper smear campaign this time around. The kids were with me three to four days/nights a week as agreed, and they loved staying over. I often took them to my parents' farm just outside of Johannesburg on the weekends. Out in nature and surrounded with animals, I kept positive and did a lot of nice stimulating things with them. Steven and I bonded strongly and he, at the age of nearly ten years was well aware of the ugliness of divorce. I never talked badly about mom in any way, but the topic of divorce did come up frequently. It's hard for kids to understand that mommy and daddy can't be together.

To make matters worse, he confided in me that mom told him bad things about me and also told him not to say anything about her, her household etc. I was aware of this and I never drove any conversation with him about the divorce unless he brought it up and needed answers. My sister bought a book for him called the 'suitcase kid'. A cute (but sad) story about a ten year old girl writing her memoirs about divorce and shifting from house to house and how that brought her down. In the end all became OK though. It was well written. Steven could totally relate to it as he felt in the same predicament as this character. Even though he knew how to read well, he always asked me to read it to him after I had put my other two babies in bed with their bedtime stories.

We'd snuggle up on the couch while I read to him. He loved the attention and absorbed my presence like a sponge in the desert, craving for water. We read that book night after the night. I felt horrible as an adult for what the kids had to endure and I so wished that it could be different.

Then one morning in August, I got a call from Steven's biological father in Yemen. I had established how Jane manipulatively cut Steven off from his own father for years and years. Since Jane had moved out, Steven and Michael were able to communicate freely whenever Steven was at my house.

They could use Skype, WhatsApp and phone calls. I promoted and facilitated the contact between father and son. Finally after so many years of missing out, they had a relationship going without any forms of blocking or alienation. Michael also appointed a lawyer to establish better contact with his son trying to block Jane from interfering. He needed to enforce his rights as a father and desperately wanted to do so.

That morning when his name popped up on my phone's screen, I answered.

"Hi Michael."

"Dude, you must see the email I just got from 'madam' he said. "You won't believe the allegations she's making. I'll send you a copy of it. You'll have to send it to your lawyer and let him read it."

Jane's email was forwarded to me. She was a brilliant writer, very skilled with words. In a 'highly concerned' and 'worried mother' sort of way she basically advised Michael that she will not allow Steven to sleep over at my house any more. Because of my past 'sexual history' and the fact that Steven had slept one night in my bed with me, she branded me a potential paedophile in that email.

This was beyond unreasonable! To me personally, paedophiles are the lowest of the lowest scum on earth and deserve every punishment and torture under the sun. A person who harms an innocent child in any way is to me the pits of the earth. I have very strong viewpoints on this.

I had known Steven since he was five years old and 'three quarters' (as he used to call it) and shared many nights with him during our marriage together, in our big king size bed, together with mom. It wasn't a regular occurrence, but it happened, especially when the boy was scared or had nightmares, he would often hop into bed with us, so it was nothing new.

Yes, he was now nine years old, but what had happened was that the very first weekend after Jane had stripped my house of her and most of my belongings, including Steven's mattress in his room (which was also mine) I made a temporary bed for Steven on the couch. In the first weekend's sleep over he had at my place, and being right in the middle of the breakup, moving houses, and arguing parents, he felt insecure and was scared that night to sleep on the couch alone and asked if he could sleep in my bed that evening. I didn't think anything of it, but my estranged ex had other plans and used the opportunity to try and drive a wedge between Michael and myself. It was a good enough trigger and perfect excuse for madam to send an extremely inflammatory and accusatory email to Michael. She obviously did not think that Michael would discuss this with me and thought she had the upper hand in the divorce proceedings this way.

At this point, unbeknownst to her, Michael and I had almost daily communication and yes, he was worried about the wellbeing of his son too. Michael had moved on in life a long time ago. He remarried and had two other kids with his new wife. He had already indicated to me that Steven was so much happier since I stepped into his life and hence he had eased the legal pressure off Jane, trying to get full custody of him, which was virtually impossible. The courts, would look at him as an absent father, overseas, not even resident in the jurisdiction of South Africa. Fat chance on him getting custody.

His main problem, however, was getting normal and occasional access to his boy. He was not allowed to see him during holidays, as all sorts of excuses were made. Calls were blocked, money sent for birthday presents was spent by his mother and not given to the child and maintenance went God-knows-where. All this money was going somewhere, but not to the household expenses, nor our marriage or the kids. I had been aware of this for a while. And I was also aware that she even used the kids ID's to open bank accounts and channel her own money through them. That information had all been passed onto the lawyers, especially since she tried to wreck me financially in her divorce papers. Well sorry honey, I'm not your mealticket!

Fourteen

An unexpected break

"Hi Mark, Jeremy here."

Jeremy was my 'modelling/talent/celeb management' agent. I used to, and still do some part-time television and advertising work as an actor. It was always fun to do and I was, even though part time, quite successful over the years.

TV work didn't pay much, but the adverts, if you landed them, paid well, considering the amount of 'work' you put in there. The hourly rate in fact is huge. I hadn't been booked for many jobs in the last couple of years, because a) I became a bit overexposed previously and b) life got busy and I didn't have time to run around to auditions all the time.

"Hey Jeremy" I answered, surprised at the call. "I haven't heard from you in a while.

What's up?"

"Ehhhm, lemme check.... Nope nothing yet. Its hanging short, shriveled and to the left. Yours?"

"Haha..." I responded. Jeremy was gay and always up for some sexually loaded remark or joke. He knew I could handle it.

"Listen, in all seriousness, can you please take some time off work and go to an audition for me?"

"Okay. What advert is this for?" I asked.

"It's not an advert. I've shown your photos and Z card to an international movie director and they'd really like to see you."

"Oh OK. Wow. When?"

"Now, if you can."

"Sorry dude, I'm at work and booked full of meetings today. Besides, the casting offices are close to my house, but it is an hour's drive from my work. Tell them to wait till after work, I'll gladly see them."

He did and although it's rather cheeky to request an international movie director to wait, especially if they called on you specifically, I went through at six pm that night. The Casting Company is literally two kilometres up the road from where I stayed, so I went straight after work.

Not expecting much to come of it, I did my audition. The casting agent and director seemed happy. I had very little insight as to what they wanted from me, and even less insight as to the role itself. As usual, I just left it at that, because if you think you did well, it sets you up for disappointment. Usually when you think you blew the audition, you get the role. My own protection was always to do the audition and forget about it. If it comes back, you'd be in for a nice surprise.

Two days later, the call came.

"Well done Mark, you got the part!"

"Oh nice, OK."

I still didn't know really what it was all about so I took in the information from my agent.

"Can you take a week's leave from work in the middle of September? You'll need to be on set for six days."

Cool. That sounded quite biggish!

"Yea sure," I replied.

I knew that I had plenty of leave built up at work and they probably wouldn't mind me taking it.

"And you also need to meet the production company, the international producer, wardrobe and make up guys in Norwood. I'll give you the address."

He gave me some more details and meeting times. It was an international movie apparently but I still had no clue what is was really about.

The production booklet was emailed to me two days after that.

Normally the dozens of people that are involved in the making of a movie are listed in this booklet. You'll find all the details and contact numbers from Director, producer, DOP, set builders, make up people, doctors on standby, insurance companies, transport people, chauffeurs, runners and you name it. Everyone involved in a production like this is listed with cell phone numbers and contact details and where you can find them. Weather forecast and location details and maps are also included.

I opened the booklet and on the first page was greeted with a full page photograph of myself with my name titled 'South African Lead Actor'.

I was shocked and phoned Jeremy at the agency.

"Jeremy, what is this? Lead actor South Africa? Did you see the booklet?"

"Yea," he said. "I'm so proud of you, you're making it on the big screen!"

"OK.. Wow." I was rather stunned about all this. Not only did I know very little about what they wanted from me, but also, reading the production booklet further, I was considered as a serious VIP on set.

Emails were flying in fast and furious. Private chauffeurs wanting to know my address for pick up. They needed identity numbers for my flight into the bush and insurances taken out on me. Everyone else from Johannesburg was driving, but no, I had to fly in with the producers and directors onto the set. An instant VIP I was indeed. It was all a bit surreal.

After my flight I arrived late afternoon at the lodge where all the crew were staying. The director immediately introduced me to a security company, specializing in guns, as well as an armourer, who was responsible for not only providing the guns on set, but also for everyone's safety.

They whipped me out to a remote area in the bush and I had to learn to shoot a specific rifle which is used in hunting elephants. It was called something like a Nitro Express 500. All I knew at this point, that was that I was a hunter and a father in the movie and I was going to shoot an elephant. Not for real of course, but I had to know how one of those guns feels, so that it looks realistic on screen.

The armourer was used to working with people on set, but the local security guys weren't. Phalaborwa is a tiny town in the east of the country near the Kruger Park, and probably the most exciting thing that happens there is when someone's cat goes missing.

So the local security company that was hired to train me, consisted of two big guys who, knew everything about guns and combat. They were real macho rednecks with cut off shirt sleeves showing bulging muscles that were pumped up to the maximum on a daily basis. They sounded like retired missionaries with many overblown stories to match. On set, their only task was to take me, the armourer and director's assistant to a local shooting range, for me to practice shooting with real elephant hunting rifles in order for me to make this look realistic on screen.

They met us outside the reception area of the lodge and were impatient to show us what they had brought.

Oh my God. Their pickup truck was an armed storage room on wheels, packed with hand guns, rifles and machine guns. They had also brought the necessary ammo to match. It was literally packed to the brim. You could probably take out an Al-Qaida cell single handedly with this set up! They had obviously heard that they had to work with an international movie crew and they wanted to make a lasting impression.

The armourer acknowledged some nice guns they had brought, but we had a job to do. Off we went to the shooting range for practice.

The 'shooting range' was really just an empty field with a derelict building on it and a couple of sparsely leaved bushes. The armourer from set picked up his guns and started preparing. One of the rednecks shoved a handgun in my hands and asked the producer if I could shoot a couple of rounds. They nodded from a distance.

"Shoot into the building over there sir". I did.

BANG

"Good," he said, "empty the cartridge."

BANG

BANG

BANG

BANG

I popped another seven bullets into the building in rapid succession.

"Wow, he said. You're good. I like your style."

This guy was a bit creepy and totally in awe of me. He came towards me to get his gun back and patted me on the back.

"Well this is how we roll here! Welcome to South Africa." A big grin exposed a row of brown and neglected teeth. He was very chuffed with himself.

"When did you arrive?" he asked.

"This afternoon," I responded.

"Oh wow, and you're not yet lagged at all?"

He was aware that I was the lead actor on set, and obviously had the impression that I was some hot shot actor that just flew in from Hollywood.

"Sorry to disappoint you, but I'm from Johannesburg." I replied, ensuring I laid on my South African accent extra thick.

I could see him shrink down. Clearly he was hugely disappointed. Maybe he was under the impression I was the next George Clooney or something.

When the armourer came out with the Elephant hunting gun, it was another story all together. I wasn't familiar with guns much, as I never owned any, nor shot any guns before either. The armourer gave me a full safety briefing on how to handle this piece of equipment. I can't recall what the gun was called, but it contained some serious bullets the thickness of an adult man's thumb and the length of a middle finger.

Firing those bullets into that same building I just shot with the handgun, was a different story all together. The kickback on launching those projectiles throws your whole body out, even when you're leaning into the gun. I was told that if you hold the butt of the gun away from your shoulder, the recoil is so great, that it can easily break your collar bone. I could believe it! Wow, I'd never experienced power like this before and I must admit, it did get my adrenalin pumping. In some weird way, I could 'relate' to the power on a macho kinda level. It was a full on testosterone kick.

The movie shoot and the days that followed were great. Long hours, I must admit, but the set was abuzz with energy and everything revolved around the director, the camera and the three South African actors of which I had the lead role.

Night times were spent at the lodge and everyone joined for these huge dinners and parties, followed the next morning at five am with rather heavy heads and tired bodies. I got to know the American director and Producer more over the next few days. They revealed more about the plot itself, of which the South African co-production was a portion of the film that goes into flashbacks of an earlier time. The rest of the film was to be shot in Canada and Cuba.

One evening, sitting chatting to Craig, the Director, he revealed who my co-actors internationally were going to be. Holy crap. These were huge and well known household names, which I will refrain from mentioning here for the sake of anonymity.

This was a mega big production with a rather hefty budget. Not bad for a part time unknown local actor landing a role like this.

I arrived home a week later, well rested from my well-paid break in the African bush. Even though it was considered 'work', I was glad to have been away from my negative environment for a while. A paid for holiday and a well deserved break.

But the movie of my own life wasn't over yet and a particularly dramatic scene was about to unfold.

Fifteen

My first trial

The court case for the protection order was initially set for trial in October 2013, but then, as with most court cases, postponed to November. Even though confident, I was still nervous. I'd never really been to court before, let alone a trial. I didn't like the fact that she had an interim granted.

When the day arrived, Jane was there with her lawyer. She looked totally confident and had an attitude to match. She and her legal representative were paging through files and papers on the benches outside court room thirteen waiting to be called in. Court thirteen would become my 'most frequented' court over the next eighteen months.

The domestic violence court is not open to the public and each case gets handled behind closed doors. When it's your turn, you get called in. After an hour of waiting, our matter was called and the magistrate agreed to go on trial that afternoon after all the other matters were postponed and heard. We were in for a long day.

It was fascinating to see the lawyers present their cases in court. Very quickly it was established that based on her founding affidavit, half of the matter she presented could not be admitted and did not fall under domestic violence. Various other paragraphs had absolutely no relevance and some other items were simply not under dispute.

Our marriage had obviously broken down irretrievably and yes, there were arguments. But the crux of the matter remained, why did she take out a restraining order? Allegations galore, but no proof!

The magistrate decided to call us each into the dock for cross examination. Jane went first under cross fire from Johan, my lawyer. She walked up, with her arrogant and sure footed way, as if to say 'I'm here to prove my demise.' Her act alternated between 'I feel so sorry for myself' (victim) to 'Mark is the biggest arsehole alive' (aggressor). But all her acting didn't help. Quite soon, because she had so many lies going at all times, she worked herself into a corner and Johan relentlessly beat her at her own game. Most of the questions presented to her remained unanswered, side tracked or twisted. It was all smoke and mirrors. In the end the magistrate herself got involved.

"Madam, you're not answering the questions—all we need is a yes or a no from you".

A simple yes or no proved to be extremely difficult for her. So much so that when she really couldn't answer any more, she'd go on the blame game, blaming others.

After Johan worked her nicely into a corner, he asked her:

"So then why did you take out a restraining order on Mr le Foncé?"

She lifted her hand and pointed at her own legal representative.

"He told me to do it."

The poor guy didn't know what to say or do and shrunk deeper and deeper into his chair.

After nearly three hours of cross examination, she was released from the dock. In all this time she remained with a steely cold look on her face and exited the dock as cool as a cucumber.

Now it was my turn! The expensive law firm she had hired didn't send the partner, but a junior guy instead. He seemed friendly enough and tried some chit chat with me in the passage earlier on that day, but I was wary of him. You never know what they're fishing for. So I kept away from him earlier on in the day. The lawyers and courts are one big psychological game. Especially if it's your rival lawyer.

The junior guy looked like he had just come out of university. He wore a very expensive Armani suit and donned a pair of very expensive glasses to make him look more heavy-weight. I got into the dock and three bundles, A, B and C were presented to me. He stood up and cleared his throat.

Silence.

He began paging through a pile of papers in front of him.

"Ehhhhmmmm..."

More silence.

"Mmmmmmhhhh..."

Besides him shuffling through more papers, you could hear a pin drop. Tension was building.

"Ehhhmmmm..."

I exchanged a glance with the magistrate. She was leaning her head on her hand supported by her elbow on the bench patiently awaiting for the show to start. I slowly raised my one eyebrow.

The paper shuffling went on for a couple of minutes.

Johan, clearly impatient started tapping his pen nervously on the desk. The magistrate shifted position in her chair. You could cut the anticipation in the air with a knife.

Ahh, hooray! Finally a sentence came out.

"Ehhhhhmmmm...eeeeehhmm..." he continued.

"If we can have a look at paragraph twenty one where you say that the applicant..."

"Sorry. Just hold a second, excuse me for interrupting," I said.

"Which annexure are we looking at?"

I needed to know which affidavit was being looked at so that I could also read it.

Totally confused, he frantically started paging again through the pile of documents.

"Ehhhhmmm.... Annex B."

Ah, I got it. Annex B, paragraph twenty one. Johan and the magistrate also had their papers open.

The junior continued: "Would you agree that using the 'F-word' constitutes Domestic Violence?"

"Sorry again for interrupting, but Annex B, para twenty one has nothing to do with that. Which paragraph are you looking at? Where are you looking?"

Further frantic paging for a minute. The magistrate buried her head in her hands and Johan was shaking his head. We all waited for the next sentence to come out.

"Eeeeeehhhhhmmm.... Ok sorry its paragraph thirty two."
We all found it now.

I asked him. "Where does it say that I used the 'F-word'?"

"Eeeehhmmm... well... w-w-w-would you agree that is constitutes Domestic Violence?" The poor guy started stuttering.

I looked at the magistrate desperately. By now I was about ten minutes in the dock and not one question had been asked of me.

"Your Worship," I started.

"Would you mind if I gave the court my version of that particular incident".

She agreed wholeheartedly with an enthusiastic nod to match.

I let loose.

"That morning, we had an argument because my wife vindictively woke up my two year old baby to get emotionally vindictive at me and in order to provoke a reaction."

I relived the moment of the infamous morning in question and could feel the tension, anger and emotions welling up inside of me.

'Calm down Mark'—a little voice in my head whispered. I had to remind myself not to become too emotional. Keep it clear and concise. It was difficult. I also had to be careful not to go into a full onslaught and blame game, but in my own way I explained what had happened and how angry I was with Jane that morning. She had set me up to be angry by being ugly to Julia, in the hope that I would retaliate and hit her or something. Jane was the type that would cut herself with a knife and blame me for it. In this instance she used (abused) our two year old daughter to get at me. I was really livid with her that morning, but never laid a hand on her. I just protected my daughter from the wrath of her own mom.

I do remember swearing something at her and slammed the door. She pretended that I slammed it on her hand, but also that was not true. I truly can't remember if I used the 'F-word', but chances were high. I don't generally use that word and especially not in front of the kids. It's not something I use or would teach my kids. So after five minutes of explanation, in the end I told the court:

"So chances are that I might have used that word in anger, but at that moment I had other things to worry about than my choice of properly selected words. Does that make sense?"

The courtroom was quiet. Again, you could hear a pin drop. I took a deep breath. I looked the junior lawyer straight in the eyes. He looked back at me a tad bewildered:

"Any further questions." I asked him.

It was the first time he started a sentence without the famous 'Eeeehhhm' and the answer was swift and clear.

"No."

"Thank you Mr Le Foncé" the magistrate said "You may step down".

The magistrate told us the judgment would be delivered in two days time, and we ordered to come back again for this. It was after four o'clock in the afternoon already. It had been a long and tiring day in court!

I stepped out of the court room and Johan grabbed me.

"You were phenomenal in the stand!"

"Oh really?" I said dryly.

"What makes you say that?"

"Because you were emotional, as humans are, but you drove the message home loud and clear and without hesitation"

"Quite frankly, I don't remember much of what I said in that box. All I know is that I was on the stand for about fifteen minutes".

"Well fifteen minutes is better than her three hour grilling!"

That was very true. But again she didn't have a case. Two days later the magistrate ruled and set the restraining order down. There simply wasn't any conduct on my side to warrant a restraining order. Plus the fact that she had tried to take out another one two months earlier, behind my back and did not succeed, did not gel with the magistrate. Jane walked out of the courtroom as if she'd won the case. She held her head up high, smiling as if nothing had happened and with a confident stride, she exited the court building. I was floored with her attitude. Things like this run like water off a duck's back with her. From that moment I decided on a new nickname for her:

The 'Teflon Queen'.

Sixteen

Manipulating the children

The communication with Michael in Yemen, became more and more frequent. Not only with him, but his wife Fleur too. Often we had Skype conversations and chatted almost daily on Whatsapp.

Calling each other overseas was not economical, but sometimes necessary to keep each other informed of the bizarre happenings. The topics were mainly about the kids and how they were coping, as well as Jane's sneaky ways and legal dramas and demands.

Out of all the kids Steven was suffering the most. He was the oldest in the mix and was well aware what was going on. His mom's pure manipulation and storytelling, as well as badmouthing me, had a grave psychological and emotional impact on him. The poor boy would sometimes come up with stories, without me asking him, telling me things like

"When I'm with mom in the car, she calls you bad names."

"I know and I'm well aware of that. Just try to ignore it."

"But she lies and I don't like it."

I never pressured him to talk as I think that's unfair on a child, especially talking about the divorce or slagging off the other parent. But hey, what could I do? That's just the way she operated and I'd just ask him how he felt when 'mom was calling me names'. His response was that he would not listen to that and that he'd keep quiet.

I was worried about him though and I could see from his behaviour, that he was becoming more quiet and withdrawn. He was shutting down communication and becoming introverted. Severe damage was being done to his mental and emotional wellbeing.

His birthday came around at the end of November and the 'huge' birthday party that mom had promised him for months already was cancelled at the last minute—on the day itself. She had told him that apparently people couldn't make it. Meanwhile she had not arranged anything for him. Just empty promises.

She had organized something though for him. She had booked a table for breakfast at Spur family restaurant. Just him, mom, Julia and Sean. You can just imagine the disappointment in this boy's mind not having his friends there, but he took it in his stride and told me bravely that it was okay.

Michael, not trusting Jane with money, sent me some cash to buy him a big Lego set that he and Steven had discussed previously on Skype. I went, prior to his birthday, to several toy shops, but none of them had that particular set in stock. Eventually I found a store that could order it and they delivered the Lego to me in time via courier for his birthday.

Steven was overjoyed with the present and spent hours playing with his Lego in his still rather empty bedroom, since Jane moved out of my house. I sent pictures and videos of him playing with his present to Michael and Fleur. Steven did in fact now realise that genuine people really cared for and loved him, but he wasn't allowed to express it.

The weekend after his birthday, as it was my weekend with the kids, I planned to go to the family farm as usual. I arranged with my mom to do something special for him after the actual birthday weekend's disappointment. I still didn't know what had exactly transpired the weekend before, because I wasn't there, but I still felt terribly sad on Steven's behalf.

Did Jane just not care about Steven's emotions? Was she financially unable to arrange something? Regardless of the reason, it was just not on. I told Steven I had arranged another party for him at the farm and he was looking forward to it.

His birthday party at the farm was a huge success. Steven always enjoyed going to the farm and being outdoors. He could really live out his boyhood there and we'd go on walks, hikes, fishing and build dams in the river. He was also close to my parents and sisters and my nephews and nieces.

It gave him a sense of family and when I took pictures at any family gathering, he'd always be first in line to pose for the photos. He had a sense of belonging, which he never had with his mom and grandparents. What made matters bad though, was that whenever he came home to his mom with stories of the nice things he'd done, she'd manage to put a damper on these things and she referred to the farm and my family as the 'enemy territory'. She was intentionally breaking him down and trying to alienate him from me. Jane meanwhile would inform Michael via mail stating things like:

Steven doesn't want to stay at Mark's place any more.

She also loved to use phrases from court like—'in the best interest of the child' and 'minor children'. Steven was being brainwashed and didn't really have a choice. He had to listen to his mom. Even though he thought differently about wanting to come and stay at my house. I could see he was suffering under the pressure. She started to keep him away from me more and more frequently. She always used the same excuse of 'he doesn't want to be with you' which I knew was absolute nonsense.

Steven still came around on some weekends though, but that started to fade. He'd remark:

"I can't stay at your place during the week anymore because it is easier for mom to drop me off straight at school without having to pass this house in the morning."

It was absolute crap of course, because his mom literally had to drive past my house every morning on the way to work in any case. She also coaxed him into believing that he needed to take a break from Sean and Julia, as they were so small and irritating. He was being manipulated beyond belief, but yet the bond between me and him remained strong, despite the nonsense and bullshit stories his mom would foist onto everyone.

Of course Jane wouldn't keep him from me at all times, because at the same time, as much as she branded me a brute and an arschole, it was also convenient for her to have me as babysitter when she needed to go out. She knew full well that the kids were actually better off and more calm with me. Despite that, her behaviour became weirder and weirder.

The one minute she was fine, the next minute she'd provoke an argument or strike up a conversation just to piss me off or irritate me. She also started stalking and stealing my post out of the postbox outside the house.

I was not allowed to use 'her' nanny/domestic worker anymore either as she had signed that exclusive contract behind my back.

Through a referral of the crèche, I obtained my own nanny. Not very cost effective, but hey, what can you do. A couple of weeks after I employed Sophie to help me out, she was approached by Jane at my gate (while I was at work) and offered her a position and said:

"You mustn't work here and you need to come and work for this other lady I know".

Sophie told me this and I even got a call from Julia's school teacher who referred Sophie to me. Agnes, the teacher told me that Jane was desperately asking for Sophie's number as she had a better job offer for her. Agnes, knowing what was going on refused to supply her with that information. Again I was livid! Sneaking behind my back and causing shit when I wasn't around. Another attempt at making life hell for me and destroying my path. I was back walking on eggshells again even though we were separated.

While she was constantly on the attack, I was constantly on the defense. Another letter to the lawyer. It all started getting very costly! This was not at all what I had in mind! I thought divorces were pretty straight forward, but clearly not with her.

Seventeen

You're fired!

My work and job were starting to suffer tremendously. I couldn't focus, except for defending myself against Jane's onslaught. She kept me on my toes and it became obsessive. By now I was now recording everything she said to me. I kept files and files with notes and a diary of exact times when the kids were with me and when not. Her lawyer's letters were piling up and the onslaught and blame game over the silliest things were order of the day.

Not only did I lose focus at work, I had to leave early because, God forbid you were five minutes late in the traffic and you picked up the kids late. The SMS's would come pouring in at five pm exactly.

"What kind of father are you, picking up the kids so late? You can't even be on time for them."

Ironically the reverse was true too. If I arrived early for pick-up she either made me wait outside the door or she'd be barraging me with SMS's again from inside the house.

"Your pick up time is five pm and not four fifty fife. You are denying me my right as a mother to spend time with my kids."

There was just no winning and it was wearing me thin.

I was damned if I did, and damned if I didn't. My mind became more and more of a fog. I couldn't think clearly any more. I was walking on eggshells—no landmines actually! I was worrying constantly. Steven's visitation became more and more erratic, as and when she felt the need. He obviously talked too

84

much to me and she didn't want me to know certain things. The control freak was in full swing!

Then one fine morning, in the middle of October, when dropping the kids off with the nanny at her house, she surprised me by being home.

She confronted me in the driveway. Normally she would have left for work already at that time and the nanny would take in the kids, but not this morning. Instead Jane stormed out, shoved the kids inside through the door into Mavis' welcoming arms and confronted me with a pile of papers. All I could see was the cover sheet. It read the following:

URGENT FASCIMILE

Atn:—Rachel Michaelson

Human Resources Dept.

BELLS INC.

Dear Rachel

Please find attached documents pertaining to your employee Mark le Foncé. Kindly treat as confidential.

"What now Jane?"

I sighed, shrugging off another threat, but admittedly I was a bit unnerved.

She rattled the papers between her thumb and forefinger as if it were a playing card deck. The pages flipped though quickly and I couldn't make out what it was.

"You should know what is in here!"

Her tone of voice was evil and sarcastic. Her eyes had an evil, yet satisfied look to them. She continued,

"And I would worry if I were you! I don't think your company will take moonlighting and conflict of interest lightly".

"What the heck are you talking about? Agh. . . . Never mind."

I turned around, walked to the car and drove off.

"Worry my boy. . . worry. . . " she shouted after me.

What was she up to now? Then I realised.

Before I started with the company under full employee status, I had my own business and was making money here and there on bits and pieces. I had files that were still open and pending until the client was ready to proceed. On employment a year and half earlier, I had discussed these files with management, as their request was for me not to carry on doing business on the side. I told them at the time that I still had these two jobs pending and that I'd have to wrap them up whilst under their employ. I had fully declared it and was open and honest about it with them.

I sent her an SMS:

Jane, stop threatening me with your bullshit.

It's not bullshit. Your employer won't like it either.

Later that morning I went up to the HR department and discussed the issue. I was so used to Jane accusing me all over the place, that I explained it to Rachel, the HR lady.

"Not to worry, she said, if I receive any fax, I'll just put it in an envelope and give it to you. I won't even read it."

Well that was a weight off my shoulders. Although I do have to add, that my performance was adversely affected by this divorce with the mind-games. I'm already not a corporate type of person to start off with, but my work was now suffering. I had previously discussed my situation with the HR director, Nelson and he was supportive and caring. I'd even gone so far as to discuss Jane's psychological profile with him a couple of months earlier, as I knew he was a fully qualified psychologist himself and worked in the army before. He was well aware.

Jane was eerily quiet for the days that followed, but as the days dragged on, I realised the documents she displayed in the driveway were just another idle threat which she wouldn't push through.

However two weeks later, I received an email from Nelson.

Dear Mark,

Can you please come to my office at 10:00 this morning. Alice and I need to talk to you. Please confirm if you can make it.

Regards

Nelson

Shit! What was this? Instantaneously I thought about Jane's threat two weeks earlier. Would she really have sent that email with nonsense again? What did that letter contain? No, they probably just want to talk to me about my performance or something. The two hours that followed were a tense debate in my mind.

At ten am I knocked on his door. Alice, my executive boss, was already sitting in his office with the door closed. They had a serious look on their faces. They clearly had had discussions already.

"Hey Mark, sit down." Nelson started with an uncomfortable and fake smile.

Alice greeted me in similar fashion with a worried look on her face. She wasn't her usual self. I tried to force a smile, but my mind was filled with scenarios. What was happening? I feared the worst.

Nelson continued.

"We're well aware of the difficulties you've been facing over the last couple of months. I know you've discussed with me the challenges of your divorce and so on. You just have to understand, and you are also well aware of the fact, that your performance is not what we're expecting from you. We know you have a lot on your plate at the moment and with the divorce proceedings, I'm sure you don't want any more blood on the carpet..."

His speech continued for a while. I couldn't absorb much of it. It was way too buttered up and flowery for my liking and my premonition was confirmed. The words finally came out

"...and therefore we believe that we should part ways. We are willing to pay you a severance package and will assist with ..."

For the first time since the divorce had started, I cracked. My mind became overwhelmed with emotions. I couldn't help but think of my babies at home, the seriousness of this situation and I, yes, I actually now really felt sorry for myself. I was always keeping my smiley face for everyone, but no one, and I mean NO ONE had an inkling of what I was really going through emotionally and mentally on a daily basis.

At that exact moment emotions got the better of me, tears started welling up and after one pathetically failed attempt at trying to suppress those, I cried and let go right there in that office.

Loudly, openly, and in front of my boss and the HR director I wailed away. I couldn't care less anymore. I didn't give a shit. I think it shocked them too, because Alice got up, rubbed and patted me on the back shedding her own tears before walking out of the office. I knew she liked me regardless of all the troubles happening. Nelson, in the interim, continued with his smoothly buttered words telling me that I'll be on my feet in no time, my future was bright and I was a strong person. I wasn't listening any more, too preoccupied with my own emotions.

It took a while before I could compose myself. I sat in silence staring Nelson straight in the face. Alice had already left the office, probably having a good cry in the toilet herself. I'm sure they could feel the pain too, but were obviously under instruction from higher powers. Financially the company hadn't been doing well that year either and they were looking to reduce costs and get people out.

"Look" he said,

"Go home and think about it and I'll see you on Wednesday at two o'clock, okay?".

In my mind I answered: 'Go home and think about what exactly?' The most terrible swear words wanted to come hurling out, but I kept my cool. I also realised I hadn't heard half of his proposal as I was too busy wallowing in my own self-pity. But it felt good to let go for once and I didn't care who saw or heard it. I just nodded. I got up from the chair, about to walk out of the door, but before I exited I turned around.

"You got a fax from my wife, didn't you?" I asked.

He nodded.

"Yes, but you got to realise that. . . . . . ."

"Realise what?" I interrupted him abruptly and continued. I was angry now.

"I will take your severance package under one condition. I get that full fax she sent you, with the time and date it was received and a confirmation report."

At that point I didn't even know what the severance package was going to be, but I did know that that fax was crucial. I needed to know what was said in it and I knew I needed it for my court case. The psycho was in full swing causing destruction and mayhem. She was instrumental in me losing my job.

I had two days to mull things over, so I contacted Johan, my lawyer, who I had on speed dial by now. We discussed the matter at length and what kind of package I should accept and what not. The company had no good reason to let me go as I had never had any warnings. I just didn't feel like taking on another fight with ex employers, CCMA, lawyers and the works. I had enough on my plate.

Wednesday came, and I signed the severance deal. At the time it came as a welcome break actually. Knowing myself, having run my own businesses before, this was actually the break I needed. I cashed in my pension fund, took the package, paid off the legal debts and I could hopefully move on.

I planned to work from home, as I had done before, look after the kids myself and was confident things would work out.

Eighteen

Picking up the pieces

With some cash in my pocket, I actually felt quite free. I needed the time to fight the case with Jane which was starting to become obsessively ridiculous and outright dangerous. I also needed the time to focus on the kids and made sure they were OK and looked after. I didn't believe much in outsourcing to nanny's and letting other people bring up your children. Although they were gems in their own right, I preferred to be more involved as a parent myself.

My days were now mine again and not hogged by eight hours of work plus an additional two and a half hours of commuting. I also had some trouble with my car and the cash that was coming in would sort out that major repair it urgently needed.

I kept quiet about the retrenchment to Jane. Our communication had already deteriorated so much. I didn't want her to know anything about my life anymore and I wanted and needed to move on, without her interference and control. Every move I made she tried to destroy. In December, about two weeks after I'd left the company, she attempted to communicate with me via my work email address.

She was advised by one of the managers monitoring my emails that I didn't work there any longer. The same day she put up a post on Facebook:

> Oh the Karma bus wheels have come off for some. Shame lol.

I mean really! How vindictive can you get? I sent a screenshot of that to Johan, for his file which was getting really thick by now. I just couldn't understand how a normal and supposedly sane person could react this way and do and say such things. I was becoming pretty immune to these kind of malicious statements and public announcements, I just took it in my stride. Reacting or lashing out at her was just going to fuel the fire even more. And I had also cottoned on that she wanted me to react. She wanted my attention for some reason. Good or bad. She was obsessed.

At that stage I didn't have her on my Facebook anymore but she had worked her way nicely into my family and contacts over the years. Roughly eighty percent of her Facebook 'friends' were actually contacts, friends and family of mine. Supportive as they were I would get regular updates on the stuff she posted, as I was blocked from viewing her profile.

Just like in real life, she liked to have an 'audience' online that would give her attention, but in reality she had no real friends or meaningful relationships with people. I learned from my psychological internet 'research' that this is a typical trait of narcissistic people.

I got a renewed zest for life and business and I was feeling good. The work incident gave me the kick up the butt I needed to start my own business again.

Within days of retrenchment I was creating websites, marketing materials, business cards and business plans. I had it going again. There was no business yet, but I knew that was going to come in. I started with my own company again under a new name and I knew I was going to be fine for the time being. I had the cash to carry me for a month or three, settled some old debts, got my car back on the road and life was looking up. I believed the universe would provide me with what I needed! With that positive outlook I carried on.

Jane's nonsense of course continued, but I tried not to react or take too much notice. As long as I was fine and more importantly that the kids were fine, things would be OK. It was just a long haul before we could wrap this whole divorce up.

Michael in the interim, had also employed a lawyer and was requesting decent access rights, communication and holidays with his son. The lawyer he'd employed was a good, albeit expensive guy. Because our case with the kids was so interlinked, we felt it important to run these cases concurrently. Michael was aware that not only was the relationship between him and Steven manipulated, but that Jane was now also sabotaging the relationship between me and Steven. As I was a strong emotional pillar for Steven, his father felt very strongly about me staying partially in his life, offering support where I could.

As I was much closer to Steven (in a geographical and even emotional sense) than him, he asked if I was prepared to take Steven on, at least temporarily, should he get the custody. Steven had built a bond with his father after all these years through me, and now of course, when Jane found out, she did her utmost to try and sabotage that relationship from happening at all costs. It didn't prevent Steven and Michael from talking regularly through the Skype platform while Steven was still at my house.

Julia and Sean were fine at that stage. Being so young and unaware, most of the drama didn't affect them and they were just being healthy, bouncy babies and toddlers full of energy and laughs. I enjoyed my home time with them and felt that I could offer them more security and healthy support in this way. I was now really a single father doing the nappy and milk bottle duties, and I loved it.

Nineteen

Rules, rulings and a Rule 43

In the interim, Jane had another plan to damage me further. She and her lawyer went the dirty route and she pulled out a Rule 43 application. Now let me try to explain, in layman's terms, what that means.

Take the following scenario: A woman is married to a well off guy for fifteen years. She has a couple of kids with him and they decide to get divorced. He chucks her and the kids out on the street as the situation becomes very acrimonious and ugly between them. She hasn't had a job in fifteen years, now has the kids to look after and has always relied on her husband for support. No roof over her head, her credit cards cancelled by him, no assets split up yet and no money for legal fees, it becomes pretty tough for her. What is she to do? An average divorce takes eighteen months to resolve. An opposed divorce longer. How is she going to live during that period? This might be an extreme example above, but people get ugly and vindictive, so this kind of stuff does happen. Regularly!

Should something like this happen, the 'suffering' party can get an interim order from the high court. It's called a Rule 43. Legally it works like this. You prepare a founding affidavit and explain the situation in a concise and precise format. The woman above for instance can claim, she had a monthly allowance in the household of ten thousand Rand, she used to have a car (which he's now taken away from her), she and the kids had a roof over her head, so she can claim rental now, and can also apply for legal fee assistance. She can also mention that she will look after the kids, the kids will reside with her under her care and her husband can see them every second weekend etc. (Or something to that extent—remember this is all just an example).

The husband gets served this document after it's filed in the high court and he has two weeks to respond. Either he agrees, and it's made an interim court order until the divorce is settled, or he can file a counter affidavit claiming that she's out of her mind and she wants way too much. Or he wants the kids living by him and so on.

You have one shot at this.

One founding affidavit and one responding affidavit. A court order is quickly made by the judge, in rare cases with some arguments in court itself. Let's say on the above claim the judge rules in favour of the woman, and she gets granted the order, gets the kids for now and the maintenance and the car to use and the lump sum for legal fees. At least she can keep her head above water until the divorce is finalised.

HOWEVER! And I say this in big letters. Generally speaking women (and sorry, I'm not being sexist here) rip the ring out of this rule and their unscrupulous lawyers have a tendency to castrate their estranged husbands in one foul swoop!

Because these kind of orders are usually not verified properly, the applicant party (again usually the women) often blow figures out of proportion so that they can benefit to the maximum on a financial level. If you are ever exposed to these, get yourself a lawyer immediately, otherwise you have a good chance of ending up in deep shit. Don't even attempt to try and answer this affidavit on your own, unless you're a lawyer yourself.

Don't waste time, this could cripple you for life as it sets the stage and status quo for the final divorce.

To continue, this happened to me and I got one of these Rule 43s served on me.

Needless to say, she claimed ridiculous amounts of maintenance for the kids and herself. More than I was even earning—previously that is! It has to be noted though that in our situation:
She was not entitled to maintenance for herself.
She was working and earning pretty much the same as me at that

stage.

The kids were shared on a 50/50 basis so she had no claim there either.

She also claimed a 'relocation' fee of around R300,000. Excuse my French but what the fuck! She moved out of my house on her own accord with most of my furniture. Not only that, but she only moved about four hundred metres away. Knowing what I know now, that was purely for stalking purposes to try and control me. According to her stories, she claimed I didn't 'allow' her to move out of the suburb.

To milk the situation even further she wanted a lump sum of money out of me to cover her legal expenses.

It was a gross misrepresentation of facts and a deliberate attempt to really cripple me financially and kick me in the nuts in the process.

It was a lengthy affidavit and not only did she claim maintenance for our kids, she also included Steven, whom I loved and cared for, even though he was not my responsibility.

Besides I knew she was already getting good money from Michael on a monthly basis. She wanted her bread buttered on both sides.

Johan had sent the documents off to Michael's lawyer, as both Michael and Steven were now implicated in her document and under oath. He jumped straight onto the bandwagon and attacked Jane as well as her expensive lawyer, Mike Vermont, in a letter intervening in this action.

He advised Mike Vermont, the lawyer, that he'd take personal action against him and his firm with an urgent high court application for being an accomplice in misleading the facts and committing perjury in court. Within two hours of that letter going out, the Rule 43 was completely and officially withdrawn, by the lawyers. Fantastic for me, because I didn't even have to respond to a shitty and fully fabricated affidavit. Not so fantastic for Jane, because the rules of a Rule 43 are, that you only have one chance! Once you've blown it, you cannot go back to court and apply for another one! Now she had to sit it out until the divorce date. Ouch...that plan didn't work!

So remember. A Rule 43 is there to protect kids, finances and issues that are real! It's not a tool to try and rip the other party off, which very often happens. What you also need to understand is that once the Rule 43 is issued, it weighs down very heavily in the outcome of your final divorce and can and will affect the rest of your life! I cannot stress this enough.

The Rule 43 and the so called Domestic Violence were taken on simultaneously to create chaos in my camp. And honestly speaking, if it wasn't for my own lawyer Johan protecting me professionally, my outcomes could have, and probably would have been very different and far from desirable. I had never dealt with legal things in my life before. But thinking and knowing you're innocent, as was the case with me, proving that fact in a court setting can be far more challenging.

Twenty

Legally Quiet Christmas Holidays

Things went relatively quiet after that for a while. The lawyers letters stopped flying in, the kids' routines were not tampered with. I wasn't being harassed as much.

But I did start receiving love letters from her.

Well not exactly love letters, but more cries for attention. Jane told me, she was supposedly writing a book about us and from time to time I'd get a passage of 'writing' via SMS. These were supposedly sent to me 'by mistake'. They were all soppy paragraphs and weirdly written pieces of writing in an overtly bizarre poetic manner. They were long SMS's and even an email with an entire chapter. And every time it was the same excuse.

> Sorry, it wasn't meant for you. This was supposed to go to my editor. Sent to the wrong Mark.

The content was really strange stuff about horses and wild stallions. About me and my sagging skin. About me not having my youthful radiance any more. About the fire in my eyes that was gone. It made absolutely no sense to me.

What I did know was that it was a direct stab at me and aimed to hurt me psychologically and emotionally.

For a couple of weeks these bizarre SMS's and emails carried on but I never responded, and as usual it would be followed up with another SMS stating:

Oh sorry, that was meant for my editor.

What planet was she living on? I was getting gravely worried about her mind. The less I responded, the better it was for me. The attention seeking behavior went up and down. A month or two earlier I received one hundred and sixty four SMS's in a single night, and she obviously wanted to drive a conversation which I tried, as much as possible to ignore. But she needed my attention.

She had the kids with her that night and at one point I told her that she'd been SMSing me non-stop for over five hours that afternoon and evening. So I asked

How can you look after the kids properly while you're so busy typing SMS's?

Just that SMS from me was enough to start up an entire barrage of further SMS's, in defense of her mothering capabilities.

Early December she was still working while I was technically unemployed. The kids were already on school holidays and during the day, they were looked after by Mavis, whom they called *Gogo*. Mavis was a wonderful woman, and I really trusted her with the kids. The kids loved her and she loved them back. She was really key in that household, and on a daily basis I had contact with her. She'd update me on things like snotty noses, bumps, lumps and general children's stuff and their wellbeing. Thank God for that, because that kind of information was never forthcoming from their mother, if she even took cognizance of it at all.

Mom genuinely didn't care. Mom only cared for money and how to either get at me, or get me back. I would have been concerned for the kids if Mavis wasn't around, as I never trusted Jane's mothering capabilities.

Julia was now at talking age, and often, when the kids were with me, I'd hear:

"I wanna stay by Daddy's house."

My heart broke every time she said it, and I carefully tried to explain to her that sharing is the way it is. A two year old toddler doesn't think that way though, but it was clear where Julia's preferences were.

Sean was still too young to express himself. He was only a year old after all and totally oblivious to the divorce and acrimony surrounding his parents. For now he was fine and happy at either place. He didn't know any better.

Steven didn't express much as he was told to keep quiet about everything. It was generally drilled into him by his mom that his feelings didn't really count. I always tried to have him open up without being forceful, but I often heard:

"I can't talk about it" or "I am not allowed to talk about it."

Having to keep secrets for his mom was a heavy burden on him and it was obvious that she had him under her control and instruction. Although he relaxed at my house in general, I felt he was starting to pine away in his own shell and was retracting himself from the world.

Sibling rivalry between him and Julia was also rife. He was very jealous of her, possibly because he was inadvertently told by his mother, that I would never love him as much as I love Julia, because he wasn't my biological son. Jane was playing very sick and dangerous games with these kids' minds. And it worried me a lot. Especially for Steven as he was so aware and conscious of the situation.

One morning, in the first week of December I brought the kids to Mavis at Jane's house. Jane had gone to work already. Mavis came out from the side door of the property instead of the garage. She asked me if I could go back home and bring back some porridge for the kids.

"Why do you need porridge, Mavis?" I asked.

"There's no food in the house for them to eat."

She sighed a deep breath. Mavis is not one of those people that would ask for much and only request things when they were really necessary. Otherwise she was a rather resigned and undemanding person.

"Whaaaat? No food? Nothing to eat? No bread?"

"No sir," she said.

Oh my God—what was going on here? I rushed home, got some bread and milk, baby porridge and formula and dropped it off with her.

"Since when don't you have food here?" I asked.

"Already for two days now! And no electricity either".

I was flabbergasted! Now it made sense why the electronic garage doors weren't working. I told her to look after the kids and that I'd pick them up later. I got in the car and immediately drove to Johan's office to meet him.

He agreed that this situation was getting out of hand and that he was going to draft a letter to her lawyers straight away.

That afternoon, I picked up the kids. All three of them. Jane was back home from work. She seemed defeated, but appeared strong. She told me that the electricity problem was being resolved by the landlord and that it wasn't because of unpaid bills but rather a technical problem. Total overcompensation on something I hadn't even inquired with her about. She also told me that I mustn't blow things out of proportion just because there's no porridge in the house. Well the electricity was a prepaid issue as far as I could see, and Mavis wouldn't ask me for food if it wasn't necessary.

The next day the electricity and food issue was still not resolved and Jane reluctantly agreed to let the kids stay at my house until it was all sorted out. They ended up staying six days in total before they went back to mom.

We had a happy time. I got us some Chrismassy things to do. We all set up the Christmas tree, baked cookies and pizzas, went to markets, lots of shopping, horse riding. The kids and I were very happy for a brief moment.

During that time, not one of them asked for or about mom once. Only Steven asked me on the fifth day:

"When are we actually going back to mom by the way?"

This question was brought forward without any sense of urgency whatsoever.

Christmas and Boxing Day was split between us parents. I could tell in the days after that the kids didn't receive much in the form of Christmas presents at her house, but knowing what it's like not having much money, material possessions are not important. It's the happiness and love that counts. Especially around Christmas. I even went soft on my side when she asked if we should combine the presents at one of our houses and I reluctantly agreed to that. But this was immediately followed by a barrage of demands from her side. I had to supply all the food, all the presents and drinks. It had to be done at a specific time at her house on her turf and I would be told what to do and when. Needless to say, I told her in no uncertain terms to get stuffed.

Her demands had nothing to do with Christmas. It was again a deliberate attempt to control me and possibly step back into my life or even get back in my pants. On Christmas morning, when she came to collect the kids from my house, she became all soppy with me in the driveway. She definitely tried to step back into my life and in front of the kids I got offered this *present* for Christmas. A special gift from my estranged wife that was now missing me so much. I didn't want to accept it, but I also didn't want to create a scene in front of the kids and Jane was persistent in pushing it into my hands. By doing it in front of the kids, she really had me on the spot.

I opened the parcel when I got back into the house. Oh God no... a little bag with our wedding rings, including mine. I hadn't missed the ring yet, but the last place I remember it to be was at my house in my own drawer, yet now it came from her house!

What was I supposed to do with this now?

In the same packet was a memory stick with all the photos she had on her computer, beautifully arranged in date and event order. In the root of the disc on top of the folders was another folder marked "Best of the best memories" with all the best photos (in her opinion).

Now I am a softie and an emotional type of guy, and even though I thought it was a nice gesture, I couldn't get the events and the onslaught of the smear campaign out of my mind.

She was trying to play with my mind again. I had to stay put and I didn't react on it as such, as I knew her parasitic behaviour would come out again. She would try to entangle me in her web. I was only just starting to clear my head out of the fog of this abusive relationship and had to stand my ground. I had to keep my head rational. I wasn't going to let her in again and cause destruction and mayhem. I had to stay strong.

The kids got no presents from Father Christmas at her house that year.

Twenty-one

The 'Lillypad' Kids

New Year's eve was a quiet one. I had all three kids at my place for the night. Most of my friends and family were either away or had parties to attend. I received a couple of invites, but I decided that travelling to a New Year's Eve party with a one, two and nine year old, was just not going to be a fun night out. The kids were just too young to drag to a strange noisy place until after midnight.

New Year's Eve parties in my book were generally a letdown in any event, and after all the busy Christmas festivities, I decided it might be a good way to have, a nice quiet bonding time with the kids. I also needed some time off and a chilled evening of reflecting what the last, super turbulent year had brought and taught me.

So I set out to make *Oliebollen* for the night with the kids. It's a Dutch thing, don't ask, but it's nice and easy to do and fun to make. The Afrikaners call them *vetkoeke*. The house smelled lovely and to me it was the perfect way to end the year.

Sean and Julia went to bed nicely on time and Steven and I bonded, chatted and got carried away doing silly stuff. I buggered around on the piano composing a new song and he liked it. I've been playing semi-professionally since childhood, so it was easy for me to entertain the kids that way and making up silly songs.

So I told him this song would be composed for him, Julia and Sean. His enthusiasm and feedback really spurred me on and gave me lots more inspiration. The tune became more and more groovy as we went along. We were chatting about lyrics for the song and at one point when he didn't hear me properly he piped up:

"Whaaat? Lillypad kids? What's that?"

It wasn't at all what I said, but we laughed our heads off and giggled like stupid teenagers for hours. Of course this became the title for the song and the words for the lyrics flowed fast and furious after that.

It took about two hours to write and compose. I was really inspired by the energy of the kids and the life we were having. Later that year I did a home recording which I made available online. I still think it's really cute and it means a lot to me.

At midnight we cracked open a bottle of sparkling apple juice and Steven and I drank our 'sparkly' out of champagne flutes watching the city skyline light up with fireworks. I will personally never forget that evenings feeling so close to my children with me at home. What was essentially supposed to be a quiet, potentially boring evening in, probably turned out to be the best New Year's eve celebration ever! I had never felt so close and connected with life and my loved ones. I was completely content for that brief moment right there.

And so 2014 started.

Twenty-two

The ex hubby is in town

On the fourth of January Michael arrived in South Africa. He managed to get some days off and arranged to come and visit Steven and he really started putting his foot down with his parental rights. It was a challenge for him to get access to his son and he had endless emails with Jane, who came up with all sorts of excuses as to why Steven couldn't spend a couple of days with him. Her biggest and weakest excuse I heard was that Steven couldn't spend time away from his siblings. Incidentally this was not the first time we had heard that excuse, and it was starting to sound like a broken record by now.

In reality, the age gap between Steven and Julia/Sean was huge! Yes they were his siblings, but the commonalities were few and far between. I remember from my own youth, my sisters who are six and seven years my junior were always 'the babies'.

For Steven, spending a couple of days with his dad and away from his lunatic pressure cooker mom and away from any divorce tension would do him the world of good. And it did!

That Saturday morning, when he arrived in Johannesburg, it didn't go so well. Michael had openly communicated with Jane (cc'd in his lawyer just in case) advising Jane of his whereabouts, which hotel he'd be in, his flight number, arrival times and the whole toot. He was very transparent and honest with his scheduling and intentions. That weekend all the kids were with me until midday Saturday which was also the day of his arrival.

He was aware of our schedule and asked me if we could meet for breakfast at the hotel in the morning. The kids were coming with me of course, especially Steven, who wanted to see his dad. Michael had called me quite early to say that he'd checked into the hotel and we could pop over any time.

Jane in the interim was extremely tense about Michael's visit and at around nine am she SMSed me that she would come and fetch Steven earlier that morning. There was no apparent reason for this, but I knew her games and what she was up to. She was deliberately attempting to frustrate Michael's access to Steven, even though he had flown in from overseas specially. I ignored the SMS and quickly put the kids in the car and got the hell out of the house before she'd be hooting at my gate. The kids were totally unaware of the situation and they were looking forward to going to the hotel for breakfast. I wasn't going to let her spoil the fun. We sped off and out of the suburb. True as Bob, the phone rang within a minute of us leaving the house.

"Where are you?" Jane said, clearly annoyed.

"We're on the way to meet Michael for breakfast" I replied calmly.

"You have NO right to take my child to Michael, I have made no arrangements with him. Don't involve yourself in my scenarios with him. I'm calling the lawyer now."

"Go ahead honey, I have the kids till midday today and I'll see you later. Bye."

I immediately called Michael and told him what had happened.

"Seriously?" He said.

"I'm calling my lawyer now just to let him know what transpired."

Ten minutes later we arrived at the hotel and we had a lovely breakfast with the kids. After breakfast we went to Michael's hotel room and he had gone totally overboard with presents for all the kids. They had a party of note unwrapping presents and jumping on the hotel bed.

Meanwhile Jane was fuming. She had her lawyer on the line and was preparing letters and doing God knows what else to try and dampen the festivities.

At midday, as per scheduled timing, I dropped the kids off at Jane's house. Michael was in tow behind me in his rental car. She opened the garage door and stood there totally unfazed. She had a big fake smile on her face.

"I'm so happy to see you Michael. Welcome to South Africa."

She addressed Steven with the same false façade.

"Did you have a nice breakfast with your father my boy?"

The honey was dripping off the intonation of her voice.

What an act!

Michael went into her house, as they needed to discuss some things. I had no inclination to go in her house, especially after her restraining order stunts. She'd probably have me arrested or cry abuse again.

Fifteen minutes later Michael and Steven arrived outside my house.

He came in with Steven.

Reluctantly, but most likely due to pressure from her lawyer, Jane 'allowed' Steven to spend time with his father, but with a whole string of conditions. I think most of them were flatly ignored, just because her demands were so ridiculous. Her main 'worry' was that Steven was going to be kidnapped by his father! What planet she came from is still a question that remains in my mind, because that very same potential kidnapping story also became a recurring theme. It was like listening to a washing machine on spin cycle.

In the days that followed, Steven had a whale of a time bonding with his dad. And so did Michael. It was a pleasure to see how the boy changed from being semi depressed to a jubilant vibrant kid in a matter of days. He couldn't stop talking about the experiences he had with his dad, visiting theme parks and doing nice things. He was certainly getting the most out of what his father and son relationship had to offer. And all that in such a short period of time. I was happy for both of them.

Of course, not everyone was happy about Dad exercising his rights. That Monday Jane had scheduled a meeting with Michael's lawyer for an hour or two to draft up a parenting plan that would stand up in the South African jurisdiction. That way Michael could at least enjoy his son more regularly and everyone was surprised that Jane pitched at that meeting. Was there hope? Did she really mean it? Was she finally getting some sense about co-parenting?

It was meant to be a quick meeting, but it turned into a five hour affair, presumably at great cost to Michael. Jane's lawyer was not present and she represented herself in this matter. I don't know if her lawyer didn't want to take on the case, or if she chose to keep the costs down on her part, but that's irrelevant.

With great and lengthy negotiations that day apparently some form of agreement had been reached, at least verbally. That, however, was another big illusion and soon thereafter it all fell flat again. Jane never signed the documents, and refused all points from the minutes of the meeting. It was a total and utter waste of time and resources. Before the week was over Michael asked me to assist in getting a SIM card for Steven's iPad he had just bought him. The iPad was provided to that Steven could connect and communicate via Skype or Whatsapp with his dad overseas at any time. Historically Michael was frustrated on all levels of communication, even with telephonic and electronic access. Michael had now provided for all the bells and whistles so that there would be no more excuses of phone lines being down, or internet not available. Steven now had his own communication device and could communicate at his own wish and time. That, however didn't last long either before mom sabotaged and hid the iPad away. She needed total control over her child and she got it!

Twenty-three

Steven's suffering

Since August when Jane moved out of the house, Johan and I had always been steadfast in our approach. Even with the attempted application of the restraining order and the Rule 43, we kept focusing on the divorce and best interests of the children. Because there was no money or assets to split at all, the divorce revolved around taking care of the kids and getting a parenting plan in place. The meetings at FAMSA all failed in that respect, so Johan requested a round table meeting to discuss this. On numerous occasions. The requests were not even answered or responded to and we decided to get a private social worker involved. Estelle Van der Merwe was her name and we issued a letter that we'd like her to come on board.

The initial correspondence received from the opposing party early on, was that they were in agreement. However that was followed shortly thereafter with a statement that they'd rather wait for the Offices of the Family Advocate. The offices of the Family Advocate are a government service and they get the divorcing parties into a meeting to settle any outstanding issues. They are the ones who actually try and prevent divorces from going to trial as it is usually a costly and unnecessary exercise.

So the meeting was set for March the year after! Oh my God, why did it have to take so long? I was seriously worried about the kids and I wanted a resolution. Now! They were the ones suffering the most and the legal term 'in the best interest of the kids' was certainly not being applied by anyone.

Of course I knew the kids well. I'm their father and emotionally committed and fully involved. In other words I was literally and in the physical sense their primary caregiver! This had been the scenario since they were born and I could see the chaos and mayhem that followed from splitting up the family did not do them any good emotionally at all. Steven's marks had dropped at school and reports came back that he was bullying other kids. His aggression also filtered through at home and towards his siblings. I tried to do the best I could and communicate with him, but over the following months he became more and more withdrawn. He was a closed book. He was being manipulated by his mom and he even told me that he could not, and was not allowed to talk to me anymore, and that he had to keep secrets for his mom. I was fighting a losing battle, because I had to tread cautiously with him. Under no circumstances did I want to force him to talk or apply harsh techniques. We were all suffering under mom's wrath. Occasionally he would let up though and open up with me. These open talks usually lasted a night or so, immediately followed by being closed up again.

I had a meeting with the school teacher in private out of my concern for him and also because I wanted to give feedback to Steven's father.

I then heard from the teacher that Jane had been losing her mind and going rampant at school. She was accusing the teachers that they were doing nothing about 'bullying' towards Steven. But with me, Steven wasn't complaining about being bullied at all and the whole story didn't gel. Jane even went so far as to cancel his four day school tour which he was so looking forward to. She broke the news to Steven the day before the trip, at the absolute last minute. He came to me in tears crying about mom cancelling his trip. When I asked him why, he said:

"Mom says I have to go to court with you guys to speak to the judge!"

Whaaaaat? What nonsense, kids that age don't go to court! Not only was Steven disappointed by the cancelling of his school trip, he was totally fearful about courts and judges. In the days that followed, his focus topic was questions about judges, courts, and what happens therein. I really had to calm him down and told him that he didn't have to go at all. And of course he didn't. The psychological damage was done. Jane had driven fear into this innocent boy just because she needed an audience. This was now becoming total mental abuse on her part, and she used her own child to get at me. This was pure psychopathy.

A day later, when I dropped the kids off at her place, I confronted her about the school trip and what she'd said to Steven.

"That's NOT what I said to you Steven!"

She shouted at him and lashed out.

"You can't go on the school trip because of the bullying that's happening at the school. I will not risk endangering you on the trip."

Her look towards him became icy and threatening and I could see him cowering at her gaze.

I protectively put my arms around Steven and asked him

"Steven what bullying is happening at the school? You never told me about it!"

Jane tried to butt in again, but I stopped her.

"There is no bullying going on" he said. There was only one incident earlier that year which was nothing more than rough play between boys.

"So, are you in any way worried about being bullied on the school trip?"

His face lit up, hoping I could convince his mom into changing her decision.

"No, I'm not worried at all. Can I go please?" he asked excitedly looking at me with hope in his eyes.

Jane again butted in.

"No you can't! And I told you why!"

Steven ran off to his room crying. My heart was in pieces. She seriously had NO emotions or empathy whatsoever towards her own child. Nor did she have any justified reason to hold him back from the school trip. I confronted her angrily.

"Who are you trying to confuse? Why aren't you letting him go on his school trip?"

"I have made my decision! The school bullying is getting out of hand and the teachers are doing nothing to prevent it. I can't risk his life as a responsible parent by sending him on the school trip."

She used her dramatic wording again, and of course it was all a fabrication, but I had no say in the matter. Especially because I'm not Steven's biological or legal father. My heart was ripped apart for the child though. What an evil move. What was her motive for this?! Hurting your own kid for what? I was sad and angry at the same time, but she wouldn't budge.

The following Monday, I followed up with the school and spoke to the school secretary. She told me that she'd received an email from Jane stating that Steven had to go to court for the divorce proceedings. Even the school administration couldn't figure what it was all about and what was going on.

The onslaught continued and furious emails were being sent by Jane to Michael saying that Steven was failing his grades at school and that it was my fault! It was totally accusatory and defamatory as usual, but I was starting to develop a very thick skin. I was becoming immune to all the nonsense allegations. Michael and I decided that I would go to his class teacher and get more information on how he was progressing and I would provide feedback to Michael directly, as the so called 'communication' from Jane, although eloquently written, made absolutely no sense.

I had my meeting with the teacher and she confirmed the worst. Since our split up, Steven had been absent minded and yes, as suspected, he was the aggressor in a couple of bullying incidents. We both agreed that this was his expression of frustration and not being able to communicate clearly at home. She recommended therapy for him, to which I wholeheartedly agreed. Michael was of the same opinion, but it was again vetoed by Jane with all sorts of excuses.

Michael started direct communication with the school from overseas and he received copies of the report cards, feedback and general information. Good, now at least his real father was getting the facts straight from the horse's mouth instead of twisted information from his ex-wife or second-hand information from me.

That arrangement didn't last long though. Both Michael and I received an email from the teacher a month later, stating that they'll not provide information anymore and everything had to go through the legal channels via the lawyers! We were both flabbergasted. Why can't a teacher send information and reports to his father at least? Michael and I discussed this strange email at length and couldn't figure out what was going on! Only months later we were informed that Jane had threatened the teachers not to communicate with either Michael or myself. According to what Jane told them, she was the sole guardian of Steven and threatened to sue the school and all the teachers in their personal capacity if any correspondence was entered into with us. Another one of her backward and back handed moves. We were dealing with a lot of smoke and mirrors here!

In the interim Johan had requested numerous round table meetings to see if we could settle the divorce amicably, which simply fell on deaf ears. He also requested numerous times to appoint a social worker to our case. The answers always came back contradictory ... Yes... No... Yes ... No.

Eventually six months after our initial request, and many delaying tactics, Jane's lawyer agreed to come to the party. I think at this stage they were driving 'fairness' into the situation and even though they were the opposition, I believe they could not listen too much to their client's instructions any more, as she was just out to be vindictive and on a path of destruction. I think they had seen the light and started 'guiding' their client.

Twenty-four

A private social worker

Estelle Van der Merwe was a social worker in private practice and came on board in February. A month before the family advocate meeting was to take place. She was employed to do a forensic legal investigation on the wellbeing of the kids and provide her recommendations in terms of their 'best interests'. Jane's trick was to keep Steven, Sean and Julia all together as siblings, even though she really couldn't care less about the kids as such. Her motive was to get money out of me and wreak havoc in my life, as I had cut off her narcissistic supply. For Estelle the case must have been rather complex and confusing to start off with.

As instructed by me, she would do an independent investigative report on the minors, Sean and Julia. For Michael, who jumped at the opportunity to employ her as well, she'd do a separate investigation on Steven. Both reports would be done independently from each other and Estelle would look at all aspects from a legal, emotional and psychological perspective. It would literally be a recommendation to the courts in the best interests of the child, who would be the better parent, or if they would be equally suitable.

The first meeting I was alone with her. Both Jane and I would each go in as parents individually, meet up and chat for an hour or so. My meeting lasted much longer than an hour, and she had a very casual approach to the matter. Her demeanour and stance were very friendly and amicable. She instantly had that 'friend'

113

kind of status. I suppose with her years and years of experience she knew she'd get much more out of people by being 'friends' than doing the whole investigation on a 'formal' basis.

Of course I had a lot of stories to tell her. I told her how Jane posted naked pictures of the kids on Facebook, how she took out the restraining order on me, how her exhusband was also fighting for his son, how she fraudulently tried to extract money from my medical aid, how she'd dose up the kids to keep them calm, how she was emotionally neglectful, how she'd threaten Steven sometimes, how she stole money from me and so on. Estelle listened with careful intent and casually made notes. Good I thought, at least she was listening even though the stories seemed like something out of a dramatic courtroom TV series.

What I didn't realise was that Jane would bring even bigger stories to the party the next day during her appointment. And being the cool, collective, believable and 'concerned' mom that she purported to be, Estelle had a hard time figuring all this out.

We were each given a set of questionnaires we had to answer individually. It was a thick pack of documents and covered a lot of areas, such as your own background, your family, how do you interact socially and how involved you are with the kids.

I completed the set in forty eight hours and returned it asap. With Jane it was another story. Estelle had to request the paperwork back from her numerous times and it took her six weeks of reminders before she got some semicompleted documents back. It was full of contradictions and a lot of areas were left blank. On the kids she said that they were happy overall and that I was a good dad, but she would then slag me off in the next paragraph. Her statements were confusing to say the least and all over the place. It didn't make sense.

Estelle came in for home visits and also requested that we come and see her in her office together with the kids. She observed the interactions between parent and child and how we operated in our home environment. Of course Jane had the whole thing rehearsed like a movie and was cooking a scrumptious dinner in the kitchen on Estelle's arrival. A total staged façade, because I knew when the kids were there, they lived on a diet of cereals, instant noodles and porridge. Cooking at her house was a rare occurrence.

In the report that followed from Estelle, she remarked that

Julia was a handful on that home visit and climbed all over the TV and Mavis had to calm her down. Sean was put in bed and she didn't see much of him. (Jane probably gave him a double dose of drowsy making drugs!)

We were also requested to supply a list of people that were involved in the kids' lives and telephone numbers of those people, so that Estelle could follow up with calls to see what stories came out there.

Jane didn't really have much family and her true friends were severely limited. But the crux of the matter was that she didn't even know the nurse where I took the kids for their inoculations! Ditto with the school teacher with whom she seldom had contact or an interest in the kids' activities. So on her contact list she mentioned a handful of names, which included people who had absolutely no interaction with the kids at all. She deliberately omitted phone numbers as well. Estelle could not contact anyone on her list!

Jane had also mentioned she had a University Degree in marketing from Wits University, but on investigation, that turned out to be another hoax. Estelle finally saw the red flags. Her report took a long time to finish. She worked on it between February and June and when the final report eventually came out it was more than fifty pages long.

Twenty-five

The family advocate

No one really explained the full process of the family advocate to me. I knew it was a forum to discuss the matters at hand and try to prevent the divorce from going to litigation. Or something like that. If it had to go to litigation, they'd supply recommendations in the form of a report to the high court based on their own findings.

Due to the fact that we were married out of community of property, and without accrual, we really only needed to look at the kids. As explained earlier, I firmly believed that the children needed a mom in their lives, but with the events that had happened since she moved out the previous year in August, I had changed my outlook drastically. I was now not only going to fight for the kids, but also for the totally unnecessary costs and suffering that she had directly imposed upon me.

The meeting was set for mid-March. Estelle had started her investigations in February and advised the offices of the family advocate that she was on board, but was still busy with her research. I had hoped she would be finished by then, but that was not the case. Estelle's job became even more complex, as she was investigating Jane and Steven's situation as well, on instructions of Michael from overseas. Obviously Jane was not prepared to pay for any of these costs and she pretended to be the 'poor' and battered mom. She became a professional victim at its best being taken to book by 'horrible enemies'.

I arrived at the Family Advocate's offices about fifteen minutes before our meeting was set. I didn't have the kids the previous night so Jane would bring them to downtown Johannesburg where the offices were situated. A pull up banner greeted you in the entrance of the building advertising their services. 'Working in the best interest of the children' it said. There was a kid friendly, glass enclosed waiting area next to the reception. There was Jane, busy on her phone as usual and Mavis, with the kids playing on her lap. I reported to reception and the kids spotted me. They went crazy behind the glass, literally trying to push through the window shouting "Daddy... daddy". The whole office noticed the warm welcome. I went into the waiting area, kids clambering all over me until we were called into our allocated meeting room. The meeting was chaired by Advocate Michaelson and Social worker Patel .

The kids were supposed to stay behind in the waiting area with Mavis, but Julia didn't want to hear anything of it. She clung to my legs and reluctantly she was given permission to come into the meeting room with us. I told Julia to behave and colour in some pictures. But she just wanted to sit on my lap to see what was going on. Cute on the one hand, but annoying on the other.

The meeting started with some general background inform-ation. Jane had that look on her face. A pasty but stern ap-pearance with dead eyes that flinched occasionally with flashes of hatred in my direction. Not a nice sight! She presented herself to the advocate in total contradiction to the 'battered housewife' and self-taught 'legal representative'. She had a massive briefcase with papers, presumable full of 'evidence' which she piled onto the table with a big bang. Quite an opening! Ironically, she didn't need or use any of this paperwork! She also proceeded to talk about me in the third person as if I wasn't there. I wasn't called Mark any more, but Mr le Foncé instead, and she substantiated some of overtly ridiculous statements with:

"As is clearly evident, Mr Le Foncé doesn't really care for the kids except for Julia!"

She also proceeded to bring out some very false and defam-atory accusations for which I actually had counter proof. At one point when her lies became so bizarre, I interrupted her and poin-ted out her lie. She banged her fist on the table and started shouting at me:

"I am talking now! YOU have had your turn."

The Advocate and the social worker exchanged some looks to each other with raised eyebrows, as if to say what the heck? Five minutes later the Advocate excused himself from the meeting. I suppose he'd seen enough and besides the matter was quite simple. There were no money or property issues to be resolved. Mrs Patel asked if we could call the kids back into the room again and she wanted to watch some interaction between parents and children. (Julia had gone to Mavis again by herself after establishing that this meeting room was far less fun than the playroom outside.)

The kids walked in and Julia and Sean jumped onto my lap. Mrs Patel spoke to Jane:

"Can you show me some interaction with the kids Mrs De Jager?" Jane got up from the chair, sat on the floor and called the kids.

"Come Sean, come Julia..." she called in a high pitched squeaky voice followed immediately by a whistle. It was almost like she was calling her dogs. It sounded pathetic and degrading to say the least and I wonder what went through the social worker's mind at that point. Bizarre! That's not the way you call your kids!

Sean clambered off my lap, but decided that he was more interested in the drawers of the desk in the office and Julia just clung harder to me the more mom whistled! They simply did not respond to mom and ignored her flat. They displayed a total disinterest.

"Could you please leave the room Mr Le Foncé?" Mrs Patel asked me.

"Sure" I said and lifter Julia off my lap and onto the floor.

"Go to your mom, Julia." I said and proceeded to walk to the door. Julia started to perform.

"I want to go with you daddy...I wanna come to your house."

"Don't worry my baba, I'm just going out of the office. I'll be back now. Daddy needs to go to the toilet."

"I wanna go with you to the toilet daddy...I need the toilet also."

It was clear that Julia was not going to budge. I exchanged a glance with the social worker not knowing what to do. She raised her eyebrows again, and nodding in agreement she said:

"Its fine, take her with you."

Julia really did need the toilet and left a turd of note in the family advocate toilet! Perhaps it was tension coming out of her or perhaps a display of what she thought of the situation! Most likely a bit of both.

I got called back into the office shortly after that for my turn with both the kids. Jane was asked to leave. I took Sean and Julia into my arms, showed them the height of the building and the street below, pointed out some interesting things in the office, drew some pictures on the whiteboard and rough housed a bit on the floor with them giggling and laughing.

Twenty minutes later Jane was called in again to wrap up the meeting, now with advocate Michaelson present again. There was nothing further to discuss, so Patel and Michaelson explained that Estelle, in her private capacity as a social worker was to complete her report and that her report would also be the basis of recommendation in the court. (Technically a pass the buck move. They'd just copy and paste the report and submit that to court.)

This whole ordeal lasted less than two hours. I was expecting to be in there for the whole day, but that was not the case! Although a weird process, I did feel good about it all and relieved that it was over and with a positive feeling, at least in my eyes, I headed home.

Twenty-six

Alienating attempts

I had to go on a business trip to Dubai in May. I had secured an agency agreement and this company wanted to expand into South Africa and sub-Saharan Africa as a whole. Not only had I secured the agency with them, but we were also negotiating a retainer for me to help them expand into Africa, from my home office in Johannesburg. Brilliant! I was securing myself financially again and could carry on my own business on the side. Through my lawyer, I had put this trip and dates of travel into a letter which he sent off to Jane. I knew the kids wouldn't like to stay with mom during that period, but I had no other options available. My parents, even though they would have loved to look after the kids, simply lived too far away to go up and down all the time to Johannesburg and I wasn't involved romantically with anyone that could possibly take over my days with the children. Jane always wanted to know what I was up to, who I was working for, and trying to break into my LinkedIn accounts and other social networks. I deliberately kept detailed information at bay, in case she'd pull stunts and allegations like she had done with my previous employer. She was out to destroy me, so it was better that she knew nothing.

Julia had just turned three and Sean was eighteen months old by now. Of course Sean was mostly oblivious to the whole divorce saga, but Julia was not only quite clever, but also very aware of the divorce in her own way. She had been very expressive towards me and her mother that she wanted me and only me. This was not a once-off occurrence, but a regular statement that came out without coaxing or anything from my side. Quite bizarre for a two year old girl, whom in my opinion should be stuck to her mom's apron strings and not daddy's jeans! She not only expressed her preferences to her mother and myself, but also to the outside world which was clearly visible and of course this wasn't taken lightly by Jane. Jane was jealous and started to take it out on Julia. In order to punish Julia she clearly showed favoritism towards Sean in the process. It was an extremely immature reaction, but also damaging for the kids. So needless to say, I wasn't happy leaving the kids with her for twelve days, but I had no choice.

Steven, being so much older, and also being close to me over the years, was being brainwashed now into believing that he was better off at Mom's place during the week without the 'irritating' little ones being around. His mom told him that he was 'free' to come and stay at my house on the weekends though. This was obviously to free herself up for dating and preying on a new unsuspecting target boyfriend.

Both Michael and I protested vehemently to these kind of moves all the time, but madam did as she pleased. Steven was getting psychologically damaged by his mom and his school results showed this clearly. (Which I got the blame for of course). I couldn't put a finger on the problem exactly, but it was clear that he missed coming over frequently. He was totally under his mom's control and was instructed not to like me or to talk to me about things. When he was with me, weekend outings were fun for him, but at home, he'd crawl into his shell and didn't want to participate in anything like cooking or other fun activities. Instead he retracted to video games and movies. Sometimes he didn't even want to talk to his own father Michael any more when I facilitated the Skype call. He was becoming a more and more troubled child, and I was powerless to intervene.

The business trip went well from a business perspective, but trying to communicate with my kids whilst overseas, was another story. Even with all the communication tools in place, from Whatsapp, to Skype, and SMS's, all forms of trying to get hold of them and to chat were being blocked by Jane. Electronic communication was intercepted under the excuse of I have no data, or the signal is bad and she did everything in her power to damage the relationship between me and the kids.

When I did get the children on the phone, the request was always "When are you coming to fetch me?" It was an emotional nightmare for me and I tried everything, while 'madam' wallowed in her power trip. After a couple of days, I even had to request Estelle the social worker and Johan to intervene just to facilitate communication. And then I got given a daily "window of opportunity" between six and quarter past six pm, which was still interfered with. She was a total control freak, damaging to say the least and loving this power game using the kids. Sick and sad! I now started seeing a much clearer picture of how Michael had been struggling for years to communicate with his own child and could only imagine how despondent you would become after a while. Knowing that the six pm calls were being manipulated by her hovering over the kids and trying to control the communication, I actually gave up trying through her and resorted to calling Mavis on her phone, so that she could let me talk to the kids instead. Bless her soul, she was more than accommodating and this was all done behind Jane's back. I had no other choice really. Michael in the interim was fuming too for my sake, and I certainly had a new respect of what he'd been through so far.

Needless to say, the reunion with the kids was one huge party. I did have to correct their beliefs though, because Julia for instance, had been told I was on the beach on holiday, I would not be coming back and when I couldn't get through on the phone that I didn't want to talk to her. She was very much in a state of trauma, and increased her own requests to me. "I don't want to go to mommy's house any more". "I want to go overseas with you". "Please don't leave again". Whatever went on in the background there, was terrible for a three year old to say the least and I had to reassure her constantly that I wouldn't be gone forever.

I was gone for nearly two weeks, which is a long absence in the mind of the child, and they had been terrorized in the process.

All these things needed to be reported to Estelle, the lawyers and Michael. Jane was so sneaky and 'credible' in her approach. She literally got away with murder every time. With her sharp tongue and clever use of words, a lot of unsuspecting people believed her stories. She managed to create allies from all walks of life, setting them up to believe bad things about me or her enemies in general. I had, myself, fallen for it for a while too, so I was just as guilty for not seeing through the façade initially. I even believed she loved me, which was, of course all part of her mask.

The problem is, if you're in that situation, you walk on eggshells constantly. You're not even aware you're doing it, because you're technically brainwashed to believe in her and as it encroaches on you over a period of time, you don't notice the change within yourself. However, now it was time to expose her. She had no right to continue using and abusing people and especially children like this. Michael knew the story well as he'd been in the same predicament and even though she tried to discredit me on numerous occasions, with him it fell on deaf ears. He knew the devil well.

Twenty-seven

Abandoned by his mom

Steven and I had less and less contact which was obviously the work of Jane. According to her feedback, he 'didn't want to see me anymore or come to my house'.

This was heavily protested and criticized by myself, Michael and the social worker. But she didn't give a hoot. It was her way or the highway.

Oddly enough, Steven did come around to stay at my house with sleepovers (usually weekends), but that was only when it was inconvenient for mom to have him around. She was back on the 'dating' scene and needed the next target/victim in her life. I was happy she started dating again, because then she'd at least be out of my hair—so I thought. I wasn't happy for the kids' sake though, because God only knew who she was seeing and shagging, and it became obvious that she was taking men home frequently.

I got wind of the fact that occasionally she even left the kids to their own devices at night with Mavis who lived on her property. Mavis would give me lots of information like this and sometimes when I'd pick up the kids Jane would step out dressed to kill, ready to go out for the night. Well more aptly, she would be totally under dressed. One day on picking up the kids, she opened the garage door in high heeled boots, a fanny pelmet and cleavage showing from the front all the way to her butt crack. A view more open than that of a vantage point at the Grand Canyon. I didn't know what to do with what I was seeing. I couldn't un-see it.

She never even dressed like that in our bedroom when we were married, let alone outside on the street! It was almost like she turned into someone else that I didn't know. I had never seen her that crass and revealing before. She was seeking attention in the wrong way.

This also coincided with pictures of her in a corset on Facebook, so she was obviously out on the town luring a suitor. It was not a pretty picture to be honest and certainly not setting a good example for the kids. One day Steven told me that mom would leave him alone in the house without Mavis even being present and he'd be up all night watching God knows what on TV until mom came home at two or three in the morning. I sent of another email to Estelle and Johan about this.

There were a lot of these what-the-heck moments, but ironically I was starting to become immune to them. It was becoming part of the daily routine. She was trying to force me into submission, while making me walk on eggshells. Attention seeking at its best. Meanwhile, I started losing my grip on reality because I started questioning myself and the line between what is normal and what is not was getting blurred. Can you imagine being a kid growing up with these bizarre changes in behavior all the time? You grow up not knowing what is OK and what is not. I suppose I had my own ways to keep a check on reality, but regularly had to pinch myself.

My psychological research online on various conditions and behavioral patterns intensified. I looked up everything from attention seeking disorders, high conflict people, personality disorders, schizophrenia and the various DSM listings. I suppose I was in no state to really do research like that, because I was emotionally so deeply entrenched, but if you ever find yourself in a situation like this, it does help to do as much research as possible. I had my 'diagnosis' on her and to this day, I don't think I'm far off: Malignant narcissism with sociopathic and delusional tendencies.

In June, out of the blue, Steven disappeared. All of a sudden I had no more contact and I didn't know what had happened. Michael went bezerk and had me on a hotline telephonically from overseas.

Steven had effectively been shipped out to the coast to his grandparents. Apparently there had been an incident at his current school and he was meant to go for a disciplinary hearing. Instead Jane had taken him out of school and he never went back.

Steven was misled and told he was going to granny for a holiday. There was no communication towards Michael or myself about this. After Steven arrived Michael received an email from Jane's mother—aka grannie—stating:

> You'll not be seeing your son again until he's twenty one. Get used to it.

Michael's lawyer tried to intercede and made everyone clearly aware that they were now in full contravention of the Children's act. Initially Jane responded that he'd be back after the holidays, but then a week later she claimed that Steven would be better off with the grandparents. She had now enrolled him in a new school there.

This situation was now becoming totally bizarre. Technically, and in my mind it was clear! Well so I thought. Steven was shipped out to non-legal guardians who were threatening the father (well at least grannie did) that he wouldn't see his son again. As far as I was concerned, it constituted blatant kidnapping now the maternal grandparents were involved in the crime too.

From Jane's angle, as a biological mother, irrespective of who the caregivers were, she abandoned her very own son.

If a parent abandons their kid(s) the other parent gets full custody, no?

Well that was my simple way of thinking. Legal systems and law are not always that simple and now both Jane and her parents were riding on the verge of the law and milking it to the maximum. They were taking fat chances, but what got me more was my emotional feelings for Steven and what were they mentally subjecting him to! He was already going through a hard time without all this added drama. I somehow felt responsible for him too and guilty for not being able to protect him more from this evil.

A few days later, I got a phone call from Steven's cell phone. A missed call actually. So I phoned back as I was glad to hear from him. This was two or three days after his move to Port Alfred. The call went unanswered and I tried again a little later. Again no answer. That evening I received an SMS from Jane.

Stop harassing my son by calling him constantly. He doesn't want to speak to you, he hates you!

I was floored, but I didn't react to that SMS.

Two days after that incident, my phone rang and Steven's name showed up on my screen. Now what? Do I answer? Yes? No? I made a quick decision. He might be trying to communicate with me. This was almost like a hostage situation. So I answered. The voice on the other side of the line was that of the maternal grandmother.

"Shit...shit...shit..." I could hear her say. "This stupid phone. Now it's calling that arsehole."

She was obviously talking to granddad and talking to him about me, not knowing I could hear everything she said.

"I hope the bastard didn't pick up," she continued.

"Hello..." I said, but she was fiddling with the phone and I could hear all sorts of beeps and sounds going on. What she was doing I don't know, but obviously she'd hijacked Stevens first cell phone and possibly even confiscated it from him, now manipulating and blocking communication channels. Like daughter, like mother. The same modus operandi. That phone and number has been 'dead' ever since. It was clear that granny was a big part of this situation.

Twenty-eight

Yes, that is my penis

I am, and have always been an open-minded person, sexually and otherwise. Maybe even more so than the general population, but I like to think of myself as a free spirited individual. Nothing sick, illegal, perverted or weird ever crosses my mind and I'd never criticize other people on their preferences and/or their sexuality. Like everyone else, I have boundaries and some of these are probably somewhat on the conservative side. What everyone else does in their bedrooms, is none of my business.

When I initially met Jane, years earlier, she appeared to be very open-minded, as mentioned earlier on. At one point between the two pregnancies of Sean and Julia she had opened up a discussion with me and said we should go to a swingers club. Big question mark for me!

She told me that she had previous experience in that area before she met me and although it tickled my curiosity on the one hand, I did not think something like that was a feasible option for me or us as a couple. I don't believe that a relationship will get enhanced by partaking in these kind of activities. As a single person, and if you're into that kind of thing, do what blows your hair back, by all means, but not when you're in a relationship. To me personally that's like walking on thin ice. I'm convinced jealousy creeps in, no matter how open-minded, liberated and secure you are in your relationship. It was maybe a nice idea or even a fantasy, but in reality that would not have been for me. Some people even call it "a lifestyle". I did my research and chatted to some people about it, but for me and Jane? No way! Our relationship was already fragile by then in any case, and something like that certainly wouldn't help in securing our situation. Plus, I didn't really feel like it was something for me.

In hindsight, I saw what she wanted to achieve by doing this. Had I had given into her requests and if we had gone to one of those "lifestyle" parties, can you imagine the comeback? Oh my God, she would have lashed out at me for sleeping with someone else and probably sued the pants off me, pretending that I was the instigator! It would have been clearly something to hold against me at a later stage. Thank God we never went that route, even as a try out for fun. It would have backfired in its fullest glory. I think it was more a case of pre-planned future litigation potential for her! Or maybe it was something that did really turn her on. I will never know.

Social worker, Estelle's final report came out early in July. She called me in for a meeting and started as follows:

"I have to apologize to you. I didn't believe your stories initially when we met and I thought they were overblown and not realistic. I thought you were a bit of a drama queen (thanks!) But you were right!"

I know my stories were large, but I never lied about anything, so I certainly had no doubt in my mind about them. An outsider obviously sees it differently and with contradictory stories and believable, cunning lies from Jane, people might have thought I was mad or simply turned their back not wanting to get involved. Estelle continued:

"In doing research for Michael about Steven, and contacting the school I found out the following information..."

She explained what had transpired at the school. Steven, as suspected and reported on already, had been a bully at school. This had increased in intensity in recent months, which coincided with Jane not letting him come to my house anymore and brainwashing him against me. Under the pressure from his mom, he was totally frustrated and could not express his feelings. Anger started taking over. His only outlet? Other kids and siblings which he bullied. Apparently he had injured another boy's arm so badly that the boy had to go to hospital and needed medical intervention. The school reacted by suspending him and requested a disciplinary inquiry for him and Jane to attend. It's a formality that needed to be documented in the school records.

The school also recommended a psychologist to come on board for Steven, which we had already requested previously, but this was again denied by Jane.

In the interim, whilst Michael and I were enquiring about Steven's wellbeing at the school, earlier in the year, Jane had all the teachers and the headmaster fooled into believing she was the only custodian and guardian of Steven. The school had taken on that information at face value, with an obvious dose of Jane's confidence, manipulation and lies. She might have even provided false documentation to 'prove' her status as sole custodian. As a graphic designer, she was very good at falsifying documents and used that trick frequently. Neither Michael, nor I had any further information about this and were totally unaware that she'd made these claims about her being the sole custodian.

Jane, obviously did not want anything to come to light about what happened at the school, nor for it to be documented officially. So she took Steven out of school immediately and moved him to the coast within a week. Before he was taken out of the school though, she'd harassed the teachers and the headmaster going crazy at the school premises with threats that no-one was to talk to anyone about the incident, especially not me or Michael. If they did, they'd be sued by her 'legal team' (she loves words like that—legal team, medical team—makes her feel important). Little did she know that Estelle coincidentally had already set an appointment with the school that very same week so Estelle got the full run down on the story, the lunacy and the threats. Straight from the horse's mouth. That was more than enough to make up Estelle's mind and her recommendation was made official in her report.

Recommendation:

It is recommended that the parties be awarded full parental rights and responsibilities and that the minor children reside primarily with Mr Le Foncé as he is the primary care giver to the minor children.

It is recommended that weekend contact be from Friday 17h00 to Sunday morning 9h00 every alternate weekend. (This is closer to the week routine and will enable the children to return to the other parent at a predictable time of day.)

It is recommended that the parties enter into a parenting plan, attend parental guidance and guidance with regard to positive communication.

Jane did not take that official release of the report lightly. It must have blown her mind and I suppose, yes as a mother, no matter how crazy you are, no mother would appreciate or like this kind of information. But according to Estelle (and various other people as well) she was just not emotionally capable to parent properly. It was becoming obvious now and it was documented.

That very same evening she went on a spin and the smear campaign antics went viral. I got a call from Michael overseas the next morning.

"Dude," he said.

"You must check the email she sent me now! I am totally floored!"

I was used to receiving strange information about her and I was expecting an allegation of sorts. I wasn't expecting what I was about to hear though.

"What did she do now?"

"She sent me an email with an attachment. It's a picture of a penis! The only thing she wrote was 'Mark's extramural activities'. I'm assuming it a picture of your dick?"

"Huh? What? I dunno!"

"I'll forward it to you!"

The email came through quickly. It had no subject matter just an email stating 'FW:_____'. In the text body it said: 'Mark's extramural activities.'

I opened the attachment. True as bob, it was a screenshot with a picture of my dick! A photo that was taken by her on her phone one silly night right in the beginning of our relationship!

I couldn't help wondering who else she'd sent it to. My parents? Sisters? Work colleagues? How embarrassing! Oh well, I took it on lightly with humour because after all it was just a picture of a dick! I felt a bit uncomfortable though as it was my dick and not for everyone's public viewing! I informed Johan of this incident and forwarded Michael's email to his offices that same morning. In my email I told Johan straight:

"Johan, Jane is now sending screenshots of my dick to God knows who in the world. I received this information from Michael this morning and although I've attached it to the mail, there's certainly no need to open it. And it's definitely NSFW!"

Johan replied later that day.

"Sorry Mark my secretary opened your mail and couldn't resist looking. She thinks it's very nice and printed it out! She even enlarged it on the photocopier to make it bigger! LOL."

Haha. Obviously it wasn't true, but we had a good chuckle about it. He told me not to worry over something stupid like this, because her uncontrolled behaviour would bite her back at some point.

Thankfully I am not a prudish kind of person and handle nudity and things like that well, but I really could not understand what she was trying to achieve by doing this? Trying to make me embarrassed? Make it into a scandal for having a dick? Trying to make me submit to her demands? She was hardcore and relentless in many areas, but all this did, was to make herself the laughing stock. Especially this email, which became evident a few months later in court! Worse though and highly concerning, was the fact that she'd also posted naked pictures she took of the kids, with full frontals on Facebook, all while trying to imply that I was the pervert!

This woman was getting sicker and sicker by the day! Thankfully I had already reported that to Estelle earlier. I found out later that she had also received the same email from Jane with my dick attached!

Twenty-nine

A beautiful mind

Technically speaking Jane had nothing on me legally, but she tried desperately and continued relentlessly to paint me with a tar brush. Sure we all have our quirks and negative sides, but she had now taken it to the extreme. Although I tried to brush it off, it affected me. It affected me badly. I could not understand why a person, that presumably had loved you, could hate you with such a vengeance just because you were getting divorced. My internet research revealed that narcissists and Borderline Personality Disordered people are like that. There is absolutely no normality, just black and white thinking. While everything was in turmoil and the divorce process well under way, she still sent me the odd love letter. They were bizarrely and poetically composed and if I didn't respond to them, which I didn't, another character assassination and an attack on my integrity would follow. On the flip side I knew that if I did respond to those, I'd be taken out the same way! There was just no winning with her. And whatever I did or said, or even if I was just being me, it was all regarded as hostile by her and criticized to the extreme. I was literally damned if I did, and damned if I didn't.

But the continuous onslaught eroded me. I was getting tired. It takes a lot for me to get angry. I'd rather walk away from a situation than confront it. But she kept on harassing and pursuing me for a reaction or to lash out at her. She was coming after me full steam in the most bizarre manner and I could not understand it. The only reason I had not moved far away from her yet was to try and keep the kids safe and in the most stable environment as possible. The kids were becoming more and more vocal, and as their vocabulary was getting better and better each day, it was clear that they did not want to stay at mom's house. As small as they were, they were being manipulated and not happy in that environment.

I was also getting frustrated with the delays, non-responses to our legal letters and the smear campaign against me. As much as I tried to keep my head together for my own sanity, it was hard. Normality was not the order of the day and I just had to take things as they came. I'd never know what each day would bring and because of this day to day living, I couldn't plan either. I couldn't plan for the kids, myself, the business and life in general. It was frustrating and I felt like life became a washing machine on a very slow and lengthy spin cycle. It was the same thing day in and day out with the odd bump or clank in between.

With regards to the kids I had excellent contact with the nursery school teacher as well as their nanny, Mavis, at Jane's house. I knew they weren't happy overall, but as long as Mavis was there, they were OK. I, however wanted the best for them and couldn't wait for this divorce to be finalised.

With all the slagging going on and having been subjected to the numerous smear campaigns already, I had actually had enough. Her sneaky ways of not returning clothes I sent the kids with, her deliberate manipulation of the kids' toys even, all made me cross and upset. When I returned the kids to her house, I felt the child should have their own possessions with them. Things like favourite blankies, toys and even bottles/dummies should pass between the two households and with the child. It's the child's stuff after all, and it belongs to them, not the parents. This turned out to be a total fiasco. I kept on buying new clothes and thankfully I receive quite a lot of hand-me-downs from my family and friends. Nice clothes! I'd send them to school like that or back to their mom. But on the return of the kids they'd come back in rags and tatters and outgrown clothing. She kept and filled up her own cupboard with the nice things and left me with the shit.

Same thing with Julia's blankie. She had a favourite Smurf blankie which I bought her, which I sent with her to her mom's house. What transpired was that when she arrived with her favourite comfort item, mom would take it away as punishment as that was an item that came from 'enemy territory'. She was involving the child in some seriously damaging psychological and emotional warfare. To me that was beyond sick! Julia in the end, even though I encouraged her to take her favourite Dolly and Blankie with her to mom's house, would hand me back the items that were dear and near to her and she'd say: "Please keep these daddy and look after them for me." She knew what would happen if she brought those items to her mom's house.

I was becoming angry but also depressed. My mood was wearing down, I became anxious and Jane's antics were infiltrating my thoughts all the time. My body was starting to take its toll with the ongoing stress and the insecure situation that I was in. I made an appointment with my house doctor to see if he could help. I explained the situation and how I felt and although I knew what he was going to do, I explained to him that I was not keen on antidepressants. But he insisted and sounded convincing. He said:

"Take these for two weeks and you'll see a definite change. Just give it a chance to work its way into your system. I'll also give you a script for an anti-anxiety. Take these only when your anxiety levels go through the roof."

I took the script and contemplated whether I should pick them up from the pharmacy. I didn't feel depressed as such. I still had a positive outlook overall, I just wanted this divorce over with and the kids safe! The kids were my primary concern and actually the only fight in the whole case.

"What the heck, I'll give it a try I thought to myself. There are millions of users worldwide. They can't all be wrong!"

I got the pills from the pharmacy. I didn't have much drive and energy in my system to start off with but, as the Doctor said, try them out and see how you feel. Reluctantly, I started taking anti-depressants for the first time in my life.

That was a big mistake. Holy crap! They zonked me out completely! Shortly after taking the first pill, I felt tired. I thought I needed to take a nap! But I didn't want to take a nap, because I felt guilty about taking naps. I needed to work and generate income. I needed to be busy! I needed to provide for my kids. Napping doesn't bring in any income! The pill took over though and rationally I thought.

"Oh well, if that is what your body needs, go and take a nap for an hour or so. Stop feeling guilty!"

I set my alarm, put my phone on silent and I lay down on the bed.

My brain and body felt weird. I was tired. More like an exhausted kind of tired, but thoughts penetrated my mind. All sorts of thoughts. They consisted of worries and anxious imagery. Like an old fashioned war movie in black and white. Lots of explosions. Flashing imagery. My thinking wasn't clear and even though the thoughts were there, I didn't care about the thoughts. The thoughts were 'just' there. I kept on reminding myself that they were 'just' thoughts.

"There's a thought for you! And here, another one see? There. You see? Another thought. That's all it is. It's just a thought. There's nothing to worry about, they're only thoughts!"

My internal dialogue became very strange and I realised my thinking was becoming bizarre. I snapped back into reality.

"Hold on, your thoughts are becoming strange!"

Another voice responded.

"That's OK it's just a thought! Maybe it's strange, but it's just a thought after all, Like all the others! Other thoughts. See, ...? There, ... there are more. Strange thoughts, worried thoughts. All kinds of thoughts. Your brain is thinking, therefore you have thoughts! Thank goodness for thoughts, what would we do without them?"

As bizarre as my thoughts became, I was also very nonchalantly okay with this bizarre scene that was unfolding in my head.

Then there was silence for a bit.

"What are you thinking? Where are the thoughts?" The voice shouted at me. I must have dropped off to sleep for a bit, but the voice woke me up. My eyes opened. The internal 'thought dialogue' continued in my head.

I was lying on my side. I was lying on my side staring at a blank spot on the wall. It was a blank white spot! Nothing special, but it was a spot to look at, so why not? Actually it wasn't a spot. It was just a white wall. Technically the wall didn't have spots, certainly not white spots. So it didn't even have spots, but it seemed like a spot. It was a good spot! It was a good spot to be in. The voices about thoughts drifted off into the background.

Four hours later, I was still staring at the blank spot on the wall. I had just woken up. No, hold on, I hadn't just woken up. Or did I? Shit, this was weird. I still to this day can't recall if I slept or if my brain went into overdrive just staring at the blank white spot.

It felt like I had just woken up from a deep sleep, or had I slipped into a trance? A coma perhaps? The pills helped me go absolutely loony! That's just great. Let's now throw in another nutter in the mix staring at white spots on the wall listening to internal dialogue about thoughts. Just what the Doctor ordered! Not!

With my mind still fuzzy and foggy, I got up and made some coffee. This was way too intense and bizarre for me and I didn't like the feeling at all. This wasn't for me! Copious amounts of coffee later, I regained some of my body and mind back. Doubts on whether to continue treatment or not became a raging war internally. I read forums and articles on the specific drug I was prescribed, and educated myself on the effects and side effects. As a 'naturalist' I decided not to continue and stopped treatment on day three. Clearly the pills didn't go down well with me and I was not cut out to be a hallucinating zombie. Besides, I really did not feel depressed as such. To me I felt more anxious from time to time, which I suppose is rather normal under the circumstances. I left a message at the doctor's office to tell him that I'm not doing this medication any more. And the voices went silent forever more!

Thirty

You're the pits!

Emotionally I needed to vent though. I needed to express myself and I hadn't seen my shrink since December the year before because of financial constraints. Thankfully I could still talk to my friends and family. They were extremely supportive and caring, but they would never know and fully understand what I was going through. Sometimes I'd get irritated with their advice.

"Oh just do this, or just do that" or

"When my friend got divorced they simply..."

"Don't sweat the small stuff..."

My hackles would go up. Didn't they understand the complexity of the situation? Did they think this was just a normal divorce and all divorces are handled the same? Did they not understand that I was dealing with a serious psycho and I had to sit things out legally and patiently?

Admittedly her capability to get into my head was worrying and there were moments that I would worry about things that were maybe insignificant. But there was no stopping her. She had managed to infiltrate herself into the core of my being and I needed to get her out.

So far the odds, legally were in my favour, but I still had months to go before the actual divorce would take place! If it wasn't going to be postponed again by her as she had a knack of avoiding all items on the divorce list—from social workers through to round table meetings. Meanwhile, the kids were suffering and

I was suffering. The only ones, I felt, who really understood most of the situation at least from an emotional perspective, were my cousin Caroline and Michael, Jane's ex-husband. He had experienced similar trauma and damage years prior and also understood what kind of beast we were dealing with and fighting against. For the rest, it almost felt like no-one could understand me fully and I needed to express myself more and better.

Thankfully, I'm a pretty creative person and I took to my piano, which was my outlet. I enjoy playing piano, and already with the Lillypad Kids and various other songs I had made, I knew I had a somewhat of a knack for composing and writing music, not just performing existing music. I explored it more and more, and found out that if you sit down and "compose" with intention, it doesn't work. The Lillypad Kids came out of nowhere on New Year's Eve and was completed in a few hours. I liked it and it meant a lot to me. It talks about the kids and bringing them up single-handedly in a humorous way. I tried to get my own emotions out into the musical form and tap into my subconscious mind, but forcing the issue didn't help. Frustrated, I left it alone.

But suddenly, one night, it jumped at me. I was fiddling with some minor chords and improvised melodies on the piano and out of the blue everything fell into place. The music, the words, the mood. This was it, again an impromptu creative experience arriving from the subconscious as if it had always been sitting there, waiting for the right moment to come out. A few minor adjustments and my song was ready. It had all my feelings and emotions wrapped up in it. It described exactly how I felt at the time, and when I completed and performed it, I started crying. All of a sudden I felt terribly sorry for myself and the ordeal that I'd been through. I just knew that this song was an expression for me. This song explained what it was all about and how I felt. It was sad and angry at the same time. Every time I performed it, it got better and better, but also more emotional. Half the time, as the lyrics left my lips, I cried. It was a deep and emotional cry. It took me a long time before I could actually record it without too much tremble and quivers in my voice. Still to this day it's my song telling her how I felt at that time. I downloaded a free trial of recording software and layered the song as much as I could in a home environment on a crappy old desktop. I think the result was OK, even though I couldn't hold the notes in the end (due to emotions and an added dose of the flu). I'd still like to record it professionally one day, and make into something smashing!

The pits is defined by the freedictionary.com as a place of pain and turmoil and the hell of battle. Quite apt in my situation.

You're the pits

I didn't lie, I didn't cheat
You show your face, but you do not greet
You're eyes show hate and so much fear,
What did I do, did I get too near?

All I gave you is love and care,
It turns out you are in despair.
You've sucked me in and you've spat me out
And I'm still not sure, what this is all about.

And you know what?
I believed in you
I've fought for you,
I've cried for you and yes
I died for you.

You gave me kids my heart to dear,
You use them now yes out of fear,
Their minds are just too innocent,
Yet you break them down till the last end.

All you want now is just revenge,
No clue for what, however meant
Delusions, fear, grandiosity,
But it's really your mind you need to see.

Chorus

Because you're the pits (x4)

You've now moved on, or so you say,
Another man for you to play.
You've wrapped him up but you played him wrong,
Now you need the next to come along.

Five fathers for your eldest son
He's only 10, but he is strong.

And all for what, I still don't know,
Please focus on your kids to grow.

All along you've played these games,
You've tried the law, to your disdain
Harassment, stalking, you've done it all,
And a smear campaign, but you are too small!

I needed strength, but that I got,
Your tricks and games, they've helped you not
Coz justice soon it will be clear
And your webs and lies won't help you my dear!

Chorus

The money spent on all that law,
Should have gone to the kids and so much more,
Instead you try your viscous tricks
And moments later you try to fix?

I'm not your ticket for you to ride
I'm in your sleep night after night.
Your blackmail and your aim is wrong
Till justice comes I will be strong.

I've been too good, I've been too kind,
A gentleman that's hard to find
You've pissed me off, yes that's what you did,
Justice will come, a final hit!

Chorus

Thirty-one

Mental abuse and emotional imprisonment

In the relationship, I had already been walking on eggshells. It crept up on me and before I knew it, I was watching all my words and actions with her. Over time, Jane had cunningly managed to emasculate me and manipulate my entire life. She was like a parasitic worm that infiltrates my mind, digging holes into the grey matter. I was not the same person any more, but an emotional wreck and a fraction of the bubbly, outgoing personality I once was. I wasn't seeing much of my friends and family anymore and it was hard to rebuild these relationships and regain their trust. On the face of things, I'd always appear cheerful and smiling and keeping a brave façade, but in reality I was stuck between a rock and hard place trying to regain everyone's trust back.

No matter how much it would cost me in litigation, I was adamant to protect the kids. It was my duty! I didn't get married to have an unhappy family and divorce was not an option in my mind at the time I got married! I gave the relationship everything I could. Support, love, compassion, trust, understanding. But it was a one sided affair. Having been brought up correctly and with the right values in life, my aim was to work through all the problems and I gave it all I could. That was not possible in my marriage though.

I was shoved from pillar to post and, talking about posts, the goal posts kept on changing with Jane. Promises weren't kept and words were just that... merely words. They meant nothing in her life. If I'd confront her about what she had promised earlier, she'd flatly just deny that she ever made that promise. She was a master at changing the reality and I figured out that she was probably delusional as well. It didn't stop after she'd moved out of my home. She lied to the kids, to me, to her lawyer, her parents and everyone around her. She was brilliant at gaining new 'friends'—or rather an entourage and getting compassion for her statements and posts on social media. She even went to a photographer with the kids to get some professionally made photographs, pretending to be a happy family. Those photos would be uploaded on Facebook immediately so that she could fuel her narcissistic supply and get the attention she wanted. It just wasn't natural. It was all an act for the outside world. With every comment or like on her Facebook pictures, she'd have another comment back, just to keep the conversation going. It was all about likes, comments and pretense. Photoshoots and statements like that didn't make the kids happy though. The real issues in parenting weren't attended to. If the kids were sick, she wouldn't care, except demanding that I deliver medicines to her house. Her favorite choice of medicine she administered herself to the kids was Deselex (an antihistamine). She'd use large amounts on the kids, probably to make them drowsy. Doctors' visits and nurse check-ups were my responsibility. So was the Medical Aid and school fees. And clothing. Of course you don't play around with things like that and even though I wanted to slap her in the face for not contributing to the wellbeing of the kids, I had no choice, but also felt obliged to make sure that they would carry on. Money was still tight, the business was up and down, but I survived somehow, taking all the responsibility in the world for my kids on a physical, mental and emotional level.

The irony was that Jane wasn't always unreasonable. There were moments of seemingly normal behaviour and rationality. If it wasn't for those moments, I would have picked up on her emotional and mental instability much earlier in the relationship and would have ended it. But believing that she could change, I sat it out. But her fluctuation and stunts were highly visible now that she was under duress with the divorce. At all times I was on high

143

alert with her. She'd flip over to the other side, out of the blue and the next minute she'd be 'normal', or even agreeable again. It was confusing to say the least and I had been exposed to this kind of behaviour for years now.

The only choice I had, was to be on my guard, at all times. Communication, since we split up was done only in writing, and I even went so far as to voice record our conversation each time I saw her in person. I didn't trust her for shit. I also started diarizing events. From the tiniest thing like a nappy rash to when the kids were sick. What clothes they arrived in and what mood they were in. What time I picked up and dropped off. What Jane had said to me. SMS's were saved and printed, emails and Skype conversations were recorded and filed. It became obsessive, but I had to do it in case she'd bring up something from the past in court. Everything I brought up was denied, opposed and slandered. I had to substantiate with proof. Proof, however, didn't mean anything to her and she vehemently defended her rights, used big words and hid behind other people's opinions. Opinions which she'd cunningly plant into their brains by feeding them twisted stories about me, with a grain of reality thrown in to make it seem plausible. She would then in turn twist these other people's words and conversations to suit herself and bring those to me. It was a total delusional mess. The long term outcome of these stories, was that she created more enemies for herself. But that didn't bother her in that moment. She would just create a new group of 'friends' and carry on feeding her narcissistic supply.

The strongest part of her focus though was money. She used the kids as pawns in her games and needed them as the meal ticket for the long run. It was always her approach from the beginning and I was starting to think that that was the only reason she had kids and married me—so that she could live and feed off me, without actually caring for the kids. I was a sperm donor and a wallet filler for her! Over time, the more substantial proof I had against her, the more she'd retaliate and lash out. However more and more evidence and reports of her bad mothering style and her manipulation would show up. She was cornered, but she had a knack of avoiding answering any lawyer's letters that came in from our side. Teflon at its best!

If she was forced to provide answers, she'd come up with convoluted and confusing affidavits, umpteen pages long, bringing up all sorts of new topics and allegations that had no relevance or substance. Her technique was to blame, shock into submission and expose. I was harshly criticized on the smallest topic, and even though I didn't really have to respond to these silly allegations, I still had a moral and ethical obligation to defend myself and the kids.

Money was tight, and I tried to avoid raking up more lawyers bills as much as I could. Although comfortable in the fact that she'd really stuffed up her case, I didn't want to rest on my laurels either. Johan had indicated that we were in a very fortunate position as we didn't really need to do anything except wait until the divorce was final.

September and October were relatively quiet months for me, but Michael had launched his high court applications, which kept her busy. Michael was sick and tired of her empty promises though and she kept on proposing and promising meetings which resulted in nothing. She was cornered. For me, the pressure seemed to be off for a little while and I could notice an immediate improvement in my mood and business success. Momentarily I had a bit of a break again.

Steven was still AWOL, supposedly with his grandparents at the coast over a thousand km away. I missed him. I missed him coming over and being around and according to vague feedback and baby talk from Julia and from Mavis I heard that he would be up in Johannesburg for the school holidays in September. The elusive grandparents would bring him up here.

An email arrived from Jane direct requesting, or rather demanding that I hand over the kids for that particular week because they need to spend time with their sibling and their grandparents.

I wondered why she hadn't copied in her lawyers. This was because the law firm, Mike Vermont, had booted her out. She was now representing herself entirely and she was under the impression that she could manage the legal correspondence herself.

Within that week her lawyer went officially off the record and didn't represent her any longer. I suppose they didn't want to have egg on their face representing an unstable person and knowing that the case was going one way. They had a reputation to uphold after all! And she still owed them loads of money.

Besides the odd email from 'madam' herself to my lawyer, things remained relatively calm and I could focus on myself, the kids and business. At the time we were still sharing them 50/50. I secretly hoped she had come to her senses, and would stop the onslaught. What I didn't know was that she was planning her next major move. An even dirtier one.

Without notice, she moved house from Garden Road to Hilma Street. A move of around four hundred metres. Four hundred metres closer to my house that is! The move must have been money driven as the house was apparently quite a small two bed-roomed place. I never had the pleasure of seeing it inside though, just the garden. What I did know, was that it was a pigsty of note. Furniture and rubbish were strewn across the lawn. There was obviously not enough space for all her things to fit inside the house.

Out of the blue, she also had a new boyfriend called Brad. Actually he was a neighbour from her previous Garden Road residence about three houses further up. How convenient! In a sub-urb of around two hundred residences, Brad and I were probably the only two single guys in this entire neighbourhood with family homes. And she managed to find him. What are the chances of 'falling in love' with the only other single guy in the area? He seemed nice enough though at first, and judging from handovers and collections with the kids, it appeared they were also fond of him. I just felt like warning him, not to make the same mistake as me, and not be fooled into believing her lies and manipulation, but I thought it better not to interfere. The fact that she moved into another residence and not into his house, surprised me a little but then again, they had only known each other a month or two. I thought he may be wise after all, but later on that appeared not to be the case!

Jane moved without any notice to me or my lawyer, which by law was required. I also had to think twice before sending any messages or communication to her, as it would just be constantly turned around and used against me!

Julia ramped up her 'I want to stay at daddy's house' scenario more frequently since the move and I felt sorry and bad for my little angels that I could not grant them their wishes and tried to explain as best as I could without slagging the mother that all will be OK in the end. Meanwhile, deep inside as a doting father I felt like a failure at times, not being able to conform to the kids' wishes.

Thirty-two

Sick kids and a sicker mom

In the beginning of October teacher Agnes from the crèche sent us both (and individually) a message. Agnes knew the communication between Jane and I was disastrous, so she cleverly kept all the communication open and transparent.

> Julia and Sean are not well today. Can one of you pick them up?

The kids stayed at their mom's house the previous night. Recklessly, Jane had brought them to the school sick that morning. I read the message and send one back to Agnes:

> I'm on my way, I'll see you in ten minutes.

Two minutes later Agnes phoned me:

"Mark, Jane is also on her way and she told me not to hand the kids to you."

As I was already very close to the nursery school, I told her I'd be there and we would wait for Jane to come through and sort it out. I arrived before Jane and Agnes gave me the rundown. We always had open communication about the kids. She was fully understanding, supportive and stood behind me on issues of the kids' overall wellbeing. Agnes was always diplomatic and tactful in her approach, but at the same time she could not believe what kind of mother Jane really was.

The kids were ecstatic to see me at the school and jumped straight into my arms. They were coughing and chesty and had badly running noses. Julia's eyes were swollen and both were obviously suffering from a bad head cold or flu. As I hadn't seen them while they were at their mom's house, I asked Agnes her opinion just to get confirmation.

"Should I take them to the Doctor?"

"Most definitely" was her reply "They're not well at all."

Jane arrived fifteen minutes later and not five minutes as she had mentioned to Agnes. She stormed in and yanked the kids away from me. All I could do, having Agnes as a witness, was to ask her if she's going to take them to the Doctor.

"I have an appointment at Eight Thirty tomorrow morning with the Doctor."

"Eight Thirty tomorrow morning? They need to go now as soon as possible."

Jane pulled a hand gesture at me and drove off. Another one of those 'lovely' interactions, this time in front of the school and Agnes. Agnes just looked at me and shrugged her shoulder as if to say:

"Now I've seen it all! These poor children."

She knew my hands were tied and I could do only so much and no more.

As it was only ten thirty in the morning at that stage, I called our house doctor and asked them if they had any earlier appointments available for the kids. Of course they had. I could basically come in at any time that afternoon and especially as it was with kids, they would slot them in any time.

I conveyed that information to Jane via SMS.

> Dr Silver can see the kids much earlier today, I don't think you should wait till tomorrow morning.

Her response was as 'charming' as ever.

> I told you I have an appointment with a Doctor at Eight Thirty tomorrow morning and I'm giving them medication.

In other word don't interfere and her 'back off' approach was on full throttle. All I could think about was the kids and how cruel she was to let them suffer unnecessarily. I asked her what Doctor she was taking them to, but I never got a reply. That afternoon I picked up the kids at four thirty (as it was my time with them) and they were as sick as dogs at my house. I did what I could with home medication and pediatric painkillers to make the night as comfortable as possible. They were gunked up, coughing and uncomfortable. I could not understand why 'mom' would not let me take them to the Doctor that afternoon.

The next morning on dropping them off at Jane's place at eight am, I double confirmed with her that she was going to take them to the Doctor. She acknowledged that fact. It was rather strange for me, as this would be the first time ever that she would actually be taking on the responsibility of taking them to the Doctor. But again, I thought to myself that maybe she's starting to take on her mothering responsibilities more seriously now that the legal pressure was on.

Later that day at four thirty, I picked up the kids again as it was my Friday night and weekend night with them. They were in a worse state than that morning. Jane vaguely mumbled some commentary in a fleeting pass at my car: She loved cutting off sentences and speaking in code.

"He said to give them Deselex three times a day for the next three months until the pollen season is over."

I instantly knew that that was an outright lie. Deselex again, her favorite over the counter antihistamine!

I SMSed her the minute I left:

Which doctor did you take them to?

No answer. I asked Julia and she confirmed that they had not been to the doctor that morning.

I didn't even bother to go home. The kids were now already in my car and I phoned the Doctor straight away.

"Come in now" the secretary said, "Doctor Silver is here until six pm today".

Fifteen minutes later we were there. He saw us straight away and I told him the story. He examined the kids and they had sinus issues as well as quite heavy chest infections. When I told him about the 'Deselex' story, he said:

"I do not believe any of my colleagues would ever recommend just Deselex for something as serious as this and certainly not for such a long time".

He prescribed medication and I got a Doctor's certificate from him. I requested that from him, as I knew I might need it to prove mom's lying and incompetence in court at a later stage. Emotionally though I was fuming. She basically had the kids suffering for forty eight hours unnecessarily, lying through her teeth, whilst pretending to be a concerned and good mother just to keep everyone else quiet. This was unbelievable.

Two days later when Jane and Brad came to my house to pick up the kids, I gave her the medication, I said to her:

"Here, take this. REAL Doctor's prescription."

She turned to Brad and said to me, making sure he heard.

"Oh don't worry, we have all that at home. Don't we Brad?"

Brad just nodded with a stupid confused grin on his face and she brushed me off. The new boyfriend was obviously under her spell already and had become a 'yes' man. I didn't argue too hard with her, because within the period that the kids were at my house they had recovered already and whether they really needed that last day of medication was debatable. At least their infections were cleared and they were not suffering any more.

Thirty-three

Smear smear smear campaign

The onslaught continued with a fresh approach.

Now that she had a new man and 'backup', the smear sessions started again. This time unbeknownst to me, she came up with another cunning plan. Madam had plotted and schemed for weeks, if not months, on how to get rid of me and had, indeed, put together a very crafty plan. She was now going to get rid of me for good.

I was of course totally oblivious to her plans. I noticed, however, (from information from Sophie and when picking up the kids shortly before November) that she was moving house again. This time she was moving in with Brad and this would basically be her fourth residence in the space of just over a year. She had managed to work her way into his life and convinced him that they should move in together. It appeared (from my observations) that she'd not paid the rent, nor water and lights, as there was a notice affixed to the garage door at her 'new' abode, that the council was going to cut off her services. I took a picture of that and sent it off to Johan. I also voiced my concerns about the fact that the house was in turmoil and that a move was imminent.

What made me worry though is that that Julia came home with stories to me that she was going to live by the beach with Steven! Even though I couldn't take a three year old's statement like that at face value, it did concern me that she was talking like that. Where would she come up with information like that unless mom was telling her bullshit and coaching her?! It did worry me, as I didn't know if she was planning on moving to Brad's house up the road or down to the coast. It weighted heavily on my mind again.

Worry, worry, worry... to the point of paranoia. What was I going to do if she abducted the kids? What and how would I, and the kids deal with that? Even though I often had to convince myself with thoughts like: 'people don't do these kinds of things' and 'keep it real', the fact was, she was, in fact, quite capable of doing something like that, because she had done exactly that a few months earlier with Steven. The grandparents were obviously just as mad for allowing this, as they had advised Michael in an email to say goodbye to his son until he turned twenty one! This whole family were looking more and more like professional sickos!

Thirty-four

A 'drug dealer' gets bust

I followed the other inmates' example and I claimed a spot in the corner of the cell eight by four meter prison cell. It was the perfect spot to check out and scan my new environment. Gymnastic type mattresses, covered in plastic were scattered all over the floor. A bunch of dirt cheap grey blankets made of felt were thrown into the mix with the compliments and hospitality of the South African Police Service. A distinctive pungent ammonia like smell of stale piss was emanating from the encrusted stainless steel toilet placed strategically in the corner—for everyone to witness in all its glory, and with all the senses. The smell got worse and worse as the day got hotter. It was one of those smells you cannot ignore, no matter how hard you tried. I had no choice but to give into my situation.

Well...

Here I was.

No phone, no email, fellow inmates snoring away or stoned and I had nothing else to do.

It was time to reflect...

* * *

On the fourth of November I was arrested at my house for suspected possession of Narcotics. The arresting officers, the station commander and my lawyer all knew this was a set-up. Knowing my innocence in the situation, I took it in my stride. I also thought to myself, 'Good, I'll nail her for this somehow.'

Having spent over six hours in the cell quietly reflecting and contemplating the scenario during that day, I knew exactly what happened and when it happened. Things became clear. Each and every interaction when Jane was physically present on handovers and drop offs with the kids, had been recorded on my phone's voice recorder for over a year now. It was partly paranoia on my part, but also for record keeping just in case! And just as well I did that.

The Thursday, five days before the arrest, Jane displayed very strange behaviour. Even more strange than usual. Firstly, the kids were not at her house when I went to pick them up. Jane was normally at work at that time, so I phoned Mavis on her cell phone to see where they were and why they were not at home. Her only answer was

"We're coming sir."

At that moment I saw Jane turning into the street with Brad's brand new Land Rover. Instead of just parking next to me in her driveway, which had ample space for more than two cars sided by side, she did a super complicated three point turn fart arse-ing around in the street. Eventually the car faced the opposite direction than that it had come from. I could have brushed it off as 'woman's logic' and driving style but this was really odd! She didn't drive that way normally. Her driving wasn't that bad!

Julia climbed out of the car with a 'Hi daddy' and clambered into mine all excited. Jane picked up Sean from Brad's Land Rover, carried him to his baby seat in my car and insisted on buckling him in.

This was odd. She never came to my car and certainly never helped strapping the kids in. Whilst fiddling at his seat she very quickly exclaimed that she couldn't get the buckle closed. That buckle was not that hard to close and you certainly didn't need to be a rocket scientist to do it, so I took over while she walked over to the other side of my car to buckle Julia in to her baby car seat! This had never happened before. Jane's normal modus operandi was to literally dump the kids outside the garage door and leaving me to sort out them out. I didn't think about it at the time, but in retrospect it was strange that she suddenly now wanted to be 'helpful' and assist. As usual I had my voice recording on in my pocket, and you could clearly hear Julia protesting against her mom saying:

"Daddy must put me in the seat".

It dawned on me this was the day that she planted the drugs under the baby car seats.

More proof came to light. She also gave herself away again on that Sunday, three days after the planting.

She had obviously tipped off the police straight away on the Thursday night or Friday morning and, she had expected the police to react instantly, but that didn't happen.

The following Sunday when I went to collect the kids from her house again, she had now moved into Brad's house. Albeit only two hundred metres up the road from my house this time, she was now forced to admit that they were staying at Brad's house and it was certainly no secret anymore. Because it was Sunday and she stayed so close, I collected the kids walking with the pram. She was out of character that morning. She reluctantly handed over the kids and said to me:

"If you only knew what I found out about you in the last week...I'd worry."

Thinking she was on some delusional mind trip again, I brushed past her and responded:

"Check the worry in my eye darling" whilst pulling my eyelid down. She walked off and responded after me:

"That's exactly what I'm looking at. Your eyes tell it all.... Extremely concerning."

It made absolutely no sense to me whatsoever and I wasn't even thinking about drugs. I was blissfully unaware. I had no clue what she was on about. I thought it was one of her famous defamatory and delusional statements again, and I shrugged it off, enjoying the Sunday with my kids instead. I couldn't be bothered with her viscous manipulative words any more. Little did I know that she had already left some parcels underneath the kid seats in my car.

Johan got me out on bail that Tuesday afternoon at half past three. Both my cousin Caroline as well as Johan were worried sick about me and the situation. The police were actually kind enough to drop me off at home and to collect my ID book they needed for the docket. Johan and Caroline were already at my house waiting for me.

As it was a Tuesday, I was meant to collect the kids at half past four for my day and night with them. Seeing that I was out of jail pretty early and in time, the plan was to collect the kids as normal. We agreed to keep the arrest saga under wraps from the outside world for now and pretend that all was cool and normal. We were going to see the reaction of 'madam' who obviously knew I had been arrested that day.

Jane was at her home, well... at Brad's house which she now claimed as her new home. I did check at the old residence, just in case she was there, but there was no one to be found. She had definitely moved. I instructed Caroline to record everything on video in case of nonsense. And nonsense was to be had!

The garage door opened and Jane came out shouting

"This is domestic violence and harassment. I'm calling the police!"

"What? Excuse me?" Both Caroline and I exclaimed.

"Where is the domestic violence? I'm here to collect the kids as per our schedule." I calmly replied.

Jane had the phone to her ear already and the cops were clearly on speed dial. With the phone stuck on her ear, she shouted:

"You were arrested for possession of drugs this morning!"

Both Caroline and I exclaimed in unison:

"And how do you know that?"

Jane had to think quickly on her feet and stammered

"An officer from CSS Security told me".

CSS is our local private residential security company patrolling the area.

Well that's very interesting indeed, as they were not involved in the arrest at all that morning and they would not just randomly advise other residents in the area who had been arrested and for what charge.

The police patrol vehicle arrived shortly thereafter and Jane had also called some security personnel from CSS. The sector policing vehicles arrived as well. It was a total commotion in the street with all these cars, flashing lights and people blocking the road. The kids meanwhile were inside Brad's house under the nanny's care, but hanging out the window screaming and crying

'Daddy... Daddy....' Internally that freaked me out emotionally, but that didn't seem to perturb Jane in the slightest. Jane was totally cold and heartless towards the kids and more concerned with punishing me than the wellbeing of the kids.

Sgt Shai, the attending police officer did his best to calm the situation down. Jane was on the attack and became aggressive towards my cousin Caroline, who was videoing this ordeal on her cell phone. She threw out threats towards her that she would take her on in court for harassment and non-consensual recording. Ironically and pathetically, Jane had her own phone recording too and was constantly taking pictures and videos as 'evidence'.

The first thing she explained to Sgt Shai was that I was arrested that morning for Drug related charges and that drugs were found under the children's seats. This was a very interesting statement as she even knew where the drugs were found! Remember that at this stage only Caroline and Johan knew about the arrest. I had told no one else about it. So how could she know?

Jane also explained to Sergeant Shai that she had been in court that same morning to take out a restraining order on me (again) and that she had launched another application with the Children's court trying to get an order to deny me access to the kids. This was all fresh news to me. Holy shit, she was really going balls to the wall now! She flat out refused to release the kids and because there were no firm court orders about access or custody in place yet, the police were not willing or able to act on anyone's behalf.

Their viewpoint was also rather traditional in the sense that the kids should be fine with their mom and the drugs arrest didn't sit well with them either. This is of course a biased opinion that carries through the entire justice system and society in general.

The police asked us to leave the area so as not to cause a disturbance. Caroline and I had no choice but to comply. I was left powerless.

The kids were still hanging out the window crying and screaming for me. As I left to get in the car I blew them kisses and shouted at them with tears rolling down my cheeks:

"Daddy is coming back for you guys. Soon! I promise!"

Caroline and I went home totally despondent and in a state.

Thirty-five

Dirty tricks and KID(s)napping

I had to appear at court on the fifth of November for the drug related charges. It was the first appearance for this matter. This had now become a case between the state and me. A criminal case in other words. From the state's viewpoint, I was indeed in possession of narcotics, so they had to press charges against me. Meanwhile, Capt. Mandell, who arrested me the previous day, bumped into me at court and was glad to see me out. He told me that he was fully behind me and his many years of being in the drug squad had never seen something as idiotic and suspicious like this. But for his own 'safety' this was all off the record.

The drugs he found in my car were totally unconcealed, without a trace of trying to hide them. This story had smelled like a rat to him. He was very apologetic in his demeanour, but explained that he had to follow the law and the procedures.

The drug case was postponed until end of January 2015 in order to complete the investigations. Johan also wanted to implicate Jane in the case and make her guilty of planting, because then it would automatically become state against her and not me.

However the very same day, while I was in court, I spotted Jane walking around the court house. What she was doing there God knows. Probably interfering with my drug case, or attempting to apply for something else.

That day I walked past her with my lawyer in the court passages. She used that fact later on in another one of her affidavits, as an allegation that both me and my lawyer were threatening and harassing her in court! Wow!

The interim restraining order she requested was granted on that same day and I was served these documents by the sheriff at my house the following Monday. The magistrate who had granted the interim restraining order didn't know at the time what she had signed, nor that this was the third attempt of Jane's to take out such an order. I suppose the mention of my drugs arrest made up the magistrate's mind. Unfair really, because you are considered innocent until proven guilty. What didn't help me either was that the state had launched an 'anti abuse' campaign for women that November and they were getting serious with offenders (and all males were automatically assumed potential offenders! Talk about bias!)

Jane in the interim firmly believed that she was on the winning streak and denied me access to the kids, which was in fact a serious offence in respect of the Children's Act, but we had no court orders in place to enforce at that time.

I went to her house every time I had my access. Thursday and Friday we had more dramas at her house with cops and the security companies present and she put me emotionally under a hell of a lot of stress. On Tuesday, the first time she denied access, I had heard the kids in the house and I had seen them briefly with the cops present. On Thursday however she had them well hidden somewhere and I didn't hear a peep from the house. I didn't even know where the kids were. Had she shipped them out to the coast to the grandparents? Had she kidnapped them? I was getting seriously worried. When I confronted her and asked where the kids were she stated:

"All YOU need to know is that the kids are fine and well."

That week Johan sent her numerous emails to tell her she was in contravention of the law, and she had no right to deny me access to the kids according to the Childrens' act, but that fell on deaf ears and was flatly ignored. Jane felt all powerful with her temporary restraining order and she was adamant to crack me up emotionally by not letting me see the kids or even letting me know where they were. She was at the top of her game and she had no remorse for what she must have been putting the kids through as well.

That week and the following was probably the most emotionally straining of all.

Jane had now effectively ripped the kids away from me and was provoking me into a reaction. Emotionally and mentally I had enough reason to commit an act of domestic violence, but I never did. But I was so fuming, I could literally kill.

How I kept my cool and my head together, I don't know, but my nightmares and visions had returned and they were not a pretty sight. Johan was busy day and night and weekends with my case(s) and the bills were piling up. Jane kept on 'waving' her interim restraining order around as if it was the be all and end all of law. In fact in the first week that restraining order wasn't even validated, because it had to be served on me by a court or sheriff before it became active.

She just kept on playing the game and by Saturday I was worried sick about the kids. Where were they? I had run daily to the cop station to make affidavits and as the events unfolded regarding the denial of access which she 'enforced' illegally on me. It was also a way of record keeping so that I had stamped evidence in case I needed it. Emotionally I was in a spin though and an SMS war between her and I endured.

The kids are sleeping right now.

She SMSed me at half past nine in the morning. Shit... no ways.

The kids never sleep at this time.'

I responded:

Did you drug them again?

I was worried about that. Did she drug them up? I knew she was quite capable to do that to keep them quiet! She used to do that with Steven to keep him calm in the car whilst driving down to the coast. Was she driving to the coast? Her pompous and arrogant statements started coming in again.

Mark, you are delusional and totally out of control

This was one of her favourite statements—and actually a full projection of what she's going through herself.

I, however had big reasons to worry. I was beside myself. I hadn't heard from the kids since Tuesday and didn't know where they were geographically. She had created a perfect hostage scenario and was goading me do something stupid, like break into Brad's house, just to see and be with the kids. Again I thank my lucky stars for my support structure, my parents, my sisters, Caroline and Johan who kept on reassuring me all was going to be fine—even though I had difficulty to believe it at the time.

I had no choice but to listen, stay within the law, keep my hands clean and be patient in the process. It was super hard nonetheless.

That Saturday afternoon, while the kids, according to Jane, were supposedly sleeping, I met up with Caroline at a coffee shop around the corner and voiced my concerns. All she could do was keep me calm and reassured me that all was going to be fine.

Driving back into the suburb, I decided in my worried mind, to drive past Brad's house and see if there was any sign of life. I drove past and by pure chance, there they were. Brad in his car, kids in the back and a security patrol vehicle from CSS on standby. Jane was chatting to the guy in the security van (obviously hanging up a huge story to them about how dangerous I was and in the process sucking Brad into the panic as well).

I drove by quite fast, saw them and I made an immediate U turn. I put my phone on video recording. It was half past three in the afternoon. On noticing my car, Brad quickly closed the back windows so that I could not see the kids, but the kids saw me in my car and they were screaming in their seats. They also had not seen me in over a week. It was a point of relief for me that they were still around and not at the coast. Jane was frantically pointing at me and saying something to the security guard who appeared totally non-phased. As I got closer I opened my window and told her:

"I'm glad to see the kids are finally awake and that you're not at the coast".

She shouted at me things like stalking and domestic violence again, which were her favourite words in the last week. She was stuck on repeat like a broken record. At least I knew the kids were still in the area and I drove off. It calmed me down a bit. Within five minutes of that incident an SMS came in.

> Mark, I will allow you to have two minutes communication with the kids. Phone now.

> I am forever indebted to you, your highness

I sarcastically SMSed back. Who the hell did she think she was?

I figured that Brad must have said something to her. The kids must have lost it in the car with them when they saw me, and he must have somehow confronted Jane about me not even being able to call or communicate. The kids' reaction to seeing me must have also had a major impact on him. Not on Jane, because by now I realised that she had no empathy whatsoever. She was brutally cold and heartless.

When I called, Jane immediately advised me that her phone was on speaker and that this call was being recorded.

"Whatever! Stop your pathetic delusional paranoia!"

Julia got on the phone immediately when she heard my voice. The only thing she could say was:

"Daddy, daddy...daddy.... please come fetch me and Sean."

Her sentences were constantly interrupted by Jane yakking in between and I told her to shut up and let me speak to my kids.

The conversation didn't last long. The kids weren't given any privacy and Jane insisted on interfering and manipulating the process wherever she could. How sickening!

On Sunday, I received another SMS from Jane, that I 'may have telephonic access' to the children at exactly four in the afternoon. I SMSed her back that if she had not promised the kids that I would phone them, I'd rather leave it be, as my voice would just make them upset. I was also pining for them and didn't want to risk a teary conversation. That very same SMS was later used against me because apparently I couldn't be bothered to call the kids when I had the opportunity.

On Monday I got a phone call from a number I didn't recognize.

"Hello Mark speaking."

"Hi, it's Jacobus Hardus, the sheriff, I've got documents for you" the voice said on the other side. "Are you at home?"

"Ehhm yes I am, what time are you coming?"

"Now, I'm here outside your gate."

"OK hold on, I'll open up."

I walked out and pushed the remote button to open the gate. The sheriff came in.

"Some more documents for you" he said raising his eyebrow with a compassionate frown.

"Yea, I was expecting those. It's the restraining order, right?"

"Yep" he said. "I've got to ask you though, what is that ex-wife of yours up to?"

"God knows" I replied "She's not an ex yet by the way. But why do you ask?"

"No, she's actually harassing me! She's phoning me every two hours on my cell phone to see if I have delivered the documents to you. I don't even know how she got hold of my number! She's also been calling the office on numerous occasions and emailed my boss twice already that we're not doing our jobs!"

"Well that's interesting to know. Now you know how I must feel with her ongoing manipulative streaks. But do me a favour, will you put that in a report or an affidavit so that I can take that to court if need be?"

"Absolutely" he replied. But it never came.

I signed his documents and he left.

Now I was rapidly learning about law as I went along. A restraining order, or an interim restraining order is only valid when the sheriff has served it. Even though it was only an interim restraining order which still had to be either made permanent or thrown out of court, it is a restraining order nonetheless. I had to be careful because madam was capable of anything and I had to keep a low profile for now. In the restraining order she had specifically said that I was not allowed to contact the nanny, as she was talking and open with me, and not allowed to contact the school. I was not to harass her or the kids (which I never did) and not enlist any help from other people. Yea, as if.

It was now the second week where she denied me access to the kids. Johan kept on emailing her about her violation of the Children's Act but those kept on being ignored. In the meantime, Michael got an email overseas from Jane's mother stating that he had to be careful who he aligned himself with. She was alleging that both my lawyer and I were in the drug business. Jane must have spun her one helluva story. But the mother was obviously just as mad as Jane, and although a laughable matter, it was quite a serious allegation again. Johan was fuming about that.

My folks, in the meantime were highly concerned not only about me, but also about their grandchildren whom they were very close to. They popped around late afternoon at my house and, worried about my wellbeing they kept me company, consoled me and made sure I was OK. We had some early dinner pizza take away.

Still not sure what Jane's aim in this whole scenario was, we were highly concerned about possible kidnapping and abduction and we discussed the various scenarios around my kitchen table. At four thirty that afternoon, I SMSed Jane again (as it was supposed to be my day with the kids) stating:

Are you denying me access to the kids again today?

Radio silence.

My parents got pretty worked up about the situation and in fact, I now had to calm them down quite a bit. I had resigned myself to the fact that I wasn't going to see the kids until the Rule 43 was enforced, which was due in High court on an urgent basis later that week.

By the time they left my house, they told me they'd drive past Jane's house just to see if they could see any life or sign of the kids there, to take the worry of potential kidnapping out of our heads. I told them that due to the restraining order, they shouldn't knock on doors or anything silly like that.

Thirty-six

My Rule (43) rules

A Rule 43 is an effective tool when you need it. Use it if you need it, but don't abuse it. Same goes for a restraining order. In fact, lying in a restraining order application can land you in jail for up to two years! That unfortunately never happened to my ex though, but that's another story all together.

I had requested a Rule 43, for one reason only. To safeguard the kids. I know I'm repeating myself, but this divorce was meant to be amicable (from my side at least). Just because the parents were not meant for each other, it didn't need to become acrimonious or costly and I certainly didn't want the kids to suffer under any circumstance. The kids had been and were my focus and initially I believed they should spend half the time with mom (as mad as I knew at that stage that she was) and half the time with me. Throughout the process I have had to deal with my kids being vocal about wanting to stay with me—strange for a two and three year old, but they obviously had emotional ties with me rather than the mom. Later on I found out that they had attachment issues with their mother. Mom picked up on this, got jealous and started manipulating the kids. That was pure emotional abuse and could potentially have serious long term psychological ramifications on the kids.

From my point of view, having had to deal with these mental outbursts and scenarios of drama, cops, lawyers and fights, I was myself losing track of what is normal and what is not. Can you imagine what it does to a child growing up and not knowing better? Can you believe that a two and three year old have attachment disorders with their own mom? Because her love and care is inconsistent, unstable and based on manipulation? I knew that this was not healthy for a child in the long run and as a seriously concerned parent, I had to put a stop to it.

The only way to speed it up now was the Rule 43. We had enough reports and evidence on file that she was setting the kids up, was creating alienation between the kids and myself. Although it wasn't working because my kids were too young, it definitely worked with Steven, and based on the fact that she had the audacity to just "kidnap" Steven and send him to the coast without any regard of the law, I launched my Rule 43.

A Rule 43 by the court rules has to be concise and short, and to the point. Mine still came in at a hefty twenty five pages to ensure all topics were covered and to really paint a proper picture to the judge in high court.

Jane had this document served on her on the 19th of October 2014. That, together with the fact that she had no lawyer herself anymore, plus Estelle's recommendation that was now validated by the offices of the Family Advocate, put her in a serious predicament. She got busy and launched her wicked 'drug planting' and restraining order plan. When the Rule 43 was delivered, she had two weeks to respond. Ten working days to be exact. She obviously thought that by having me arrested for drugs, she got rid of me and thus the Rule 43 as well. By quickly moving into Brad's house, she could continue to live her parasitic lifestyle off of him, drive his car and deplete his money. Plus she could quickly disappear off the radar as she wouldn't be at her legal residential address any more. By hook and by crook she managed pretty well with all her wicked plans.

The timing was there, she managed to move, got me arrested and got the restraining order out. Oh and Mavis, the nanny got fired during that same time, because she knew that her and I talked a lot about the wellbeing of the children, and therefore became too dangerous for Jane.

Jane was busy, very busy. She was so busy plotting and scheming, that she forgot to respond to, or flatly ignored the Rule 43 altogether. She obviously thought it would just fall away automatically the minute I was arrested. Either way, she hadn't responded and the court date was due on the 14th of November. Because she didn't respond in the allotted time frame the case was now uncontested.

I went with the advocate and Johan's assistant to the high court. It was more out of curiosity, as there was no real need for me to be there. I met Richard at the court building and he explained the process to me. Because he is a senior advocate, we were attended to almost immediately. It apparently works like that in high court. The more grey hairs you have on your head, the quicker you get served and the more serious the judge takes you!

The judge had already read the file, prior to proceedings and the order was granted without further delay. All we needed to do now was to get an official order typed out and stamped.

So that very same day I had the court order in my hand and I was ready to get the kids with an army of police in tow. By now, I hadn't seen them for nearly two weeks and I was adamant to get them out of this situation. I had enough of being polite and chivalrous. I was done being Mr Nice Guy. Now I had the court order in my hands and the cards had turned in my favour. It was such a relief. Finally I could shove that under her nose and bring the kids to safety. I cannot describe the feeling it gave me that day. Relief, elation, pride, happiness and power all mixed in one. The whole situation was pretty much all over now. This was going to have a major impact on my final divorce as well! The divorce date was set for end January. A mere nine weeks away.

Johan was just as elated. He called me and proudly announced:

"Congratulations Mr 'Sole Custody'. Hope you're relieved! Well done. Now you know what to do. Go and get the kids and give her a copy of the order. If she gives you any trouble, call me and don't hesitate to bring in the cops."

My ordeal was over! I drove home from the high court in town, got some food out the freezer to thaw for supper that night and the kids would be with me! We were going to celebrate! Yay!

I called Caroline with the news straight away. She knew every thing about my life and had been my support pillar and confidante on an almost daily basis. She was also elated that it was over now and wanted to pop in immediately. I said it might be a good idea, especially as I needed a witness while picking up the kids and in case Jane gave me uphill.

Just to make sure we had another witness I decided to flag down a security patrol vehicle and asked them just to be there as an impartial witness.

At exactly half past four, that Friday afternoon, we arrived at her house. I saw the kids playing outside in the courtyard behind the driveway gate. They literally went crazy with joy and happiness when they saw me and started screeching, crying and laughing at the same time with emotion. We hugged each other through the metal bars of the gate, little hands grabbing and pulling me wherever they could reach. Hunched down on their level on the other side of the gate, I tried holding them as tight as possible. Tears of happiness and relief were flowing down my cheeks as the emotions got the better of me. We hadn't seen each other for such a long time now. Sean tried to squeeze his little body through the bars of the metal gate and Julia, after attempting to squeeze through as well, realised that that plan wasn't going to work. She quickly ran inside and grabbed the padlock key and attempted to open the padlock from the inside. (She was a clever little girl already then.)

Jane, hearing the commotion, came out of the house, snatched the keys out of Julia's hands and pushed her aside. She immediately started shouting domestic violence again and screamed:

"I have a warrant for your arrest! I have a warrant for your arrest!"

Both Caroline and I responded in unison:

"For what?" as I passed a copy of the High Court order through the gate to Jane. She went as white as a sheet, but quickly composed herself and retaliated with:

"You're going to get arrested".

I calmly replied

"Jane open the gate and release the kids to me as per the court order."

All this happened while I was trying to calm Julia and Sean down as they were now in hysterics, crying non-stop trying to grab me through the bars with their hands.

Jane was frantically dialing on her phone and within minutes the cops arrived. Without me being able to explain anything, they grabbed me, handcuffed me in front of the kids and arrested me!

What the fuck?

The arresting officers were relentless and rude. They treated me like an animal and I was forced into the van. There was no need to be that violent with me, as I wasn't going to cause a scene in front of the kids. Both Julia and Sean were still crying and screaming for their daddy, and although I did my best to reassure them in the pandemonium that unfolded in front of them, the emotional damage that was done in that exact moment would take years to heal.

I managed to shove a piece of paper that Jane handed me earlier and my car, keys, wallet and some other things into Caroline's hand and instructed her:

"Get hold of Johan. Now!"

The kids were completely traumatized. They were just babies still, hysterically crying and still trying to escape from behind that fence, while their cold hearted psychopathic mother just stood there gloating at the scene unfolding in front of her. She was totally oblivious and ignorant of the children, preferring to admire her proud handy-work and craftsmanship. Caroline was in tears and went into total panic mode. She couldn't help the kids that she was so close to and neither could she help me at that moment.

Shit, what a day again. From a total high to a total low in two seconds flat!

The arresting cops were absolute bastards. They drove me five km to the nearest police station. The word driving wasn't appropriate though because they made sure I was treated like a dog in the back of the metal van. They drove like maniacs cutting corners with screeching tyres, ramping over pavements, they slammed on brakes all the time and pulled off like idiots. I tried to hold on for dear life, but there was nothing to hold onto. Like a rag doll bounced around in a washing machine I arrived bruised and shaken at the cop shop. Before I knew it, I was back in jail for God knows what.

"Not to worry," I thought to myself, Johan will resolve and will get me out of here. He did, but it took longer than expected.

Thirty-seven

Some perspective

Now at this point I have to put everything in perspective time wise before it gets too confusing. It hopefully gives a better overview of what she planned and what her motives were:

July 2014—Estelle the social worker releases her final report and recommends that the children reside with me on a permanent basis. In the recommendation, access is granted to her on an alternate weekend basis. That same evening, Jane in her uncontrolled anger, sends a picture of my penis by email to a whole bunch of people. For what we still don't know.

August 2014—I have it on good authority that she was sending (or rather bombarding) Estelle's office with countless emails daily, slagging me off as a father. Pretty much a separate case of harassment really. Apparently, with Estelle, knowing the beast by now, it fell on deaf ears and eventually the emails were mostly ignored.

September 2014—it was relatively quiet on my front. Jane was preoccupied with Steven for the school holidays and her parents 'supposedly' visiting, in Johannesburg, which never happened. I think her parents gave her the boot as she was likely lying to them too. They just dropped Steven off and left within a day.

October 19, 2014—The sheriff delivers my Rule 43 application to Jane, in which I request the kids to come to me on a full time basis and also apply for maintenance.

October 30, 2014—She plants drugs in my car thinking that

I'll be out of her life for good.

November 1, 2014—she moves house without notification to anyone (also so that she can duck and dive from the authorities as well.)

November 4, 2014—I get arrested for drug possession. The same day she is off the Domestic Violence court to obtain, yet again, for a protection order against me. Based on her affidavit and theatrics at the court, together with the mention of my drug arrest the same day, her application for the restraining order is approved on an interim basis by the magistrate. The magistrate did not delver deeper into the topic, nor were her historical applications looked at.

The sheriff delivers the interim restraining order a week later and within two days of that delivery I got arrested—again.

Thirty-eight

Jail time

So there I was again. Straight back in the hole. At the 'check in' counter I had to take out my shoelaces, remove my belt, smokes, lighters, cell phone and anything else that was loose on me. I knew the drill by now, signed the documents and was escorted to cell number two. It was probably built for a maximum of eight inmates, but the general average population in there fluctuated in numbers between ten to twelve men. Sometimes more.

Oh well, back again in a familiar and extremely hostile environment. No contact with the outside world. I knew my family and my lawyer were frantically panicked and busy on the outside, but from within, there is absolutely nothing you can do. I was completely cut off from the world. I didn't get updates on what was happening on the outside which was the most frustrating part for me. The best approach while in there is not to expect anything and I quickly resigned myself to the fact that I was locked up in a cell again.

My fellow inmates were all moping and feeling sorry for themselves. Most of them had been arrested that same Friday and were sitting in the small outside courtyard not talking to each other. It was a weird vibe.

I went to the inner cell, or the 'sleeping quarters' and picked the best spot in the corner. I needed to be patient, compose myself and just wait for my lawyer to get me out. I was arrested on a 'violation of an interim protection order'. I still don't know what that meant, coz I didn't violate anything and the protection order wasn't even confirmed or made permanent by the court. It was just an interim order!

Within twenty minutes 'dinner' arrived. If you could call it dinner as such. A couple of plastic plates with maize porridge and sauce were handed through the bars of the cell. I hadn't eaten the whole day as I was in the high court that morning and simply forgot to feed myself with all the events happening that day. But now I was hungry, so the tasteless dinner was palatable and I ate it all. After dinner my fellow inmates started chit chatting a little.

The obvious opening question and curiosity was:

"What are you in for?"

Minor offences really for most of them, but a couple of hardcore cases too. Theft and drug possession were the most common and one other guy pulled a gun in someone's face and had threatened to shoot his opponent.

Everyone pulled up a mattress inside as it started raining. How appropriate to end the day with rain! For me personally it washed the stress and emotions away. Each guy claimed his spot in the eight by six meter cell. The cell and the bedding itself wasn't too dirty, but the toilet and shower were another story. Especially the toilet! The toilet area had never been cleaned properly, if at all and I think most guys just piss and miss the bowl. The surrounding floor and walls are layered with a yellowish white crust of urine crystals that have formed over years. I'm sure you can imagine the odor of stale urine wafting into your nose from time to time. It was rather sickening, but your brain's wiring starts accepting the fact that you have no other choice but to get on with it.

My fellow inmates came from all walks of life. Some homeless people and unsavoury characters to small business owners who had gotten themselves into shit.

Later that night Johan came to visit me. With a concerned look on his face he advised me to resign myself to the fact that I was going to stay for the night. Thankfully being there for a couple of hours already, I had no expectations of coming out yet because if I had done that, I would have set myself up for disappointment. He said:

"My entire office, my junior assistants and I have been busy for over five hours now. A police docket hasn't been opened and no one can find your warrant of arrest or any other paperwork. You're actually in here based on an illegal arrest."

Apparently, which I heard later, he had taken the matter up with the Ministry of Justice already that day as something very dodgy and corrupt was going on in the station.

He had brought along some take away food my parents bought for me. They had driven all the way from the farm that night to Johannesburg, in a panic of course, thinking they could help in this drama somehow. I believe Johan did a good job at explaining the situation to them and helping them understand what was actually happening. They were worried sick. Luckily for me the warden/constable on evening duty was a friendly chap. For some reason he liked me a lot, heard about the controversy surrounding my arrest and he allowed Johan to take the bag of food in. I wasn't allowed to take anything into the actual cell though, so I had to eat it in the visitors area. Underneath the food there were two packets of Marlboro. I shoved one packet into my back pocket and asked the night cop on duty if I could have a quick smoke there. He agreed, but told me I was not allowed to take any smokes into the cell. I 'agreed' and handed him the opened pack back for safekeeping. I had my smoke and after saying my goodbyes to Johan, The officer on duty escorted me back to the cell.

When I got back to the cell, my fellow inmates asked what happened, I told them briefly and I whipped out the full box of cigarettes. They guys were impressed with my smuggling abilities and were overjoyed. Our Friday night 'party' had started and I received instant hero status based on such a simple luxury.

The party didn't last long though. An hour later, it was lockdown. The inner cell and outer courtyard (or rather cage as it was even covered overhead with metal bars and grills at six metres height) were locked up. Me and guys were now behind two gates and two metal doors. I lay down on my 'mattress' and exhaustion took over.

Worry did creep in again though. I had never spent a night in a cell! Was someone going to try and rape me? I had heard so many horror stories about those kind of scenarios. I suppose it wouldn't have made any difference, but I made sure my butt was well pressed against the wall that night. I fell into a deep sleep out of sheer emotional exhaustion.

Day two.

After our night (without rape incidents) all the inmates started to get more relaxed. I did some yoga and stretching exercises. Breakfast in the form of four slices of brown bread and a sweet tasting sort of tea arrived. A bit more chit chat and most of us were back on the mattresses snoozing again. It was a bit weird, because I slept the night before and not doing anything shouldn't make you tired!

In retrospect I heard that the tea is laced with something called blue stone which is a drug to make you relaxed and is also an anti-aphrodisiac. In other words you don't get a hardon or horny. I suppose it's a good thing for everyone's safety, but I certainly couldn't see myself feeling sexy in that kind of situation! No matter how much pressure or hormones!

In the afternoon, most of us had now been "in the hole" for twenty four hours or more. You lose all your inhibitions basically as you sleep, eat, drink, fart, shit and snore together in the same cell. Our chats became more personal and it turned out that yes, all the guys (and I'm talking soft and hard criminals with experience) were all somewhat worried about the jail rape thing. The guys with previous lengthy prison sentences actually told the non-experienced ones amongst us, that yes it does happen in jail on a consensual basis, but real rape is not that common. Well that was good to know and we could sleep safe and sound that evening.

I saw Johan again that day and he advised me that no dockets had been opened yet and that all the documents were still missing. Someone had planned this very well and I now had to resign myself to the fact that I'd be sitting in jail until Monday at least!

Oh well. I was now used to my situation. I didn't have to worry about my fellow inmates as they were all quite supportive and humbling. In a strange way, without my cell phone, emails, calls and Whatsapp's blinging in my ear the whole day I was also having some seriously good rest and relaxation time. It goes to show that we are actually prisoners within our own society outside of the cell with all these gadgets, phones and privacy invaders. I was starting to enjoy having a digital detox.

My parents visited later on and even though they came outside of visiting hours, the nice cop on duty allowed me, as an exception to the rule, to see them. They brought me more smokes and chips, chocolates etc. My mom and dad visibly relaxed in the knowledge that I was in pretty high spirits and feeling OK. They had been on a permanent hotline with Johan for a day and a half now and they appeared more worried about the situation than I was. I managed to smuggle some more smokes into the cell as well as some chocolates. Party time again! The inmates loved me and hailed me as their 'white leader'.

Being in the cell now for a day and a half, unavoidably, everyone started emanating some serious body odour in varying degrees of offensiveness. That, mixed with the smell of the corner toilet, was now becoming a serious fiesta of heinous attacks on the olfactory senses, especially when we were all locked in at night without access to the open courtyard. At six am in the morning, you could almost cut the air with a knife in there.

However God was with us because one of the inmates, in his boredom was playing with the open shower. It has one of those push buttons that switches off automatically after fifteen seconds. It was cold water of course and the outside temperature wasn't that warm. The question remained. Do I dare shower in cold water and freshen up? Or do you carry on with stinky armpits and other body parts?

Up until this point the odour wasn't bad enough (on me at least) to warrant a cold shower, but some others were certainly in desperate need of it. Vusi, however, discovered that if you turn the tap on and let the water run for a longer period, it became scalding hot!

Yay, another jubilation in the cell. Once he went in, the others, including myself had a good scrub with the bits of scrap Sunlight soap hiding in the corner of the shower and I felt a hundred times better. Having established earlier that day that no one is really interested in your butt in any case, all modesty went out of the window. There were only two guys out of the ten that were too shy to have a shower in the open and preferred to carry on stinking in their own body odour. The overall smell in the cell improved dramatically though. What I found amazing is, what little luxuries like sweets, smokes and a hot shower can do if you haven't had it for a while. We take so many things for granted in life.

That night went without a hitch and we all slept better. We were now 'brothers in crime' or fellow 'bandiete' as they say in Afrikaans.

Day three.

In the morning, we showered again to try and keep the armpits clean at least and I called the boys out to the little courtyard for a yoga lesson and stretching class. You can just imagine these thugs in the cell courtyard doing the 'downward dog' pose followed by a 'salutation of the sun'. The officers on duty couldn't believe what was happening in cell number two, called in their colleagues to come and look, and just shook their heads from the other side of the metal bars. This was followed by a brisk circular walk in the courtyard to get the heart pumping and after our four slices of dry brown bread for breakfast everyone chilled again. It was probably the blue stone in the tea doing it's magic.

Myself, and the only other white guy, in our cell Jason, decided to catch up on our suntans and we lay shirtless in the courtyard, while our African brothers were snoozing inside. This was actually starting to turn out to be a really relaxing weekend!

That afternoon as time was ticking closer to our court appearances on Monday, for some, worry crept in again. We heard a lot of stories from our more hardened brothers in crime about 'Sun City'. 'Sun City' is the nickname for Johannesburg's largest prison close to Soweto. If you get sentenced or your bail is not granted, you go there for a more permanent transfer. They described the prison in detail. About the gangs, the wardens, the life inside in general and what you got to do and not do as a new arrival. Some of our inexperienced weekend inmates were getting visibly worried. I was in ignorant and naïve bliss with the knowledge that I was not only innocently locked up, but I also had a good lawyer, plus the support of my family. But I suppose not all the guys in there were that lucky.

Before dinner, and to lighten the mood, we did a push up competition. One of the buff guys managed to do a hundred and twenty five but another pot smoking, skinny and over the top hysterical drama queen dude couldn't even do one. All he was interested in was pot and women. He was a comedian of note though and had everyone in stitches. That night my folks came around again and brought more supplies. Some of it I managed to get into the cell including a bar of Dove Soap for some proper showering. We decided to keep it until the morning to smell good for the magistrate. After I read out a bit of bedtime stories from my Wilbur Smith book on lockdown, snoring and farting took over the rest of the night.

Day four.

Court day! With nervous apprehension and anticipation we woke up and started the day. Most of us cleaned up the best we could and showered with the luxurious Dove cream bar that my parents supplied the night before. Jason decided to call the gang into the courtyard before breakfast and did a generalized prayer without focusing on a specific religion. The youngster was surprisingly good at it and we all joined in wishing each other well for the outcome of the day and the future. It was almost sad to know that I'd probably never see these people again, as we had gotten to know each other well over the last few days. I couldn't help but wonder who would walk out of court, or who would be transferred to 'Sun City' in shackles later that day.

Everyone was called out of their holding cells into the large courtyard and we lined up in rows to receive our confiscated property back. All in all I think there were about thirty five people coming out of the various other cells too.

I still didn't know specifically what I was in for as no docket had been opened for my case. I got pulled out of the queue by a detective and was hauled into a little office where they press charges.

Miraculously and all of a sudden the cops had 'found' the warrant earlier that morning and a docket was opened hastily half an hour before being transferred to court. I got cheeky with the guy and I certainly wasn't going to make any statements. In our constitution you cannot hold a person innocently for longer than forty-eight hours. I was in for nearly seventy hours by now!

"So you're the guy who disappeared this weekend with my file and documents and let me rot in jail." I announced.

He was a bit taken aback by my question and started mumbling something about other detectives and he didn't have a car to come back to Randburg over the weekend. What a bullshit story. He took my fingerprints and I told him I'm not making statements whatsoever as my lawyer would do this in court. The official paperwork was done very quickly and I joined the guys back in the courtyard.

Breakfast was served. Two slices of brown bread! I actually lost weight that weekend, but I suppose it was a good detox as well. It was coffee I missed the most.

They gave me my bag with the confiscated items back. I put on my belt and shoelaces and powered up my phone. Thank God I had some battery power left. It was enough to make a call and a selfie—or rather a 'cell-fie'. I gathered the troops from cell number two and asked them to do come and do the 'cell-fie' while we had the chance. Amongst roars of laughter and cops shaking their heads again we took these photos of us.

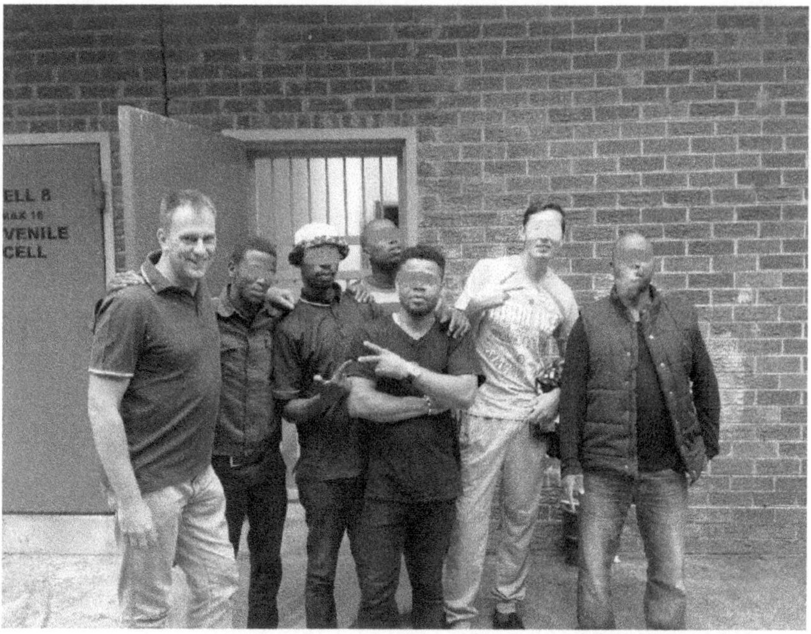
ELL 8
VENILE
CELL

Thirty-nine

Back in court again

I was getting used to the court processes by now, and I actually felt confident about going there. I knew I had a good lawyer and all the support from my family. I was just going to pay my bail until the court date and walk out later that day. Simple no? Apparently not!

We were transferred from the police station by truck to the court building next door. Silly system, but hey, that's government for you. They should just build a tunnel or a cage you can walk through. After the hundred meter drive the truck reversed back into the court doors and we were all 'offloaded'.

A friendly cop, a Will Smith look alike, briefed us about the processes and instilled confidence in all of us that ninety percent would walk out on bail. (I think he was lying, just to make us calm). Although I knew that court building well, I never realised the extent of the 'machine' underneath it. My God, it's a maze of cells, holding areas, more cells, cells next to the courts and so on. A bunch of police and admin people work there releasing or detaining those for transfer to 'Sun City' who've already appeared before the magistrate.

Phones had to be handed in again and they would keep them until after your appearance. My name was called and I was moved to another holding cell just under the court. Some other people joined me who had to appear as well. We were ordered to keep quiet and we just sat waiting. One by one the detainees were called up to appear. Some came back smiling. Others, however, were not so fortunate and were taken back to the cells downstairs for transfer to 'Sun City' or another prison.

From time to time a robed lawyer popped down from the courtroom above, talked to one of their clients and went back up again.

With its flickering neon lights, the continuous sound of slamming metal gates in the background and green Novilon floors, it became a tedious and long wait. Much less pleasant then the actual holding cell at the police station.

It was a somber and clinical environment down there compared to the wood cladded court upstairs, which, on its own was bad enough already.

My lawyer's junior guy, Raymond, all of a sudden, came down the steps.

"Can you sign these affidavits quickly?"

He presented me a bookwork of note and I didn't have the time to read it. I have full confidence in my lawyer and didn't bother to check anything. They prepared the affidavit that very morning and I had to initial each and every page with its attachments and annexes. It was about fifty pages all in all, if not more, and in triplicate and with a cramping hand, I quickly signed off about a hundred and fifty pages in total. The policeman watching over us was a commissioner of oaths as well, and kindly commissioned the documents for me, all while I remained in the holding cell.

The wait continued. At around eleven am Johan himself came down to the cell.

"Sorry I couldn't come earlier." He continued "we've got a problem though. Your bail application is being opposed."

"What do you mean? What does that mean?" I replied.

"Jane has been in court this morning and is opposing your bail".

"Why? What? What is she thinking? Is she out of her mind?"

I had never heard of someone opposing bail, but I could just imagine what that meant! It makes your bail application a lot more difficult. Especially in light of the fact that the state arrested me with drug possession charges a week earlier and I was out on bail already for that.

"Shit.... What are my chances?" I asked him.

"I don't know, but your case has just been postponed for a formal hearing at the end of the roll. At the earliest you'll appear after lunch at around two o'clock."

Holy crap! Panic engulfed me. Because I didn't have to appear yet for a while, they put me into another holding cell. But this time I was alone!

My mind started spinning in overdrive. I was now imagining getting transferred at the end of the day to 'Sun City', preparing myself for the worst. Shit Shit Shit... How dare she? What a bitch. Opposing my bail application! This was some serious psycho stuff. The work of a seriously sick and evil monster! How does she know all this stuff? Who's advising her about these legalities? To calm my nerves, I started humming and singing the song Amazing Grace. If there is a God, please be with me now. It didn't help much. I feared the worst. I didn't understand what was happening. I don't know law but this just didn't gel with me at all. I didn't have much faith in the justice system any more, and the three hour wait alone in the holding cell seemed to drag on forever with the imaginary movies playing over and over in my mind.

They brought some lunch—if you can call it that, but I was too tense to eat. The knot in my stomach was tightening.

Finally all other cases had been attended to. 'Will Smith' came to my cell and with his dazzling white teeth and with a friendly smile said:

"You're up next big guy!" as if it were a theatre production.

"Good luck!"

He escorted me upstairs into the court. The Magistrate took a quick glance at me and I positioned myself into the dock. Johan, stood slightly in front of me in his robe. He turned around, looked back at me and winked as if to say 'It's gonna be alright'.

I wasn't so convinced but smiled back at him with nervous anticipation. Looking back into the gallery, I saw my parents sitting there with concerned looks on their faces as well. They gave me nervous smiles. I returned the feeling with an equally fake and worried smile. It was nice to know I had a support system around me, but this was pretty much out of their hands. It felt good to be loved and supported though.

There were some other people in court, but I didn't see Jane. I kept thinking that, surely if she was opposing a bail application she should be present to state her reasons for the motion. I just didn't get this whole system anymore. In this case I was thankful for the support of my lawyer.

Johan opened the case and mumbled something to the magistrate, requesting permission to present the entire case to the court. With a disapproving and reluctant look, the magistrate agreed.

I mean why should she let a druggie with a restraining order and two offences in one week get out on bail? Why should she even listen to the story? But she allowed it. Was this the justice system at work or my lucky stars?

She opened the case by making the court session 'in camera' and threw everyone, who had nothing to do with this case, out of the courtroom. The only ones allowed in court were my parents.

Not knowing what it meant, and in my naivety, I actually looked around for cameras but I didn't see any there. Later on I learned, that because it was a sensitive issue and children were involved in the matter, the courts close these sessions from prying ears and eyes. They make it a private session to protect the innocent parties. *In camera*— another legal term learned.

Johan presented his case and read the affidavit I had signed earlier that morning into the record. The magistrate read along with him and listened intently. I saw her shaking her head from side to side from time to time as if to say 'Oh my God what a story'.

Occasionally she looked up at me empathically and I could see a concerned frown on her face. I was starting to ease up a little and looked back at my parents, who were listening to the proceedings just as intently. Bravely, I gave them a wink.

Within half an hour she released me on bail of two thousand Rand and read out her "interim verdict" into the court records. She made it clear and was well aware that a lot of people abuse the Protection order and she found it extremely odd that I was all of a sudden arrested for drug possession whilst having clean blood, and a week later arrested for a violation of an interim protection order. She looked up at me and gave me a lecture.

"Mr Le Foncé, I am aware the predicament you are in with your divorce, but I am now ordering you now not to communicate with your estranged wife."

My head just nodded in agreement and she continued.

"When I say not to communicate, I mean NO communication whatsoever. Let the lawyers handle the communication. Do not call her, do not send her any Whatsapps, SMS's, emails, NOTHING. Do you understand me? This is for your own protection and interests!"

I understood full well. And I also understood from that statement that the magistrate had seen the dangerous predicament I was in.

With a big sigh of relief I knew at that point everything else, and all my other cases would fall into place soon. I had hope at least.

The court session ended quite late in the afternoon. My parents, Johan and everyone else (from a distance) had all been highly involved and worried about what had transpired that weekend. The world was living it with me. Even my friend James took the day off work and came to court to offer moral support. Unfortunately for him, he wasn't allowed in due to the *in camera* session.

I had to go back downstairs to the cell area to get my phone. 'Will Smith' smiled with his dazzling teeth and wished me good luck as he handed me my phone.

"I told you you'd get out! Your story is quite sensational! Just be careful with that ex of yours. She's a woman scorned and appears to be very dangerous and on a revenge path."

Gee whizz, how fast does news spread around these courts!

I walked back upstairs to open arms and hugs, phone calls and well-wishers.

"I think it's time for a beer" Johan proposed.

"I think it's time for a coffee" I responded.

I hadn't had a cup for four days now and I love my coffees. After four days I was suffering from some serious cravings and withdrawals! I had a mild headache as well. Maybe from stress, maybe from caffeine withdrawal. We all headed to the nearest restaurant around the corner from the court building.

I had a double espresso followed quickly by another and felt a hundred times better, but the reality and stress was still all too surreal for me. I had a lot to process in my mind. I was glad

to be out though and we had some good laughs. My mom was fielding the calls and SMS's. I told her I just wanted time out and not to talk to anyone at that moment. As much as everyone was calling and wanting to know how everything was, I just wasn't in the mood to explain the same story over and over again.

Johan said he was going to talk 'business' (i.e. law) for five minutes with me, but obviously that turned out to be the topic of conversation for the next hour! He had started to take my case very personally and he felt I needed protection.

"I want you to start watching your back." he said.

Blazé as I was, I told him:

"Why are you so paranoid? What else can she come up with now?"

"Take out a hit on you perhaps?" he said.

He looked me deeply in the eyes. He was being earnest and his tone of voice had a serious ring to it.

"Remember Mark, we are not dealing with a normal person here! Look what she's done to you already! Please start watching your back. I mean it! You never know what she can come up with next."

I pondered those words for a bit. My mind wanted to deny that statement in ignorant bliss. But I had to take notice. I don't believe in being paranoid, but Johan had just confirmed what Estelle had mentioned to me earlier in the year. Estelle told me that she had picked up psychopathic tendencies. I didn't want to make up 'movies' and horror stories in my mind, but I had to start taking this information serious. I wasn't being warned for nothing. It was after all the second time someone mentioned it. And it came from two different, and unrelated sources.

When I got home, the first thing I did was take off my stinky clothes and threw them in the wash. I soaked in a bath with probably a litre of disinfectant plus a kilo of bath salts and scrubbed myself down enthusiastically from tip to toe. Just to make sure I was clean, I rinsed off, the now dirty bath water, by jumping in the shower. I suppose it was a bit over the top, but at least I felt rejuvenated and clean. Much better!

The days that followed were difficult again. I needed to process the bizarre happenings of the last three weeks mentally and emotionally. Not only that, but the legals went onto a full spin as well. Jane had borrowed twenty five thousand Rand from her new boyfriend and sold her car to raise cash. She put a deposit down with a new lawyer, a relatively unknown firm apparently, who came on record on the 18th of November 2014.

Jane must have bombarded them with tons and tons of paperwork. They frantically scrambled to get their ducks in a row and familiarize themselves with the case. The first thing they did, as a priority, was to apply for a rescission application on the Rule 43 which I had secured. The documents they submitted were an interesting batch to say the least.

Instead of being clear and concise, her new lawyer decided that a hundred and fifty page document would help. This was submitted to the high court just in the nick of time, before the dies would expire. The dies had in fact expired, but at least it was a reaction.

Needless to say the document was full of lies, fabrications and allegations. There was no merit to it whatsoever! What made it interesting though was that in cross referencing her own versions of the events, she was now in direct contradiction with her other cases and affidavits!

Forty

By her own admission

On the drug related charges, Johan had, two weeks prior to my arrest, sent an email to Jane requesting an explanation of how she knew about the drugs in my car and the fact that I was arrested. The fact that Jane did not respond to that at all, was already highly suspicious on its own accord.

Meanwhile, her lawyer must have explained to her, that she needed to respond in order to avoid further and deeper legal dramas.

So finally after three weeks, an affidavit came in. It was handwritten this time and stamped by the police on the 18th of November. The fact that it was handwritten indicated to me that her lawyer was not involved in this at all and she was handling her own matter on this. The affidavit proved to be a convoluted concoction of lies and fabrications that she'd made up. She 'explained' how she knew about my arrest and the drugs. The affidavit was so delusional and surreal in parts, that she had just proven herself guilty by her own admission.

The affidavit read (verbatim except for names) as follows:

> I hereby swear under oath the following statement

> On October the 19th I noticed some small clear plastic knotted packetsin the back of Mr Le Foncé's car under the child's seats as I was buckling in my son Sean into his car seat behind the front passenger seat. As was

confused as to what they were. I described the capsules in small knotted or bow tied packets to a friend. They suspected narcotics.

On October 20 I contacted our residents association for direction on how to handle this issue. She immediately put me in contact with CSS.

I spoke with Jan de Cock and he recommended I monitor the situation and advise him if I saw similar packets again. He also advised me to go to SAP and speak to inspector XXX.

I went to Randburg SAP and spoke to inspector Maghlangu who gave me his cell phone number and the number of the Bordeaux area sector vehicle.

For at least a week I saw no further suspect packages.

On Thursday October the 30th I saw again small packages under Sean's seat. Mr Le Foncé prevented me from looking further by pushing me out the way saying he would buckle Sean into his seat. I then walked around the car to buckle Julia into her seat, and there were further under her seat. I tried to retrieve one of the packets, but was unsuccessful. There seemed to be a mix of small packets of a whitish powder and small number of capsules bowtied into little 'parcels'. As soon as Mr Le Foncé drove off with the children, I phoned Michael de Cock and inspector Mahlangu. Inpector Mahlangu returned my call and he was in Limpopo but he advised me to continue to work with CSS. Mr de Cock ask if I could try and photograph the packets or retrieve one the next morning when Mr Le Foncé return the children to me.

At 8am on Friday October 31 I was able to pull out a package of 2 (two) white capsules, wrapped in a white clear bowtied bow tied package. I hid the packet in my hand and walked into my residence. At 8am I called Michael de Cock at CSS and advised him off the capsules. I placed the package in a blue/grey nappy bag and waited for Mr De Cock's response.

I moved myself and the children to 1 xxxxxx drive, at 8:19, Mr de Cock confirmed that he was enroute to meet me with a SAPS representative.

At 8:30 am I handed the packet containing the 2 (two) to the police officer and Michael de Cock, they would take them for testing.

I was not to provoke or do any changes to the children's routine until he had confirmation as to the contents of the capsules.

On Monday 3 November contacted me and confirmed that the narcotics team was enroute from Langlaagte with a narcotics dog and if I could confirm Mr Le Foncé was home.

Mr Le Foncé was not home as of 8:30 when I drove past. On Tuesday 4 November, Mr de Cock called me and asked if Mr Le Foncé was home. I confirmed this by driving past after dropping the children at crèche.

I met with the police officers doing the raid and based on the fact that police can do an ~~anonymous~~ search based on an anonymous tip off, they would follow that route as I feared reprisal, intimidation and harassment from Mr Le Foncé.

I then left Bordeaux around 830 am and went to work. At approximately CSS informed me had been arrested for possession of suspected narcotics.

I was at that point on site. When I returned to my office we were without power. I drove home and proceeded to contact Mr Le Foncé's attorney, Mr Johan du Randt and the social worker Estelle van der Merwe and advised them that I was suspending Mr Le Foncé's access to the children until this matter was resolved. This communication was sent at 16:20 PM.

Mr Le Foncé appeared at my gate at 16:30 PM demanding access to the children and accusing me of "planting drugs. This was in front of the police officers I had called to assist. The officers eventually convinced Mr Le Foncé to leave, after about an hour, during which he ensured he traumatized the children.

Signed stamped and dated.

Now if the roles were reversed and had I noticed suspected drugs under the baby seats in her car, I would have had a wobbly on the spot! My reaction would have been:

"What the hell is this? Are you carrying drugs UNDER the baby seats? Since when are you into drugs? I'm calling the cops right away!"

I would have bust her on the spot, and hauled in the cops. Who on earth contacts the residents association? Who on earth would have, as a parent, let the other parent drive around with suspected drugs under the baby seats within the child's reach and endangering their lives? Can you imagine if Sean or Julia grabbed these packets under their seats and started chewing on it? It could have resulted in death!

Her crucial mistake in this set up was that she forgot that sometimes I walked with the kids to her house to either collect them or drop them off After all, I only lived a few hundred metres away in the same suburb. On three occasions she claimed that she 'saw' the parcels. Firstly on the 19th of October, the second time 30 October and the third time on the morning of the 31st when (she claims) she even 'collected' a sample from my car!

When I went through my voice recordings, which I had on my phone, it turned out that on both the 19th as well as the 31st, I had collected the kids on foot with the pram. This was clearly audible and without a doubt. On those two days, my car was not even near her house! She had just perjured herself even more!

I reported it immediately to Johan and he was elated as now she'd clearly lied again under oath and was making up stories to suit her own case, even going to the point of implicating other people's names and where they work. She needed allies, but to this day I doubt that a security company would just take 'samples' from her for analysis. The whole story stank. Either way, I had the evidence to counterproof her claims and it was not going to go down well.

Meanwhile, with the interim restraining order still hanging over my head, I was advised to 'behave' and keep my hands squeaky clean. I had a couple of court cases to clear and the next appearance would be on the 9th of December. Finally her newly appointed lawyers advised her not to hold the kids back illegally anymore. They did, however request if we could hold off on the enforcement of the Rule 43. For some reason, Johan had agreed to this, but I was not in agreement with his decision. He told me that we would give them two weeks, to respond in 'good faith' and to try and keep things civil. Being civil was a hard thing to do for me personally. I had just been jailed twice for nothing! I just wanted the kids out of there and exercise my rights, but Johan kept me in check and had his reasons.

In that two week 'good faith' period I had to bite my tongue and had to listen to the lawyers. The magistrate who released me on formal bail for the 'violation of the protection order' had also instructed me not to communicate with Jane at all. All correspondence was now to be handled by the lawyers until my appearance for the restraining order which was set down for the 26th of November 2014.

In the interim I had the kids back on their old access schedule with me and on initial arrival on the 18th of November, although happy and over the moon, they were totally bewildered and manipulated.

It took them hours to settle in at home and they were extremely clingy. I could see that they had attachment disorder issues again, and their behaviour clearly projected their insecurities. Julia kept on asking me about the police as they witnessed the arrest first hand. Mom had apparently poisoned her mind and told her that I was a baddie and I was locked up in jail because I was naughty. This was a lot of information to process for a little three year old girl. She asked me at one stage:

"Daddy, were you crying by the police?"

I told her that the police were actually good guys and that they are here to help us against bad people, but I did't know what she could absorb and understand from that.. The topic weighted heavily in that little mind as this was followed almost immediately by another question:

"Daddy, do you think Mom is bad?"

I was a bit lost for words, but knowing that Jane was still her mother, I responded:

"No Julia, mommy and daddy are just not getting along very well. I just don't agree with some things that she does."

Knowing full well that with the emotional disorder Jane had, she probably really didn't know what she was doing.

However, having said that, Jane was still responsible and accountable for her actions and justice needed to be served. My diary was full of court appearances. The first one booked was to try and squash the interim protection order she had applied for.

Johan and I worked frantically on the affidavits and responses.

I wanted this matter out of the way, and we were ready to proceed. I was also ready, but the applicant for the restraining order was not! Jane's lawyer was not up to speed and they attempted a delaying tactic under the banner of 'We're too busy and haven't familiarized ourselves with the matter as yet'.

The magistrate wouldn't have it. They asked for an extension until January or even February, but that would mean I'd still have this interim protection order hanging over my head with potential further arrests based on fabrications. Johan fought tooth and nail and questioned them as to why they couldn't be ready as they were the applicants in this matter. The magistrate clearly wasn't impressed either, but under law, as it was the first appearance, they had the right of a postponement. It was clearly a delaying tactic to keep me squashed under the interim protection order, so the magistrate gave them three weeks The magistrate warned both parties that nonappearance would result in arrest. I wasn't happy with this postponement, but I had no say in the matter.

Due to the animosity of the situation and also for my protection, the lawyers instructed us that the kids' handovers from now on would only take place under camera at the petrol station a block away from us. The situation was getting more and more bizarre. To add insult to injury, Jane had spun huge stories to the local security company and community. She played the damsel in distress and asked for a security patrol vehicle with security guards attending at each handover. Just in case the monster (me) would lash out! So we handed over the kids under heavily armed guards and under camera at her request. I just kept quiet hoping that the long arm of the law would eventually do its thing.

At the same time I also started getting feedback on stories she was throwing around in the suburb and at the kids' school.

The smear campaign was again in full swing. The same week I got out of jail, I received a phone call from the nurse at the local clinic. I got along well with Sister Desiree and she always attended to inoculations, or she would quickly do check-ups on the children when they were under the weather. She worked at the local pharmacy at our nearby shops. Often when I went grocery shopping with the kids we ended up chatting with Desiree. She cared for the kids and knew my story well. I had seen her just after my second arrest and had told her what had happened. Desiree was flabbergasted. She was quite a character, British by origin and she was rather rough with her tongue. Needless to say she let out some hefty inflammatory words about my estranged wife.

The day after I saw her she called me on the phone. I saw Desiree's name appear on the screen. Surprised to see her call me, as she never did that, I answered:

"Hi Desiree."

Her voice was raised, loud and thick with a heavy British accent:

"Mark...I got yer foocking wife sitting here in my office with yer kids and she's refusing to leave!!"

"What? Why? What does she want?"

"She wants the fooking inoculation certificates for the kids."

"Well I have those in my office" I said to her.

"Yer I know" she said. "But she is demanding them from me and I can't give her any!"

"Well, why doesn't she ask me for them? What does she need them for in any case?"

"Because she tells me you're still in chookie and she doosn't know when you're coming out. Thank God I saw you yesterday and I know the story. The lying bitch!"

"Holy crap...okay," I said. "So Jane is telling you that I am still in jail? In front of the kids? In your office?"

"Yes...she's being an absolute bitch! I could see your daughter cringing when Jane mentioned the word jail!"

"This is insane. Let me phone Johan. I'll call you back just now."

"Yer please hurry, because she is refusing to leave, she's a fooking psycho."

I called Johan immediately and luckily he answered the phone. Although he didn't intervene with Jane directly, he did speak to her newly appointed lawyers, MNM who in turn got hold of Jane. They advised her to leave the nurse alone and remove herself from there.

Forty-one

'Cop' of Coffee?

I planned to meet up with my mom for coffee. She had come to Johannesburg for a dentist appointment and we arranged to meet at 'Muggs' coffee shop near her dentist. At around lunchtime I SMSed her.

> I'm a little early. I'll go to Muggs so long. Meet me there when you're done.

The place was busy and bustling. I spotted a table in the chaos and I sat down at the only available table. My mind was busy with all sorts of things so I didn't take much notice of of my surrounding. I didn't notice the two guys in blue uniforms at the table next to me. I took my laptop out of my bag to check for emails and do some work.

After I'd just settled and plugged in, I heard a voice call me:

"Mark.... Hey... it is you!"

It was Captain van Tonder, station commander of the Police station where I was locked up just two weeks earlier. What a coincidence!

"What are you doing here?" He asked.

"Having some coffee!" I replied dryly. What else could I say really!

"Tell me, what happened with your case in court?"

"Well, as far as Johan tells me, I was arrested illegally and under very dodgy circumstances two weeks ago, without dockets being opened and the warrant going missing!"

"Yea I know, I was on leave at the time but I heard about it. I've already been in contact with Johan and we're doing an internal investigation. Something is not right here."

Interesting! Things are not only happening behind my back with the 'madam', but now the cops are doing investigations without my knowledge too! Capt van Tonder reassured me that they were working on getting to the bottom of certain irregularities.

He asked some more questions about the restraining order and told me he'd talk to the prosecutor. Mhhh.... I wasn't quite sure what that meant, but trusted and hoped that he was behind me. He'd obviously seen some stuff I wasn't privy to and I should probably keep my nose out of. I never heard anything more about it though.

A week later I was in court again. I had two cases in one day! The one case was in criminal court for the 'violation' of the protection order, for which I had sat in jail. The socalled violation was based on my parents driving past her house. (I apparently used a third party to harass her—that was the 'violation'.)

The other case was in the Children's Court because she had also submitted a request to legally deny me access to the kids. This was done the same day she applied for the restraining order, but the magistrate had not granted her that request immediately as the magistrate wanted both parties to be able to explain themselves. Even though the Children's Court didn't grant her the request, Jane felt she was within her right to deny me access to the kids regardless. It was an absolute violation of the Children's Act.

Although by then, I was getting fairly clued up and familiar with the court processes, and knowing my rights quite well, it was a tense and daunting situation. What if a magistrate has a bad day? Or hasn't read the documents properly? What if the courts are biased? We're all human after all and mistakes do get made.

Worries aside, Johan decided to tackle the violation of the restraining order first that day. Although my name and case were on the roll, my file was not in court.

According to the court clerk, the docket was with the public prosecutor, Mr du Randt. Johan knew him and asked me to come with him into his office. I stayed behind in the doorway because the office was chaotic and buzzing. It was full of people already. Du Randt and Johan chatted and Du Randt advised that he'd sent the file back to the court.

He told us my DV case had been dropped as there was a reference in Jane's application to a certain act 2.1.2. (something like that). It appeared that this act, or that point within the act at least, did not exist! Charges were dropped based on a technicality! Cool. That was easy! She shot herself in her own foot. There was going to be no trial, but as a formality we still had to appear in court. Within half an hour, the magistrate read the 'verdict' and case was closed forever.

This was the same magistrate that had handled the previous criminal court proceedings when I had to do a formal bail application. She was well aware of what was going on. After she read the case as dismissed, she gave me a huge smile from ear to ear, almost as if to say. It'll all be OK, don't worry! I liked her and my day was starting off well.

We weren't finished yet though. We still had to see the Children's Court Magistrate, Mrs Labuschagne. Due to sensitivities of cases involving children, this is usually done in closed chambers (in 'camera') and we waited for her in the waiting area until she could see us. Half an hour later we were escorted by a security guard to her chambers and she beckoned us to sit at the boardroom table.

Mrs Labuschagne is a burly woman who doesn't take nonsense from anyone. She'd been handling children's cases and court issues as a magistrate for many years, and although strict, she was apparently very fair when making judgments. She was definitely there in the best interests of the children and simply did not care about the parents emotions. Parents should sort out their issues amongst themselves, and she tried to make sure that the children did not get hurt in the process. She had no tolerance for mudslinging parties. Common sense really.

She started off with being apologetic, as she hadn't had a proper chance to look at the file yet. They had a power failure the day before due to an electricity load shedding schedule.

Before looking at the papers she addressed me directly and said:

"So you're the applicant in this matter and you want your wife to have no more visitation rights to your children?"

Johan intercepted:

"No your worship, it's the other way around. The applicant is his estranged wife." (Just goes to show how even magistrates can misread or misinterpret documents.)

With a quizzical look she opened the files and the affidavits contained therein. After reading for a minute or so she looked at me:

"Where is your wife?"

"I don't know your worship" I remarked.

"So, are you telling me that the applicant isn't bothered to be present in this matter? She wants to deny you the right to see your children, yet fails to show up for the hearing she applied for herself?"

The agitation was clear in her voice.

"Ehhm it appears so, yes. . . ."

She took a few minutes to read through some more documents in the file and glanced at me again pensively.

"OK this is bizarre" she continued. "I am closing this matter with immediate effect. I cannot make a cost order in your favour, because the applicant is not present, but I will note on file that the cost of this application may be added to the cost in the actual divorce."

She made some notes on the file, looked up again and smiled empathetically.

"Good luck and all the best Mr le Foncé. You are dismissed."

The day was done. Although I would not wish anyone to ever have a day like this, it was a good one for me. The courts, magistrates and justice system seemed to be coming full circle slowly but surely.

However, nine days later I was in court once again!

This matter was important. This case was to confirm or set aside the interim restraining order that had been granted on an interim basis erroneously.

Janc was adamant to get this order taken out on me and her lawyer had submitted further affidavits on the court file. They were, as usual, obvious and blatant lies and baseless allegations. She had attached a falsified statement from Mavis, the nanny, who was fired a few days later. She had also attached a new affidavit from her boyfriend Brad, but the writing style was totally Jane's as well as the types of allegations contained therein.

It was like a novel. All to paint me with the same old tar brush and to try and convince the court that I was a criminal.

Jane had her 'entourage' and (limited) fan club playing the court's emotional strings. The boyfriend's affidavit was pathetic to say the least. Not only did he claim that my lawyer's letters were falsified and full of errors, (as if that had anything to do with him in the first place) he also had a paragraph in there stating that he had never been so scared in his life as when I confronted him at his house picking up the kids.

I had never raised my voice at him or threatened him in any way. This just reeked of manipulation and pathetic cowardice. I joked with Johan that Brad had probably received a blowjob in return for signing that affidavit. Not only that, but the guy looked a roughish type, covered in tattoos and piercings! And he was scared of me? It made me laugh!

The affidavits didn't matter. We were called into the court-room. The magistrate asked us to come back at eleven o'clock as she wanted to prepare for the case and go through the documents on file in her chambers.

Something you don't see in the movies and on 'courtroom TV' series is that in reality you spend most of your court time waiting and wasting time in the corridors. It's an extremely boring and usually tedious environment to say the least.

'Madam' was present, waiting in the corridors as well. She appeared over-confident as always with an arrogant attitude. She was dressed to kill and ready to put on her pity party performance in front of the judge. Besides her files and files of evidence stashed in three separate bags, she had her new lawyer in tow. Even though this lawyer was from the same law firm, MNM, they had sent a twenty-something year-old junior who was going to handle her case. I couldn't help but wonder if the more senior staff were too scared to pitch as they knew they were going to have egg on their face?

A 'little birdie' had also told me the day before the court case that this law firm had advised their client (Jane) to withdraw all the charges against me and come to her senses, however they were unsuccessful in that attempt! She had to have her show snd would rather continue in her path of destruction and mayhem. An utter waste of time, money and resources.

Jane was becoming increasingly delusional with her allegations and was incapable to see the path of destruction she was creating for herself. Jane was now not only fighting me, but she was also going against the advice of her own lawyers. In her affidavits for the high court as well as this one, she carried on playing the same tune over and over again and implicated more and more unwilling and unknowing parties.

In her affidavits she was criticizing judges, the sheriff, the social worker, her own lawyer and implicated the police, the security company and other people without any proof or substantiated documents. She loved dropping names and played the game of: 'He said, she said.' But had nothing to back it up. Her own delusional-mind-movie was now in full swing, yet in her voluminous documents, written like novels, she was continuously contradicting herself.

Her junior lawyer approached Johan in the corridors. She wanted to speak to Johan privately. He excused himself and went with her. Two minutes later he came back with a big grin on his face.

"They want to settle" he exclaimed.

"Whaaaat?" I said to him.

"Yes, the proposal is that you can have the kids as long as she doesn't have to pay for them!"

"What kind of patheticness is that?" I remarked.

"I've asked them to put it in writing asap."

"Yea, but hold on, I need to think about this. I'm not just going to make quick decisions in a court corridor like this."

"I agree" he said, "but it's still brilliant! The fact that they want to settle is a step forward. The fight is obviously over for her. Maybe she realised she's not going to win."

"Don't sell the skin before the bear is shot. I know her better than that. This is an impulsive decision that is going to change in an hour. Look what she did to Michael earlier this year. With this chick even a court order is not going to put her in line. She believes she's God herself."

It had to let it sink in for a while. I can have the kids, as long as she doesn't have to pay for them! I mulled it over.

"So actually" I said to Johan, "what she is saying here is that she as a mother is willing to give up her kids as long as I pay? In other words she is selling the kids to me?"

"Yup...pretty much..." Johan smiled. "Why do you think I want that in writing?"

Unfortunately that 'settlement' letter never came of course. In fact there was absolutely no more mention of it.

Shortly after eleven o'clock we were summonsed back into the court room. My parents also arrived. They were so worried about me and the whole situation that they insisted on being there. Even though I told them that I didn't really need them, they still wanted to support me morally and to make sure that everything went well. Their poor nerves were shot and bless their souls for being so supportive. For them this was also all new and worrisome, but they wanted to see how things got handled and settled. None of my family had ever been in a litigational situation like this before, so for everyone it was also an interesting scenario to witness.

Johan wanted her in the dock, no matter what, and bring her to trial. He was ready to pounce and eradicate her crap for once and for all and make her stew in her own lies and manipulation. He was ready for the kill.

"All RISE!"

The door behind the bench opened and the magistrate walked in.

She looked at the lawyers and told everyone to sit down. She cleared her throat.

"I've read the affidavits" she started "and have come to the conclusion that this restraining order is to be set aside. There is no reason for a restraining order."

She had made up her mind. No trial, no arguments, no cross examinations!

She continued:

"And I'd like to let the parties know that your conduct in this divorce is not helpful to anyone and your kids are suffering under the circumstances."

She was visibly angry, but I whole heartedly nodded in agreement as if this was a church sermon. Although the magistrate addressed 'both of us' I knew this was directed at Jane. The magistrate also only looked at her as she delivered these words. Not that that helped much, as Jane would not take no for an answer. From anyone!

The matter was closed. Johan, standing in front of us, looked back directly at Jane. He gave her the most evil look imaginable. I had never seen that expression in his eyes before. Jane got up without being excused and stormed out of court. She didn't even say goodbye to her own lawyer. I think she understood what the magistrate had told her. Regardless, the opposition lawyer approached us in the corridors to say goodbye to us and wished us all a Merry Christmas with a smile.

The most important thing was that the restraining order was set aside. The third one I had had to deal within the space of a year.

Forty-two

Holiday time

With all the nonsensical court cases behind me, restraining orders being squashed and allegations thrown out of the window, it was time to relax. Or was it?

Emotionally I was strong but the last two months of worrying, arrests, smear campaigns and character assassinations had exhausted me. My family was super helpful and also assisted me financially in order to keep my head above water. After all I hadn't had a chance to pursue new business and my regular client was shutting down for Xmas. Cash flow was a problem. Johan assisted me a lot as well and I hadn't even seen his bill yet. (I wasn't particularly interested either, because I knew it was going to be beyond horrific!) When I asked him about it, he said, "It'll come, don't worry."

The Rule 43 had now been implemented but because holiday times had started, I had to stick to the order of the Rule 43, which stated that the holidays were to be shared. Johan had drawn up a schedule which we had to obey. 'Madam' Jane had to have the last word on this of course and was of the opinion that the kids could not be with me for such an extended period of time as they'd 'miss' her too much. She was obviously flatly in denial of the Rule 43 order and she still tried to control a sinking ship instead of bailing out.

With the restraining order squashed, I could or she could, easily hand over the kids at my or her house, but the lawyers decided for the time being it was better to do it under camera at the petrol station. I didn't trust her one bit. With her new boyfriend she had obviously played the sympathy card and she was the 'fearful' separated wife of a dangerous and abusive convict. When we met to hand over the kids at the petrol station, her car was usually surrounded by three security patrol vehicles to add that dramatic effect. She still had someone under her thumb at the security company and carried on portraying the 'damsel-in-distress'.

I approached one of the guards and showed him the letter from court that the restraining order was no longer valid and that there was no reason for them to be there to intimidate either me or the kids. Although the guards were never nasty or harassing to me in any way, or at any time, I did explain that it's not good for the kids when they were constantly there. The kids were getting phobias about police and men in uniform. It rattled them in spite of my reassurances that it was all okay.

He softly responded to me

"Dude, don't stress. I don't understand, but I know women well enough to see that this is nonsense!"

He rolled his eyes back, saying that he was under instruction from his manager.

The kids were happy to come to me and we spent a good couple of days together setting up the Christmas Trees and visiting Santa at our nearby shopping centre.

For me it wasn't a case of bonding with the kids, as the bond was there, but I almost felt like I had to do exciting things with them in order to compensate for their stressful life and experiences at mom's house. One of the conditions of the holiday period was that we could phone and have reasonable telephonic access to the kids and calls were set for six pm. But Jane didn't bother. There was radio silence for now.

Five days later the kids had to go back to her house. It was just before Christmas. At breakfast time I sat them down, to explain that they had to back to mommy that afternoon for a few days and then they'd come back to me. I showed them the letter from Johan with the roster for the period, but that probably went right over their heads. They were too young to understand rosters and holidays. I felt that it was important to explain things though and be as consistent as possible, no matter how small they were.

Just before handover at around four pm, I got them dressed and told Julia to put out the cookies and milk for Santa at the fireplace. I explained that when they'd come back, Santa would have come and brought lots of pressies for them. Excitedly and in a hurry she got milk, cookies and carrots for the reindeers. She also ran to the kitchen table and picked up Johan's letter and the holiday roster. She ran up to me and said:

"Daddy, Please can you put this letter in my stocking. I'm going to give this to Santa and tell him I want to stay by your house. He must change this."

Tears shot into my eyes. I had a hard time fighting my emotions and hugged her so hard. My little innocent three year old 'poppet' had always been vocal as to where she wanted to be, even with her mom. This was so unfair on these little babies. I knew that Julia was getting the brunt of the emotional abuse from mom, purely because she was so innocently honest with her feelings. Even her teacher, Agnes, had picked that up at school and advised me of mom's manipulation and favoritism.

Whilst the kids were at Jane's place, I phoned every day at six. Calls were generally cut short by Jane or simply not answered. This was usually followed with a set of abusive SMS's. She was taking full control of the calls and of the kids whilst in her care.

One day before Christmas Eve, when I called, her phone rang, but it was not answered. An SMS came through shortly thereafter:

> They have both dropped off to sleep. Will let you know in the morning.

Sleeping at six pm? It was clearly a lie again, as the kids would never be asleep at that time. Of course, I didn't get any feedback in the morning or a message to call back either.

On Christmas Eve, I couldn't get through at all. Her phone was switched off. Eventually, after trying a couple of times, at six thirty that night all of a sudden her phone was on again. It rang, but there was no answer. I sent her an SMS:

> Jane, I tried to call, but I can't get through. I didn't hear anything this morning either as you promised.

The response SMS that followed astounded me. It read:

> "It is way past six pm and they are in bed. You are supposed to call at six."

This SMS was followed by another one immediately after.

> Are you high again and in a time lapse Mark? The agreed time was six pm, not when it suits you. Please respect the agreement that is in place as per attorneys.

I just responded

> CC Johan Brooks

I was instructed to advise him of any shit happening during the holiday period.

Another message came through from her:

> I am only asking you once not to harass me and my family on Christmas Eve. It is now seven pm and I am not tolerating you spinning out of control and affecting our evening.

The best thing for me was just to keep quiet and I did. Feeding a narcissist with more SMS's or correspondence was just going to add more fuel to her delusional mind and I would be the only one ending up getting wound up. Johan, in the meantime, sent me an SMS shortly after.

> I'll call you in five min.

I told him not to worry over Christmas eve, but he called regardless.

He advised me that she's aware that her days are numbered and that she's losing it. Expect more flare ups and allegations like this. And the fact that she had surrounded herself with three security vehicles at the last handover was indicative of serious paranoia she was dealing with internally. No shit Sherlock!

The kids were with me the next day. Her boyfriend Brad who worked away from Johannesburg every week on site, was home for the holidays. Somehow, I was glad about that. Even though I was pissed off with him for sending out false affidavits, I was also realistic and hopeful that he was saner than her. The kids seemed to like him more than their own mother and I could only imagine what kind of stories he must have heard about me being a drug dealer and so on. He was totally under her manipulative spell. I gathered that he was being kept in the dark, just like I was initially. The kids liked him so much in fact, that they'd run straight into his arms, instead of hers at handovers. They developed a closer bond with the new boyfriend then they ever had with their own mom. That alone just showed how emotionally stuffed up mom really was.

Jane never came out of the car anymore during handovers. She would just sit there in the passenger seat like 'Miss Daisy'. She made Brad now in 'charge' of the hand-overs and parenting duties. Although reluctant and never saying much, he always wished me a nice day, and greeted me with a "Hi, how are you?" He made sure that the kids had their shoes with them, jerseys, if necessary and said his goodbye's to them. Jane would just sit there watching and gloating, admiring her new found slave.

I was hoping by now, that Brad, although hugely manipulated by her lies about me, started seeing things more clearly. Surely he had heard the kids talk positively about me. Surely he had seen that there really was no aggression in me, contrary to her statements. Surely this was amplified by the setting aside of the restraining order!

He'd also seen the letter about the drug charges, which Jane had claimed, was a letter falsified and written by me! I think he must have been confused and somewhat worried. He'd only known her for a few months. She'd already moved into his house with two kids and occasionally Steven as well, when he was up from the coast. He had already lent her twenty five thousand Rand. She "lost" her job the day she moved in with him. He was now paying for groceries for everyone, dinners out, the household costs etc. Things were starting to pile up on him and red flags must have started to show. She was starting her abuse on him and he must have felt it deep down. Surely he was not that stupid?

I took the kids to my parent's farm for a couple of days just outside of Johannesburg. As per the lawyer's letter, we had to give each other notice if we were intending to leave the province for holidays. The farm was situated just outside the border, so technically we were leaving Gauteng. I sent her an email and copied in Johan.

We'll be at the farm if you need us for any reason.

That's all I legally needed to do and say. Giving her any more details would only ensure she would find fault and stew over them.

An email immediately followed back addressed to her lawyer:

Dear Bronwyn,

Please see below. So much for his attorney's letter regarding pre notification as per his lawyer.

Regards.

Jane

Another email followed five minutes later:

Like I stated last week when meeting with the advocate, he would escalate over Christmas and do as he wishes, despite any written agreements.

Wow what a projection! She must have been holding up a mirror to her own internal self. She was frantically typing emails and continuing her smear, without really thinking about it.

Again the best response from my side, was no response. I was fed up trying to defend myself from this madness and left it at that. I certainly wasn't going to allow it to ruin my Christmas.

I think I had finally come somewhat to my internal senses as well, and these kind of allegations didn't really bother me so much anymore. Her allegations and nonsense was starting to fall on deaf ears . I was comfortable and hopeful in the fact that others saw it loud and clear too. Her lawyer also didn't follow up with this kind of crap. My confidence and self-esteem was finally starting to come back.

We had loads of fun at the farm. My dad had bought a new Jeep. We took the roof off and went for some serious off roading. I took the kids to the various neighbouring farms with cows, pigs, horses and the works. We had mud fights, swimming, lots of sunshine and Julia, Sean and me were having a good break. They relaxed more by the day and so did I.

Jane called the kids daily at six. And I mean exactly on the dot at six pm. I always answered the phone, but I never had a desire or inclination to talk to her. On Boxing Day, I called Sean and Julia to come to the phone but they refused to speak to her. I told the kids not to be rude (and I meant it), but convincing the toddlers to "talk" on the phone when they didn't want to, was no easy feat. After a minute or so, I gave up, put the phone to my ear and said:

"Sorry, I tried, but they won't come to the phone."

Jane tried to have a conversation with me, but I rejected her outright and told her to send me an email. I was beyond oral communication with her as it would be turned around in any case.

Jane had access—just for three hours the next day. We would meet at a local kiddies restaurant to hand them over. When I met them at the restaurant farm the kids ran straight past her again into Brad's arms. This was becoming a regular thing. And worrisome at the same time!

Again he greeted me nicely and said,

"We'll see you later at one o'clock."

As usual, not a word of communication took place with her during the handover.

Three hours later at the same location I picked them up. Brad handed me Julia and Sean. They were cranky, whiney, crying and visibly upset over something.

"Great," I thought to myself. They were so chill and within three hours they returned a nightmare and uncooperative. Thankfully their 'crankiness' didn't last long though. Back at the farm they continued playing and going on with their own business. We spent another couple of days with their grandparents, and went home to my house in Johannesburg two days later to continue the holidays there.

I had some work to do still and had to tend to the pool, garden etc. The kids kept themselves busy with their new toys that they got from Santa and over the period I taught them to swim in our pool. We spent lots of time playing in the pool and I was super proud of them that they were so confident in the water. We also did fun activities like painting, going to feed the ducks, visiting the

botanical gardens, and shopping. The joys of single fatherhood.
These were all little things, but nice for them and uplifting. I
regularly had friends over, either for dinner or just a drink and
yes, although we didn't really go away on a big fat holiday, we
had a lovely time and a good break all in all. Jane made only two
attempts to call during this period, but both times I failed to get
the kids to talk to her. I actually sat them down afterwards and
told them:

"No matter what your feelings are towards anyone, when mom
or anyone calls to talk to you, you at least say hello and goodbye."

I didn't want my kids growing up to become rude and obnoxious. They needed guidance and order.

New Year's Eve arrived quickly, as it tends to do in December.
I spent it alone with the kids, who were still too young to stay up
until midnight. I had Caroline over for a drink early that evening,
but not one of my friends and acquaintances were in the mood
for any festivities. It was almost like everyone wanted to get rid
of 2014! And the same rang true for me. The kids went to bed
in time. I followed suit at ten pm. It was the first time ever in
my life that I had slept through New Year's Eve. And ironically
I felt good about it too! No champagne, no fireworks, no parties!
Sounds depressing, but it really wasn't. I was refreshed and fit for
the upcoming New Year. Welcome 2015! Let the real fireworks
begin.

Forty-three

Rescission application—the response

When the courts re-opened after their Christmas break, we had to attend to the rescission application. The rescission application on the Rule 43 was niggling me and hanging over my head. Was it still going ahead? As far as I'd heard, she was out of time to file her paperwork in the court. These were technicalities really, but the high court is quite strict regarding this.

From my personal perspective and opinion, responding to her hundred and fifty page rescission application in December was basically a waste of time and money. Neither Jane, nor her lawyers had followed it up and she was again working against court rules.

Courts and their rules are funny beasts though. Sometimes things make sense, and sometimes not. I was getting good at it, but by no means did I understand the law and its rules like a lawyer or legal professional would. I don't believe our response on the actual rescission was a waste of time, as it probably stopped her right in her tracks by trying to push the application forward. In this document Johan laid it on thick and included my various arrests and the alleged drug possession case. He pretty much put on the court file that there was no doubt in my mind that she'd planted the drugs and that she had set me up. It was time to expose the beast!

He chronologically stated all the events in his affidavit as follows. This section was the 'meat of the affidavit', the crux of the matters at hand and the total undeniable truth as well (verbatim).

> To prove to this Court the mala fides of the Applicant, I will now turn to the chronological sequence of events since 17 October 2014:
>
> a. On 17 October 2014 the Applicant is served with notices in terms of Rule 35, 37 and 43 of the Supreme Court Rules. The subject matter of this application is the Rule 43 application, which the Applicant denies to being served on this day;
>
> b.   The Applicant, in terms of her statement of 5 November 2014, declared that she noticed parcels under a child seat in my vehicle on 19 October 2014, while buckling our son into his seat. Noteworthy of this statement is the fact that I collected the minor children from the Applicant on foot and with a pram. I pause to state that the applicant at that stage lived a mere 300 metres from me. The events of this day was recorded with my telephone and I will avail the recording and the phone to this Court if required.
>
> c. The Applicant's statement relating to the events of 19 October 2014 is therefore rejected as an outright lie.
>
> d. What should also be concerning about this fact is that the Applicant failed to raise any concerns with me in this regard (although she would refuse me access to the children from 4 November 2014 onwards). Instead she states under oath that she discussed this with a 'friend". She would then proceed and state that she phoned the head of the Resident's association on 20 October 2014.
>
> e. For the next week no parcels were noticed by the Applicant. She however then again noticed, and described the parcels found in my vehicle on 30 October 2014. She also stated that she attempted to take a sample but failed.

f. On 31 October 2014 the Applicant 'succeeded' to retrieve a parcel from my vehicle. This parcel collected was handed to the SAPS according to the Applicant's statement. The concern that I have with this statement is the fact that I again, on 31 October 2014, returned the minor children by walking from my home to the residence of the Applicant. I have a further recording to this effect, and will follow the required procedure to make available this recording if required.

g. I also at this stage pause to confirm that my attorney of record recorded on 7 November 2014 that the Applicant had access to my vehicle on 30 October 2014, a letter that she conveniently exclude in this application. It was alleged in this letter that the Applicant 'planted' the illegal substances in my vehicle, an allegation which the Applicant never explicitly denied to this day.

h. What I find peculiar is the fact that the Applicant still deemed it not necessary to raise any concerns (on her version), and she still allowed access to me for the weekend of 31 October to 2 November 2014.

i. I was then on the morning of 4 November 2014 confronted by Const. Mandell of the Randburg SAPS who informed me that they suspected that I was in possession of illegal substances. I was completely surprised and taken aback, and even more so when substances which could be drugs, being found in my motor vehicle.

j. I was arrested, and after about 6 hours in custody released on prosecutorial bail in the amount of R1,000. After my release at about 15h00 attended to my home, and then proceeded to collect the minor children from the Applicant as I was entitled to have the children with me for the evening.

k. The Applicant refused me access to the children, and called the Randburg SAPS. The events of this afternoon is properly ventilated in my attorney's letter of 7 November 2014, which I pray be incorporated herein as specifically pleaded. A copy of this letter is attached hereto marked Annexure 'MLF ...'.

l. At my first appearance on the charge of possession of illegal substances, both my attorney and I noticed the Applicant being in attendance to the Randburg Magistrates Court. Afterwards it became clear that she attended Court to obtain an interim domestic violence order;

m. From the affidavit supplied in the Domestic Violence application it is clear that the Applicant now, 14 days after she first noticed the suspicious packages on 19 October 2014 (on her version), deemed it necessary to suspend my access. The interim protection order did not suspend my access, which lead the Applicant to approach the Children's Court section at the Randburg Magistrates Court;

o. The Applicant here applied to the Children's Court, again on an ex parte basis, to suspend my access. This application was denied and notice was issued to attend to the Children's Court on 9 December 2014. On 9 December 2014 my attorney and I had to attend Court, only to be informed that the Applicant attended to Court on 8 December 2014, informing the Clerk of Court that there is now a Supreme Court application pending. At no stage was my attorney nor I informed about the fact that the Applicant would not be attending Court, and the application was accordingly dismissed in the Applicant's absence. This is just another example of the lack of respect that the Applicant has for the legal system.

p. Noteworthy from both the domestic violence and Children's Court applications are the fact that the Applicant fails to mention or make any referral to the Rule 43 application, which on her own version had at that stage already being served;

q. The argument followed by the Applicant in both the applications was that I was arrested for the possession of illegal substances; and that she believed that I should not be granted any access to the children until finalisation of the criminal charges against me.

r. In the domestic violence application the Applicant further stated that I, on 4 November 2014, harassed her, her nanny and the children when I attempted to exercise my access.

s. On 4 November 2014, after my release, I attended to the new premises of the Applicant to collect the children. On my arrival the Applicant informed me that she did sent a letter to my attorney informing him of the suspension of my access. When I contacted my attorney at 16h30 he indicated that he was not aware of any correspondence, but would investigate same;

t. After about 5 minutes my attorney did contact me and informed me that he had received an email from the applicant, transmitted at 16h20 (thus 10 minutes prior to the agreed hand over time). A copy of this email is attached hereto marked Annexure 'MLF?' ;

u. The email received from the applicant on face value further indicates the mala fides of the Applicant, as she clearly took her time by submitting this email, as she firstly addresses various issues raised in a letter of my attorney of 3 November 2014, and then only turns to the issue of the suspension of access;

v. Although the Applicant was well aware that no order existed to suspend my access from 4 November 2014, she refused access up to 18 November 2014 without any such order or responding to any demands and requests for such access.

I have no doubt in my mind that the Applicant placed the drugs in my vehicle on 31 October 2014.

I haven't included the entire affidavit above, because Johan basically responded to a hundred and fifty page document, so the response was rather hefty. I do believe panic broke out at enemy camp, specifically pertaining to points b and f above where it stated that I had proof on my phone (voice recordings) about walking to her house. Not only was her own affidavit regarding the drugs pathetically written and an obvious attempt at covering up in a highly fabricated manner, but I had serious proof that she was not even near my car when she 'noticed the parcels' and 'took a sample' out of my vehicle. It was game over for her and jail time was surely going to be the outcome of this. Even if I didn't lay charges, the state could go after her. That also meant that for the divorce case she had surely blown her cover into smithereens.

I still cannot fathom as to why someone would do that to themselves. Was winning so important to her? She was seriously injuring herself trying to damage me. The list of criminal offences was starting to pile up.

Lying in court

Character assassination

Defamation of character

Planting of drugs

Drug possession

Endangering minor children

Denial of access rights

Illegal arrest

Taking out restraining orders for no reason

Involving others and making them lie on your behalf

Falsification of documents

Possibly bribery of police officials and court personnel.

If each of these would carry a minimum of two years in jail (which most do, I believe) and if I had to tackle her on these one by one, she could potentially sit for a total of twenty four years! And lose all rights to the kids in the process. Unfortunately our system didn't work that way though.

Remember also that at this point I had not opened a single case against her, except for the Rule 43. With all the other cases, I was only defending myself against her vicious and heinous attacks.

Forty-four

Malignant Narcissism

I needed to know more about what she was suffering from and started some more research again into the psychology behind it all.

Armed with more behavorial patterns and knowledge, and, myself being more calm now that the restraining orders were out of the way, I had the time to spend some nights on the internet and came across the term 'malignant narcissist'. Basically the most dangerous type of narcissist you can have in society a.k.a 'psychotic'.

I found out a lot about this disorder and it is more prevalent than we think. Generally malignant narcissists are clever, with high IQ's, they are cunning, charming and witty, and they deliberately stalk their prey to get them entangled in their web. On one of the sites called the `narcissistschild.blogspot.com` I found the following article blog and I could totally relate. Although not a pure definition, other accounts of malignant narcissism were mentioned. It's a very interesting read nevertheless:

> An elderly woman visits her doctor for a check-up after
> a mild heart attack. While in the examining room she
> has a sudden stroke and the doctor immediately ad-
> mits her to the hospital to which his clinic is attached.
> The following day her sister-in-law, a registered nurse
> who is the executor of the elderly woman's will, calls

the small family together for a conference. The hospital will not turn off the woman's life support without the consent of her next-of-kin, who are the nurse's two sons, the old lady's nephews. One son votes to turn off the life support—oxygen and IV fluids—while the older son advocates waiting until his aunt regains consciousness and then ask her. Because the family does not unilaterally agree, the life support remains in place and when the old woman regains consciousness a few days later, she opts to keep it going.

At a family dinner two months later the nurse castigates her older son for voting against pulling the plug. The old woman is now in a nursing home and the cost of maintaining her is eating away at her (not inconsiderable assets. "This is your fault!" the nurse screams at her son. "I should take the cost of this nursing home out of your share of the estate! She is using up all the money because she's taking too long to die!"

Another malignant narcissist plotted for more than two years to steal her grandchildren from her daughter so that she could give them to her childless brother to adopt. She sends her son to the daughter's house to spy on her and, after years of ignoring her daughter and grandchildren, she begins dropping in unexpectedlyladen with gifts for the childrenand snoops in her daughter's cupboards and rooms. She even calls Child Protective services and makes baseless claims so that there will be a record of the daughter being investigated. With her son's corroboration, the woman then spreads false tales of drug addiction, prostitution, child neglect and other horrifying stories among the extended family, blackening the name of her daughter and turning the family against her. In a court hearing in which the young mother's uncle (brother of the grandmother) perjured himselfhe had not seen his niece in more than five years, yet testified he had witnessed events in the last few monthsthe judge gave the grandmother a one year temporary guardianship, admonishing the stunned mother that she had a year to 'clean up her act'. Visitation was granted, but when the young mother arrived to see her children several weeks later, grandma's house was empty and a 'For Sale' sign stood in the front lawn.

The grandmother took the children to another state where she obtained a permanent guardianship of the children by telling the court their mother had abandoned them. She got around the requirement to notify the mother of a court hearing by saying she had no idea where her daughter was and publishing a notice of the hearing in a newspaper in a city in which her daughter had lived several years prior, calling it the young mother's "last known address." The court terminated the mother's parental rights and gave permanent guardianship of the children to their grandmother whereupon she uprooted the children yet again, moved them to the state where her childless brother lived, and gave the children to him for adoption. The children's mother did not know where they were for eight years.

Yet another malignant narcissist, on admitting her terminally ill husband to the hospital, lied to her brother and sister about the nature of his admission, knowing the word would get back to her estranged daughter: she said he fell off a ladder at home and injured his back. When the man died of his illness a few weeks later, his daughter was not notified and she eventually discovered the fact of his death through a cousin, weeks after he had been cremated: her name was left out of his newspaper obituary as well. There is no gravesite for the bereaved daughter to visit and his ashes, according to a family member who has visited, are kept in a plastic bag in the closet of the spare room of the late wife's home.

Another daughter worked for more than 30 years in the family business, side by side with her father. On the few occasions she considered going out into the general workforce, her father convinced her to stay.

"I need you here," he told her. "I can't run this place without you." When he died unexpectedly, her mother inherited the business and promptly fired the daughter without notice, severance pay or references.

At Christmas dinner a woman who was the executor of a relative's estate thrust some legal papers in front of her son, one of the heirs, demanding that he sign them immediately. The son, who suffered from dyslexia and for whom reading was difficult, politely demurred, saying he would take them to a lawyer to review when the holidays were over. She began screaming at him in front of the assembled guests, saying that if he didn't sign the papers immediately, he was "stupid." This insult cut him to the quick, as she knew it would, because he had struggled with feeling stupid for a lifetime because of his dyslexia, even though he was of above-normal intelligence. The man's fiancée stepped up and told his mother "He's not stupid! Do not call him that!" to which the mother replied, eyes narrowed and mouth twisted triumphantly "I am his mother and I will call him anything I want!"

The man took the papers and immediately left the dinner with his fiancée. The mother loudly blamed the fiancée, screaming that she was a bad influence on her son. She ignored his wedding five months later, as did the rest of his family. Early in November, however, the mother called her son to invite him and his new wife to Thanksgiving dinner, as if nothing had transpired between them over the past year.

Another woman received a series of disturbing letters in which her mother threatened to go to a lawyer and have the daughter brought up on criminal charges for defrauding the government. She claimed she had proof and she was just waiting for the "right time" to instruct her lawyer to proceed. The daughter spend weeks in a state of anxiety, not knowing what her mother was talking about, but fearing that the police would be knocking on her door at any time. It was not until she conferred with friends and sympathetic family members that she realised that a private attorney does not have the power to bring criminal charges against anyone, and she was then able to write it off as yet another random, unwarranted attack by her malignant narcissistic mother.

Yet another woman began spreading malicious rumours about her mother, calling her a liar, after reading her mother's blog. The blog contained some ugly truths about her own mother (the young woman's grandmother), a malignant narcissist who had disinherited her daughter in favour of her granddaughter, guaranteeing continued family discord. The young woman told the extended family about her mother's blog, saying it was nothing but lies (although the majority of the entries were about events that had occurred before the young woman's birth and about which she could have no first-hand knowledge) and suggesting that the family cut ties with her mother. Not only did the young woman cut off all communication with mother, so did many other members of the family, fearful they would be recognized in the blog and be shamed or held up to ridicule or public embarrassment by her revelations. Nobody, least of all the young woman, stopped to consider that if the blog was a lie, as she contended (and no real names were used), nobody could be recognized since the stories would not be true. It was five years before the writer of the blog learned why her family had shut her out.

A man sat with his soon-to-be ex-wife, signing papers.

"Why have you been so angry with me?" she asked. "You wanted this divorce as much as I did."

"Because you stole my thunder," he answered.

"I don't understand," she replied.

"I was planning to go out to do some late Christmas shopping," he told her. "And never come back."

They had separated in June—he had been planning an exit guaranteed to make her and their 13-year-old son frantic and ruin Christmas for them—and he was planning it more than six months in advance! Why? Because the first Christmas they were married, when the boy was just an infant, she had bought a Christmas tree, ornaments and gifts and he was outraged that she would not return the purchases for a refund. He did not want to spend money on—or celebrate in any way—Christmas, he considered it a waste of money. She refused, saying he didn't have to participate if he didn't want to, but she was not going to allow him to ruin the holiday for their child. He had waited 13 years for his opportunity to retaliate.

Malignant narcissists are the personification of human evil. Well-known psychologist and author, Erich Fromm, coined the phrase 'malignant narcissism' back in 1964 and characterized it as the 'quintessence of evil'. Psychoanalyst Otto Kermberg claimed that the antisocial personality was essentially narcissistic and lacked morality, indicating that malignant narcissism includes a sadistic element, which serves to create a sadistic psychopath. In 1984, Kermberg proposed malignant narcissism as a psychiatric diagnosis. Writer and psychiatrist M. Scott Peck (People of the Lie) identified malignant narcissism as 'the primary root of most human evil'. Peck further characterized it as 'militant ignorance'.

According to Wikipedia and Richard N. Kocsis in Criminal Profiling, 'malignant narcissism can be described as 'an extreme form of antisocial personality disorder that is manifest in a person who is pathologically grandiose, lacking in conscience and behavioral regulation, and with characteristic demonstrations of joyful cruelty and sadism'.'

'As a syndrome, it may include aspects of schizoid and narcissistic personality disorder, as well as paranoia— recent 'contributions have confirmed the importance of malignant narcissism and the defense of projection' in the latter syndrome, as well as 'the patient's vulnerability to malignant narcissistic regression'.'

"Malignant narcissism can be comorbid with other psychological disorders such as borderline personality disorder, sociopathy, even psychopathy. Malignant narcissists, however, cannot be helped by therapy. According to Jacques Lacan in Écrits: a Selection, 'the patient attempts to triumph over the analyst by destroying the analysis and himself or herself.' The patient cannot stand the idea that anyone other than his own lofty self has the power to free him from his condition which, all too frequently, the narcissist sees as being preferable—even superior—to being mundanely normal."

In What Makes a Narcissist Tick by Kathy Krajco, it is stated that while a personality disorder is a psychiatric diagnosis, in the law the narcissist's behaviour is viewed as 'premeditated and volitional'. She later opines '...it is quite likely that psychopathy (Antisocial Personality Disorder) and malignant narcissism are one and the same. [They] go through life doing their thing by laying waste to lives in other ways like malignant narcissists do, as 'love thieves', parasites, gold diggers, climbers, slanderers, verbal abusers, child abusers, wife beaters, pied pipers (i.e. religious and political messiahs), and the like... leaving poverty, destroyed careers, ruined potential, lost nest eggs, psychological injury and even suicide in their wake.' I can personally attest to poverty, ruined potential, psychological injury, and even near-suicide as the result of relationships with malignant narcissists. These people are just plain dangerous. They are evil.

Peck says that evil has to do with killing, it is that which is against life and liveliness. 'When I say that evil has to do with killing, I do not mean to restrict myself to corporeal murder. Evil is also that which kills spirit. There are various essential attributes of life—particularly human life—such as sentience, mobility, awareness, growth, autonomy, will. It is possible to kill or attempt to kill one of these attributes without actually destroying the body.' Emotional abuse, manipulating and controlling another person, denying them autonomy and freedom: these acts, common to narcissists of all stripes, are acts of evil.

Evil, however (according to Peck) is not so much the sin itself but the refusal to acknowledge the sin, to admit you were wrong and seek to make amends. So while any person may do something that hurts another, like participating in the bullying of a co-worker, for example, the truly evil are those who refuse to acknowledge their wrong-doing. This is the difference between having a conscience, knowing remorse, and the narcissistic lack of conscience, even going so far as to blame the victim for his feeling hurt: '...he was asking for it, wearing those pink socks with yellow pants, dressing like a geek—we just gave him what he had coming...'

Malignant narcissists take it one step further: instead of waiting for an opportunity to ride someone, they make their own opportunities. They stalk, cyberstalk, harass, bully, and even plot against their targets for extended periods of time. There is nothing too low for them to stoop to, no behaviour too extreme for them as they pursue their goal of power and dominion over those around them. A malignant narcissist will do anything she thinks she can get away with in order to get what she wants. There is nothing they will not do to get their way, to create ways to get gratitude and admiration from others, to punish those who thwart them. From intentionally digging at someone's emotional tender spots to stealing their children, to keeping a terminally ill man home until he collapses on the way to the bathroom and breaks a bone, then concealing both his illness and death from an adoring daughter (who didn't so much adore the narcissistic mother), these people have no boundaries, no sense of shame, no limits to what they are willing to do to get what they want.

Malignant narcissists: they are the evil that walks among us.

That particular article was a serious eye opener for me. I could so relate to that. Under no circumstances can I or may I make a diagnosis on my ex. I'm not qualified to do so. But it seemed that was exactly what was happening to me. I got too deeply sucked into the madness of it all and kept on giving her the benefit of the doubt. This was another awakening for me and I started putting things into perspective without giving her that benefit of the doubt anymore or making excuses for her behaviour. Because in reality:

I had my kids held at ransom,

I was arrested and locked away,

Bullied, and attacked legally,

psychologically,

emotionally and

mentally.

I was in a living nightmare just as bad or even worse than the stories from the above article!

But with all the odds piled up against her, Madam still didn't give up. With all the confessions against herself, her contradictory affidavits, her nonsense bullshit stories and in the face of blatant proof, it wasn't good enough for her and I got a call from Johan.

"Mark, when can you meet up with her lawyer? They now need to verify that the voice recordings you made are real, not tampered with and made on the date that you claim."

"What? I have to now prove that my own proof is proof enough? This is getting pathetic!"

"I know" Johan said, "But let's just do it. They're grasping at straws. Let them have the straws. They're obviously panicked."

So mid-January, two weeks before the high court divorce trial was set, I now had to prove to the enemy that my recordings were real! How ridiculous. More wasting time and resources! At least I understood that the recordings were obviously causing panic and mayhem, as they should. The crimes committed were serious and even though I didn't really need the proof in the form of a voice recording as such, it was the cherry on top and made her plotting and planting undeniable.

Bronwyn, the opposition lawyer, wanted to meet me at the iStore the next day. I had to go in with my iPhone, so that they could verify that the recordings were not tampered with. I got there slightly early and so did Maria, Johan's assistant who would be present as a witness. Bronwyn arrived shortly thereafter, but the technician she'd booked was still out on lunch. Whilst waiting for him, she started chatting to me. I was in no mood to chat, especially in light of the fact that Jane was not present either and I knew opposition lawyers would chit chat nicely just to extract information out of you.

She started:

"Just between you and me, and off the record..." I raised my hand to Maria in a 'come hither' motion to witness was about to be said.

".... I'd like to know if you're amenable to settling this matter out of court."

I frowned at her.

"Who actually requested the court date?" she said.

Was this woman daft or what? She didn't even know who requested the divorce court date? Had she not read the files properly? I know there was a load of paperwork and she was after all the third lawyer in the last year, but surely she would have familiarized herself with the case before she asked questions like that?

"Ehhhm , well that would have been your client" I responded. "She's the applicant in this matter."

"Oh, OK, well, just so that you know, if the divorce does go to court on the 28th of January, you have to realise that there are no winners in these kind of things."

"Thank you for your advice Bronwyn, but please pass that information on to your own client, my estranged wife, accordingly." I responded dryly.

"Well I do believe that we should have a round table meeting and agree on a settlement."

"Ehhm, we've requested numerous round table meetings with your client, but they fall on deaf ears. In fact, if she had attended FAMSA's meetings last year, we would have been divorced already and would have been able to share our children for a total cost of around two and a half grand. I'm now in the hole for hundreds of thousands of Rands because of your client's antics. And I don't believe you should be discussing out of court settlements and round table meetings with me in a public iStore. I don't know what you're trying to achieve. Contact Johan rather."

Maria rolled her eyeballs at me and Bronwyn fell silent. The tech guy arrived and we went to his workstation at the back of the shop.

He explained that voice recording dates could not be changed after the recordings were done. You can however change the date and time settings on your phone, start recording and reset your phone into the current time and that recorded file would show up on the false date recorded.

In other words, if I'd really wanted to, I could have set up a scenario with the kids, change the time and date settings on the phone, started recording and submitted that as evidence. Seriously and highly unlikely and based on the fact that I had sent that particular recording to Johan, the minute the dates came up from Jane's side, impossible. I was pissed off though with the tech guy for even suggesting that option, but I suppose it was possible, though highly improbably. You'd need to think like a criminal to do that.

The minute we were finished, I phoned Johan. He could hear I was pissed off, but responded:

"Mark... calm down. You're forgetting one thing. They are literally fucked! (It was the first time I ever heard him swear) You sent me that file in November already. They are creating the most pathetic scare tactics now and the fact that Bronwyn is discussing round table meetings and settlements in the open just shows their panic. These are desperate moves. They are cornered and have nowhere to go."

Yea, I suppose he was right. They had nowhere to go and they were grasping at straws. I just felt like I had been wasting time whilst 'madam' didn't even bother to pitch. All the time wasting was on my clock. But their clock was ticking too. Tick tock... tick tock...

Forty-five

Becoming the primary caregiver

The 13th of January was D-Day. The Rule 43 was officially implemented and the kids were handed over to me at the garage as usual. The school holidays were over and the arrangement according to the court order was as follows:

She had visitation rights on Wednesday afternoons for three hours.

Every alternate weekend.

Half of each school holiday.

Regardless of my victory now being implemented, I couldn't help but think of what Jane, a mother must be going through mentally and emotionally. It's exactly this empathic nature—that has gotten me into so much trouble before. I had to pinch myself to stop doing that. Johan phoned me late that afternoon.

"Have you got the kids?"

"Yes" I replied.

"Congratulations" he continued, "you've now won the battle."

I wasn't sure what he meant exactly, but the kids were, in principle better safeguarded from her daily antics by having the Rule 43 enforced. I suppose with the actual divorce date looming a mere two weeks away for which she had not complied with the court rules, and cooking her own soup, she was literally 'toast' now.

My head went into a spin and the next two days, I couldn't think clearly. Was this really it? Was the battle indeed over? I had fought for the wellbeing of the kids so hard and for so long, it felt a bit surreal to now be officially declared a single dad! Holy shit! What's going on!? I had so much to organize to get myself and the kids stabilized! My life was in a mess still work wise, financially and emotionally. But could I call the shots now? Technically yes, but obviously not in madam's mind. She was scheming again and still in her control freak mode.

On collecting the kids from her that Wednesday night she remarked:

"Don't forget to bring them to school tomorrow. I'll see you there at half past seven."

"Oh really?" I responded. "And you signed all the school paperwork and commitments on that?

"Yes, as per my correspondence with your lawyer" she snapped back.

She had, on her own steam and without my consent or input, enrolled them at a pre-primary school three months prior. The school she had enrolled them in, was probably the most expensive pre-school in town. Although a lovely Montessori set up, I certainly couldn't afford it on my own and neither could she! Knowing how she operated, I was convinced that she hadn't put any signatures on file in order to avoid any responsibility. She manipulated the administration to push that financial burden on me.

Johan advised me to meet her at the school she had enrolled them in, even though I had a cheaper daycare option available for them.

The next morning, I drove the kids to that school which was literally down the road. She was clearly in a vicious mood! She got out of the car, approached me and started an attack on me right in front of the children—in the middle of the street.

"Just make sure YOU sign the papers in the office" she barked at me.

Her tone and demeanour were nothing short of disgusting. Jane's eyes were possessed by the devil himself. In that moment, she launched herself at me as if she was going to punch me. I had to step back to avoid her onslaught. I got very scared by that behaviour. It was a totally different personality coming to the fore.

I had seen this in the parking lot at FAMSA once before yet she was different again. Was she demonically possessed?

The kids felt her aggression coming from a mile away too. They clung onto my legs and held onto me tightly. When Julia saw her mom she exclaimed:

"I don't want to go to mommy's house."

I had to reassure her that that was not the case. Julia, in her own mind had already somehow figured out that she was going to stay at daddy's house now, but, having waited so long for that to happen, she (just like me) couldn't actually believe that that was now the case.

I grabbed the kids and hurried them across the road to go inside the school. Jane was hot on my heels snapping remarks which I ignored. She was livid and her behavior in front of the kids was nothing short of scary.

Once inside the school, her behaviour made a complete U turn and she changed her tune completely to become the 'responsible' and 'happy' mom for her audience. Jane introduced herself to the teachers beaming with a smile as the children's mom and as if nothing had happened outside. She was radiating an aura of control and calm, but I knew inside she must have been a wreck. In her sweetest and buttered up voice she approached Julia's teacher.

"Hi, I'm Jane and these are Julia and Sean, my children."

I obviously didn't feature and she didn't introduce me. I had to do that myself, while the kids were still clinging onto my legs. The teachers in turn approached me separately while Jane ran around the school trying to look important, but doing God knows what in her frantic mental state. I took the kids on a guided tour and settled them in as much as I could while their mom was trying make friends with all sorts of other moms and teachers all over the place.

In the playground 'uber-mom Jane' approached me while I was talking to the owner of the school. She snapped:

"Make sure you sign the paperwork!" then approached Sean and Julia in the sweetest voice. "Mommy will call you from the 'bushhouse' later today. OK my baby?"

Julia hid behind my legs again.

"Ehhm hold on... what about seeing them for three hours later today?" I said to her, referring to the fact that she had the right to see them for three hours on Wednesday.

She looked at me sternly with piercing and intimidating eyes.

"Well I've seen them now, haven't I?"

Okay! She didn't give a shit about the kids and it was clear. That fact was now amplified a hundred times over.

Truthfully, I suppose any mom, crazy or not, would not want to hand her kids to the father and lose them voluntarily, but she kept the 'bravado' and supposed 'good mom' status up towards the teachers and other people. But in reality it suited her quite well that she didn't have that 'burden' of her kids. She had more leverage and time for herself this way. And less responsibility.

The headmistress told me to come back later to discuss the way the kids were enrolled with her. She was rather busy taking in the new kids on the first day of school, so I set up an appointment. I went back there slightly early before the kids were due for pick up.

The school administration was of course totally sidetracked by Jane! When pulling out the file from the admin department, all the forms were there, but there were no signatures on file. They couldn't believe it. Jane had effectively enrolled the kids, without my consent and without her own signature! They were baffled, but I was not. I told them:

"I was expecting something like this. I have been through similar things before. Many times!"

It was time to tell the truth. Jane had to be exposed. I told them the whole story. I told them how I was blacklisted for Steven's school, how she planted drugs in the car, how she emotionally and cleverly manipulates people, how she emotionally abuses the kids etc etc. They sat there listening in awe as the story unfolded! When I was done with my tale, I leaned back and said in a very quiet tone of voice:

"You may choose to believe these unbelievable allegations or not. That choice is yours, but I know I'm telling the truth."

The headmistress and the admin staff sat in stunned silence trying to pick their jaws up off the floor.

I always loved parenting, but now having the kids around eighty percent of the time, I loved it even more. Everything was still chaotic and stressful to say the least, but the kids were my bundles of joy and rays of sunshine in the otherwise psychotic fiasco of the divorce process.

We started settling into quite a nice routine slowly but surely. Julia needed a two week period to get acquainted with the new school, but Sean settled right into his new environment. Being a Montessori school, it suited them well and they really started to blossom. The teachers did pick up that they had experienced some trauma though. I was hoping it wouldn't be a long term thing for them.

Although, I still got the regular,

"I don't want to go to mom's house."

Telephone calls from Jane were mostly being ignored by the kids to the point that Julia even covered her ears when mom was on the phone. But after repeatedly telling them and coaching them that it's rude not to at least say hello to mom, eventually they became a little easier with that, albeit under protest every so often.

Jane had the kids on Wednesday afternoon from three to six pm and every alternate weekend. As the kids were starting to trust that they'd come back to me, the handovers at the petrol station became a bit easier and less tearful too. They had obvious separation anxiety. Jane still arranged for the security guards to be present initially, but also that stopped after a week or two. Most of the time either on the Wednesday or the alternate weekend, the kids would be returned sugared up and quite mentally frazzled. They always needed a good hour or two of whining and being impossible to get back into their normal calm selves. After visitation, Sean, who had just started using his words, would come back with a very monotone

"Mommy...mommy...mommy". It was like a game to him but it wasn't like he was hunkering for his mom. The tone of voice, the smiling face and the repetitive nature he was doing it in, and only after his visitation with her indicated to me she had been brainwashing him to say that. It was a rehearsal that his mother put him on pretty much like teaching a parrot.

Julia, being able to speak better due to her age, came back with sentences like 'I love mommy and Brad' but refused to speak to either of them on the phone. The poor kids were totally confused.

I suppose even healthy parents and kids have to adjust to a new life during and after divorce, but it seemed that the manipulation and desperate attempts of alienation on her side were rather extreme and most concerning.

But otherwise, both the kids and myself were starting to settle in nicely. Business was still up and down and whatever work I had, I tried to do early in the morning while they were at school and later at night after their bedtime. The afternoons I kept open for the kids generally and ran errands such as picking them up from school, feeding them lunch, doing the bread and milk run and making sure they had all the attention they needed. My social life picked up, but not like it was before. After all I was a bit housebound now, especially at night with the little ones in bed. Being alone a lot had its good sides too. I slowly found my old self little by little and more frequently had people over for coffee, drinks and dinner parties. My house had an open door again and the vibe improved a lot. The interaction with my friends was also good for the kids. In themselves, they became more open and chatty and I started receiving compliments on how they'd improved so much from being so clingy to well adjusted, happy and free spirited children.

After five weeks of being at school Julia's school teacher approached me. She said:

"I have to tell you as a teacher, you're doing a fantastic job at parenting. The difference of Julia between when she started and now is phenomenal! And I'm not saying it to compliment you, it's because I mean it! You're doing a fantastic job."

Wow, well that was nice to hear and it definitely made me proud as a parent. Especially a single one without much support! I needed to hear that and it gave me a big boost in morale.

In the background the court cases and legal battles were still going on. I wouldn't say I became complacent with the situation, but it appeared that I was on a winning streak.

Legal matters are a funny thing though. If you are ever in that situation, be prepared for endless postponements, appearances, affidavits, paperwork and so on. Patience is of utmost importance and in family law, you have to allow the dust to settle on some things. Time is also a great healer and things do come out in time too. Never act prematurely and keep your emotional side away from it all where possible. Knee jerk reactions can only get you into trouble. I kept on learning, sometimes the hard way, as I went along.

Forty-six

The divorce is cancelled

The divorce was set for the 28th of January. I was so looking forward to that date. So looking forward to having this all behind me and moving on. I had positive vibes and hopes of having this all resolved, picking up the pieces and going forward in peace.

Jane's attorneys, MNM requested round table meetings to see if we could settle out of court, but no concrete proposals came forth. I turn appointment dates were proposed from our side, but we never received any answers or further correspondence. The divorce date was looming and we still had no meeting as is required by law.

I was used to the delay tactics by now, but I never expected the call from Johan the day before the divorce date.

"Hi Johan."

"Mark, are you sitting down?"

"Yea why? What's up?"

"You're not going to believe this. I just had a call from MNM attorneys. They've somehow taken the divorce off the roll."

"What? No ways! What the heck is going on? They can't just do this! Tomorrow we're getting divorced! They can't just cancel it!"

"Let me find out with the advocate what he says. I'll get back to you."

Somehow it was taken off the roll in high court for God knows what reason! To this day I don't know how or why.

237

Another delay! Another frustration! It was clear neither my ex nor her lawyer wanted to face the judge as no new trial dates were being issued either! Was she trying to get me to submit by carrying on with her onslaught and wasting resources and time?

The answer to that was a resounding yes! The narcissistic beast was furious and adamant to get me down. Not only that, but she knew how to play the legal game in a very dirty way. She was avoiding accountability and used the legal system to stretch it out as far as possible, to the frustration of all involved. Her lies and contradictions were becoming more and more obvious as time went by. She had opened herself up completely and her lawyer was helping her along to stretch this process further. Jane needed to punish me, and now even more so for taking her kids away. Jane was now obsessed!

In the middle of February, shortly after the cancelled divorce debacle, Julia started coming home with stories about visits to her mom's friend called Michelle. This was always on a Wednesday afternoon when Jane had her access for the three hours. I had never heard of any 'Michelle' before, so naturally I got curious. Who was this mysterious Michelle that Julia praised and liked so much? Not much information was forthcoming from Julia and I didn't want to push her too hard either. The only thing I could gather was that 'Michelle had a nice house with lots and lots of toys. A whole room full of toys!'

One afternoon at the end of February, I went to pick them up at the petrol station up the road after their visit with mom. Julia was in a state. She was crying hysterically and clung to me as if she wanted to get under my skin. Her sobs were painful and I couldn't figure out what she was on about. What had her mom done to her? She just couldn't get the words out and explain it to me.

My mom, who was visiting that day, came with me and was as horrified as I was. It took Julia a good half an hour to calm down and eventually come out of her shell. Peace had returned somewhat, but she remained tight lipped about her emotional freak out.

I had both my parents and my cousin Caroline over for dinner that evening. They were sitting outside by the pool chatting and playing with the kids whilst I was busy in the kitchen cooking and getting dinner ready for everyone. My mom walked into the kitchen.

"Julia was chatting outside to us about this 'Michelle' woman she's been visiting. It looks like she's a psychologist."

"Oh really? I'm not surprised" I responded.

My mom continued:

"She told us that she goes there and mom and Sean wait outside in the waiting room and she and Michelle play games with Dollies and make drawings."

Okay right.... Now my suspicions were getting confirmed by my three year old daughter via my mother. How could Jane take Julia, in her three hours a week visitation, unanimously and without notice to me, to a child therapist? This on its own is already absurd if you think about it. You get to see your child for three hours a week and you spend half an hour each way there and back driving, one hour waiting in the waiting room which leaves you with only an hour of 'quality' time with your child?

When I had asked Jane for the kids to go to play therapy five months earlier, it was denied by her, saying 'they didn't need it'. I also couldn't enroll the kids for therapy on my own steam, as the psychologists needed both parents' consent prior to treatment.

I needed to identify her motive in this behind the scenes operation. I needed to know what for? What were her secret games about? What was she trying to do?

I reported it to Johan the next morning and I started searching for child therapists called Michelle all over Johannesburg. But I couldn't find anyone called Michelle on Google. This made me worry even more. Who is this mysterious Michelle woman, and why was Julia going there?

Johan immediately sent out a letter to her attorneys requesting details and ordering clarity, but they didn't provide answers. A common tactic, it appears, with unscrupulous lawyers and their narcissistic clients.

In the interim work was still going slowly, as I was preoccupied with the kids, doing absolutely everything I could for them. I made sure they were well looked after, happy and healthy with the help from my cousin Caroline who was by now an almost daily visitor (and surrogate mom). Cash flow was tight, but with the help of my family who were fully supportive emotionally and financially, I somehow managed to get by. I was wangling between raising kids, protecting them as much as I could from mom's brain-washing and mental escapades, but at the same time I was also trying to get the business up and running again. It's handy and convenient to work from home and for yourself, but cash flow wise it's not always easy. One of my biggest clients, who gave me regular business, and was my main source of income, suddenly dried up out of the blue, and ceased business altogether. It was only a temporary lag for four months, but I didn't have the cash to carry me through that period. My tenant in the cottage defaulted on her rent which added to the aggravation and put things under severe strain. From treading water, the boat was now leaking slowly and starting to sink. Having the kids under my roof full time now, and not getting in the maintenance payments as ordered by the courts, didn't help much either. Banks and debtors started calling from their irritating call centres and didn't give up. I had to keep explaining my situation to them, but the institutions just didn't care. Pressure was mounting and the wolves were at the door.

Forty-seven

Sexual Molestation?

About two weeks after Julia spilled the beans on the psychologist, things got worse. I picked them up from the regular garage handover on a Wednesday at six pm, under camera of course! The problem I had in general with the kids, that due to the absolute non-communication between me and their mother, I didn't even know if they had eaten, drank, and bathed or where they had been. As much as I would have loved to parent with an ex who was cooperative and communicative, it clearly wasn't an option with Jane. As proven in the past, anything I said, whether positive or negative would always be ripped out of context and held against me. I was therefore literally forced into a silent submission with her.

On numerous occasions I received lawyer's letters complaining about things like a mosquito bite or allegations that the kids were over or underdressed on handovers. Meanwhile she'd literally steal the clothes off their backs that I bought them and she'd send them back in outgrown or torn clothing. I had to continuously defend myself to the point where I got sick and tired of the game. The accusations were beyond bizarre and she was grasping at straws. There was many a time where I called Johan and told him:

"Do we even have to supply an answer to this kind of crap? This is becoming beyond absurd."

In the first week of March, Sean and Julia came back from mom at six pm and after establishing that they hadn't eaten at all whilst

241

under mom's care, I quickly whipped up some dinner as they were cranky, 'hangry' and ravenous. I put the kids in front of the TV. I had two massive beanbags in my lounge which they liked to lounge and chill on and I put on their favourite 'Dora the Explorer' DVD. Because my lounge and kitchen were all open plan, I could keep an eye on them that way and went about cooking duties. Julia was not her usual self and fidgety. Not only that but she had her hands in her pants and was scratching herself down there.

"Julia! What are you doing?"

I asked from my vantage point in the kitchen. I walked up to her noticing her discomfort.

"I'm ouwie and itchy!" she exclaimed.

"Why? Whats wrong?" I asked her.

"I don't know."

I told her to show me where she was itchy and ouwie and she pulled down her panties pointing at her vagina. It did appear to be a little bit reddish, but I couldn't immediately establish what the cause of her irritation was.

"Why are you sore there my girl?" I asked.

"Mommy touched me down there."

Internally my world froze up and crumbled. I was beyond stunned, but quickly had to regain my wits in order to support my daughter! Panic engulfed me. I didn't know how to respond, but this needed more discussion! I managed to grab my phone off the kitchen table and opened the recording app and pressed the 'record' button to witness this.

Julia was reluctant to talk, but I needed to get to the bottom of this. I was aware of the brainwashing and parental alienation that was going on, but THIS? OMG!

I didn't want to be a cause of panic for her, so I proceeded with caution, whilst trying to be as calm as possible myself. My mind was in total denial. This is not happening! This isn't possible! No mother would ever do this to her child. EVER! Shock, horror, denial!

Carefully I probed more and asked her questions.

"Julia, show me where mom touched you!" She showed me.

"Why did she touch you down there?"

"I don't know daddy."

"How did she touch you?" I said

242

"Finger inside!" she responded.

Oh my God! Oh my....! Oh shit...shit...shit...Would a three year old lie about something like that? Did this really happen for real?

I tried to keep my wits about me and my rational mind kept pushing harder and telling my conscious that this isn't real. This can't be true! No ways. Julia is talking rubbish. But why? A three year old child would not know about fingers inside unless it happened or she had seen it somewhere. Children that age are not sexual at all! I was floored, concerned, panicked and my mind in a spin.

"Did you tell mom to stop it?" I asked.

"Yes."

Her responses were coming out, but she wasn't comfortable talking about it.

"Did you cry?"

"No she said, but it was sore."

"What happened when you told mom to stop it?"

"Mom said that she'll touch Sean's bum!"

Oh my fucking God! What's happening, this was becoming more surreal.

"And did she?" I asked her.

"Yes."

"And then what happened?"

"Seannie cried."

Holy crap! I decided not to push the issue too far. I needed to clear my mind as well and get a grip on myself. This is not the kind of stuff that happens in my world!

I hugged her and said:

"Remember Julia, we've spoken about this before, nobody, but NOBODY touches you down there! These are your privates for you only. If anything happens, you tell me about it OK?"

"Yes daddy."

"I love you my baby."

"I love you too."

Although she was reserved in her talking about anything that happened at mom's house (grooming), it didn't seem that she was overtly abused and besides a bit of redness, I didn't find any other signs of abuse or penetration as such.

I didn't know what to think any more, so I called Caroline. I needed to get this off my chest. It felt like I was losing the plot and going paranoid.

I had Caroline on the phone for over an hour. She agreed with me that a child that age would not make a statement about 'fingers inside' if it had never happened. And also the statement that she'd touch Sean's bum as well, was just as concerning. Sean couldn't talk yet at his age, so had that happened for real, he could never report that information to me. This was too sick for words and I felt sick in my stomach for real. Right down to the core of my being.

"You have to send that recording to Johan, now! Don't waste time. Let him listen and see what he says." As soon as I put the kids in bed that night, I emailed the recording to Johan. I didn't want to make any allegations in my emotional state, but I requested him to listen to the recording urgently and make the call on what to do.

The next morning, both Sean and Julia were in a good mood and happy to go to school. I didn't pick up any signs of discomfort, and brushed off the evening's discussion as a figment of my and Julia's imagination. I preferred to stay in denial.

Just after drop off at the school Johan's email came in.

"I've listened to the conversation. I'll call you just now. Going to consult with the advocate on this! Speak to you later."

The previous evening's panic set in again. So it's true! Johan is just as concerned. This is for real. It did happen. Are we failing to protect my kids? My poor babies! Thoughts were racing. The mind went busy. The rest of the morning I spent going through possible scenarios and accepting the fact that this was happening for real! I called Caroline for support. She came over immediately to support me emotionally. When she arrived, I broke down and cried. Tears were streaming. My mind was so confused and worried. It felt like I was going crazy and I had had enough.

My emotions and imagination fluctuated up and down. I went from furious to despondent. It was a rollercoaster which wasn't stopping.

Legally the lawyers had decided to deny access until further investigation from an organization called the Teddy Bear Clinic. The Teddy Bear Clinic are specialized in protecting children from physical and sexual abuse. As much as this organization probably has all the good intentions in the world, they were absolutely useless. Johan had set up an appointment with a social worker there, and I needed to go in to get the ball rolling. Over the next week I had called these people about a hundred and fifty times, but no one was available to take my calls or set up the appointment. If I did manage to speak to someone, I was told that the allocated social worker was on a course and not available. Endless messages were left for her. They were absolutely totally useless and inundated with work.

Johan had, in the interim, denied access for the weekend following and sent her lawyer the recordings.

The response came in quickly, for a change, and we were getting answers albeit in a screwed up manner.

Jane started with a counter claim that Julia was severely constipated and had blood in her stool whilst visiting the psychologist that last Wednesday, and that Julia's psychologist was 'witness' to all this. Julia had never been constipated at my house before and I found this psychologist story all a bit dodgy. In his letter, Johan had also demanded to know who this 'Michelle' person was that Julia kept on talking about. We still didn't know this and Jane was now implicating the psychologist as a third party in the battle without the psychologists' knowledge.

The psychologists' name and contact details were released the same day. The psychologist's name was not Michelle, but Marianne. It was no wonder I couldn't find any therapist in town with the name Michelle. Julia was groomed by mom to believe that this was mom's friend and that her name was Michelle. This was totally sickening. Psychotic mind games going so far as duping shrinks into the mix for your own gain.

Jane had quickly requested a progress report from Marianne before Marianne had the opportunity to speak or meet with me! Marianne had issued one even though she wasn't even aware that I was the primary caregiver.

I immediately started communicating with Marianne in the interim and raised my concerns with her. Especially the fact that she was seeing a child without both parent's consent. Marianne had sent the report off to Jane but no copy to me! I had received a copy of it via the lawyers, but it didn't mean much. Marianne had only been treating Julia for a short time and had limited information to work with.

One of the crucial items of concern for Marianne was that Julia was displaying tendencies of splitting which could result in a personality disorder later on in life. I wholeheartedly agreed to that statement, but Marianne was still in the dark on the history of my child and the façade that Jane displayed in front of Marianne. She hadn't heard my side of the story yet. Jane's cunning ability to lie and sidetrack people could fool anyone, which made her so dangerous for all concerned.

Meanwhile I kept on trying to get in touch with the Teddy Bear clinic but calls were still not being returned weeks later. I was getting nowhere with these people.

We went into the Easter period and April was filled with public holidays and school holidays. The legals were also not going anywhere fast and the 'non-availability' of the clinic didn't help at all. I had no choice but to go the private route again and get help from Estelle Van der Merwe, our previous social worker, who was familiar with our case.

Legally I had no choice but to release the kids back on their visitation schedule with their mom as no progress was being made elsewhere, nor did I have actual proof that sexual abuse had indeed happened. I had to stick to the law and orders that were issued. It was a totally shit scenario to be in. Releasing the kids back to that monster whom I believed was trying to set me up on allegations of molestation (hence Marianne's involvement, so she had an 'alibi').

Interestingly, even though I blocked access for a while and she had heard the recording from Julia, she never took me on for me 'making allegations' from my side, which indicated to me that I wasn't wrong. She loved turning things around in her favour even though it was truth. The fact that she constantly sent me lawyer's letters about mosquito bites and similar crap, made me wonder. I believe she tried to abuse the kids so that she could set me up on false allegations, making out as if it was me.

She had a very similar approach to the drugs scenario five months earlier. She went for testing (three weeks late so that all the drugs were out of her system) and didn't do bloods, nor did she include Khat which we specifically requested as well. She also insisted on being re-imbursed for the drug test, but didn't follow it up because she came out in the 'clear'. She never bothered to follow up with her 'cost' claim, wheras normally she'd hound me for any moneys due.

I started seeing a pattern here. As bizarre as it seemed, for her this was about creating costs, mayhem and chaos and using the kids in her sick ways to get to me and at me. It was all about drama, creating drama, smearing me with it and using everyone in her circle (triangulation) to get validation and sympathy.

By now I was a regular in court. Even though all child cases and restraining orders she applied for were thrown out, she was still pushing through for the rescission of the Rule 43. That was in high court though and mainly dealt with by my advocate. He had committed to resolve that case on a probono basis, knowing full well my tight financial position and probably also because this case was not only interesting for him, but becoming a high profile case in the legal fraternity.

The drug case, State vs me was still open and I kept it open on purpose in order to have my day in court. The prosecutor wanted to drop the charges against me already, but we turned the cards around. Jane was declared a hostile witness based on the evidence we had. Johan wanted her in the dock at all costs. She was issued with a summons to appear in court and we applied for a trial date which was granted.

The state, however, wasn't ready to proceed as they did not have all the documents in place, nor could the arresting officers be found to be called in as witnesses. Case postponed until two weeks later. Two weeks later it was the same scenario and the magistrate told us this would be the last postponement she would grant, as they were inundated with similar cases and she could not keep on postponing. Jane was in court that day, even though she was not required to be there. I can only guess what she was doing there! And my suspicions were confirmed when Johan and I went outside for a cigarette.

One of the junior prosecutors was also outside smoking and started chatting to us. He knew Johan. "Oh, how's that case going with the drug planting?" he remarked. "We're all waiting with bated breath on what's going to happen with that. That witness has been a regular in our offices the last few days requesting details and files. She's a piece of work and is harassing anyone she can in our offices!"

Oh, interesting! Jane had been lurking in the prosecutors' offices? Nice! She obviously had a desperate desire and need to intervene in the proceedings now that she's been declared a hostile witness! It was getting too hot under her heels.

The next court date was set for early April. Jane was in court again (not as a witness, but just present in the public stand). The same public prosecutor in the smoking section approached us again prior to the case and told us that Jane had been in and out of the courts for three days solid again and also arrived at their offices early that morning approaching employees and clerks again. Obstruction of justice by any chance?

The magistrate handled some minor cases and postponements and called our case forward. The public prosecution advised the magistrate that they couldn't proceed because the police docket was missing. Again! When asked why this docket was disappearing all the time, he even went on to explain that the information he had received from the witness(!) that the last person who had the docket was a tall Indian police officer! Question mark, question mark, question mark!

How does a witness supply information to the public prosecutor, who in turn presents that to a magistrate? What for and why? How does she know about some Indian police officer that had the docket last? Was this perhaps the same Indian police officer she had on speed dial and who arrested me in front of the kids without a warrant on an interim restraining order? The story stank from here to Tokyo!

The magistrate threw the case out of court as the prosecution also didn't want to proceed.

On one hand, good! I was off the hook for possession of drugs. But on the other hand, she had effectively managed to get herself out of trouble as well, because if she was found guilty, she would surely go to jail for planting! Shit shit shit! This was, again, going nowhere fast. She was a sneaky, clever manipulator, now manipulating actual court processes! This woman was not to be underestimated.

Johan consoled me that we'll get her on perjury charges and she'll get what she deserves. But it meant opening a new case against her with the evidence we had.

More time and more money which I didn't have. And who was to say that she wasn't going to manipulate the system even more? So far this year I had suffered legal disappointment after legal disappointment. There was simply no justice. The divorce postponed from her side, and now she slipped through the cracks on her drug planting as well. What next?

In the meantime she must have been ecstatic and her abuse directly towards me flared up that same afternoon.

Quite frankly she had been relatively quiet the last couple of weeks, probably because she was so busy making dockets disappear and manipulating public prosecutors. She had the kids for the three hours that afternoon and I received an SMS whilst they were with her.

> Dear Mark. Julia is severely constipated and bleeding again at Marianne's office. I've taken pictures and Marianne has noted her ordeal. I have advised my attorneys accordingly.

Oh my God. Now what? Another backhanded allegation thrown at me for possible child molestation? I contacted Johan immediately and he gave me swift instruction on how to handle this. I responded to Jane via SMS:

> OK. Take her to Dr Silver's rooms at quarter to six this afternoon. He has an opening. I'll meet you there.

I must have called her bluff, because I didn't get an answer. Twenty minutes later I sent the next SMS.

> No response! Is that in the best interest of the child?

She was very quick to answer that one:

> Firstly watch your tone, secondly I was driving and busy with the kids, thirdly I will be there. This is from my attorney—Fine make sure he pays and you go in together.

So now, mulling this over in my mind, according to mom her child is severely constipated and bleeding from the bum, and all she's concerned about is my 'tone' and who is paying for the bills?

That should be of last concern! As a mother she was prepared to send her three year old daughter in for an invasive examination while nothing was wrong with her? Was she trying to reverse my allegations from a few weeks earlier and create 'proof' of potential abuse on my behalf? It certainly seemed like it. It was total projection happening here.

True to her word for a change, she arrived at the doctors' office at quarter to six. I had already arrived earlier and was waiting for them. My cousin Caroline jumped to the rescue hearing of the story and came to the doctors' practice for back up and support. When the kids arrived, they were clearly unsettled and confused. I did not get my usual excited greeting and they appeared 'off-ish' towards me. Mom had gotten to them quite severely that afternoon probably saying all sorts of bad things.

Not only were the kids offish, Jane was as well. There was nothing new about her not greeting me or looking at me, but she proceeded to be over the top loud and obnoxious in the waiting room. The waiting room had some toys for kids and she was hopping around calling the kids from the one toy to the next. She called them by name in a shrill high pitched tone of voice that was piercing enough to cut holes through concrete. Occasionally she'd do that dog whistle thing in between as well to get their attention.

"SEAN, come look at this train!"

"Oh look Julia, a book!"

She appeared very nervous, jittery and upset. She was possibly in a severe mental and delusional state as well. But that's beyond comprehension to mere mortals like you and me. The kids were uncomfortable as well and quickly found refuge on my, and my cousin's lap. I got a raised eyebrow and frowned look from the receptionist behind the counter as if to say 'what the heck is going on here?'

Thankfully the ordeal in the waiting room didn't last too long and Dr Silver called us into his examination room within a few minutes.

Jane, Sean, Julia and myself went in. Quite a gathering in that cramped office.

"So how can I help you today?" Dr Silver said with a friendly smile.

He knew me and the kids well. I'd taken them in there a couple of times for minor things, but he'd never met Jane before. Besides 'diagnosing' illnesses and dramas, she had never actually attended to medical matters pertaining to the kids since their birth. I was always the one taking care of these things.

I responded:

"Well, according to my estranged wife here, Julia is suffering from severe constipation and excreting blood."

The tension in the air was visible in Technicolor and you could slice it with a knife.

The doctor remained calm and in a nurturing tone of voice and manner, he said:

"Well let's go into the examination room and find out."

Julia clung to me and demanded that I sit next to her on the examination bed. The Dr proceeded to check her eyes, ears, throat and the usual stuff. He asked her to lay down and he pushed various areas of her stomach to see if there was any blockage and or pain.

There was none. He asked her to turn around and cautiously and with the utmost care proceeded to examine her anus visually.

"Well I can't see any traces of blood or fissures from straining."

Jane intercepted and whipped out her phone. Clearly she had a problem with her volume button (or 'inside voice as I call it with the kids') as her shrill and agitated voice echoed through the rooms again.

"Hold on doctor. Here. I have the proof. Here! Look! Do you see it?"

Proof? Proof of what?

She grabbed the doctor and showed him pictures she apparently took earlier that afternoon at Marianne's practice.

I, of course, never had the pleasure of seeing any of the photos and neither did I have the desire to see them really. I believe what she had was a picture of a piece of toilet paper with some blood on!

Dr Silver just calmly nodded with a 'mhhhh...' and an 'aha...,' but never commented. It was clearly not the reaction she anticipated and Jane decided to leave the office with Sean. When I was alone with the doctor and Julia, he said to me:

"Look I'll give you an over the counter medication in case she's straining a bit, but there's nothing serious there. Give the laxative to her if you really think she needs it."

Of course I knew that there was nothing serious going on in advance already, but it was good to hear from the doc himself.

He continued,

"And make sure she eats regular roughage like apples and raisins, just in case."

She does in any case as I always included these items in her school lunch box. I asked him for a full Doctor's report and he gladly obliged.

It stated exactly what there wasn't!

No blood in the stool or evidence thereof. He even wrote that she had shown him some pictures. But that could have been toilet paper with tomato sauce on for all we know.

Again the situation was beyond bizarre and was now effectively creating a neurosis in the child about her toilet habits, all for the sake of trying to make me look bad or setting me up. She was building a case against me again on manufactured evidence, photographs and with alibis. But it wasn't working! The only result was that the children suffered in the process.

Internally I felt extremely uncomfortable. I felt anger, sadness and confusion. So many whys and what for? She was creating dramas and nonsense, got everyone walking on eggshells around her, it was clear as daylight and noone, from social workers to lawyers could do anything about it. I just wanted to protect my babies from this insanity, but I had to stick to the court order in the interim, and hand her the kids every second weekend and Wednesday afternoons while she was continuing relentlessly with her smear campaign and onslaught on me. Not only that, but it was now becoming clear that she was manipulating the kids and in my opinion this was mental and emotional abuse. What mother with normal maternal instincts would stoop so low as to hurt her own babies like this? Did she not see it? Was she that evil? Would she seriously play these games to the kids' detriment? All to get at me? What obsession was this? What illness? I didn't know any more other than that it was pure insanity.

Forty-eight

Shit happens

After that failed attempt of a molestation allegation, she kept a low profile for a few months. It was just enough to take a bit of a breather for me. She was like an incurable rash on my back. Or a painful throbbing hemorrhoid that would flare up every so often. Ok, I've never had one of those in real life, but I've heard they can be agonizing.

Emotionally it was hard to get on top of things. It was a constant barrage of attacks on me, so much so, that every time I felt myself perking up and getting a zest for life again, I either got smashed down with some legal stuff, or I, myself would feel down in the dumps again, because of depression or whatever. It wasn't easy going through this all whilst looking for work and doing my utmost to care for my toddlers as much as I could.

Whilst having a bit of a 'break' so to speak, my body started to give in physically too. Stuff needed to come out. Tension was built up and, knowing from experience, in the quiet times, your body starts releasing on a cellular level from all the build-up of stored stress. I'm a pretty esoteric guy and constitutionally a strong person (thankfully) but at that point, my constitution was worn out.

I had just dropped the kids off at the playschool in the morning and on my way back home when it happened. My stomach was aching and I needed to fart. You know that feeling? It's one of those things we all experience from time to time.

I could feel the buildup before I got to the school, but brushed it off and thought it would pass. As the teacher was handing over some drawings to me to take home and settling in the kids, my stomach had a big cramp. Oh shit. This was gonna be a big one. The cramp was very painful and the blood drained from my face.

"Are you okay?" Agnes asked.

"You look a bit pale!"

"Yeah I'm absolutely fine."

I lied externally whilst fighting off another cramp internally. I tried my utmost not to show the pain on my face. With a grimaced face, I quickly said goodbye to the kids, waved at Agnes, and ran outside. Well not really ran, but walked as quickly as I could, just in case, you know?

Obviously, I couldn't just let rip whilst dropping the kids off. The 'mommies' at school would be absolutely mortified. So, like a good well-mannered boy I managed to squeeze my gluteus maximus and sphincter with enough force to keep the gas from escaping. My colon felt like it was about to explode.

"Where did that come from so quickly?" I wondered.

I had to make it out of the driveway. And fast! I squeezed my arse as tight as I could and walked in short quick steps out of the school property. I must have looked really funny. Short strides. Maybe it was because I was squeezing against the pressure build up behind my sphincter, or hadn't I noticed before how long the driveway really was. But it felt like I had to walk a kilometer. A bit of wind managed to escape the death grip I had imposed on my bottom half, but there was more to come. Not yet... please not now!

I managed to make it out of the property without incident albeit under great duress. Phew... I was finally in the clear. I was well out of ear and 'smell' shot of the other parents and as I got to my car I could finally relax the tension of the muscles a bit.

Needless to say, it all came out. A whole heap of smelly gas managed to escape its pressured confines.

Aaaaaaahhhh... much better! I breathed a sigh of relieve as the cramp in my guts quickly subsided and immediately ceased its cruel and painful onslaught on my colon. What a relief. I hope no one heard that.

254

But the relief was short lived. Within a second of the gas escaping:

"No! Shit...No!"

The relief on my face dissipated at once and the relief gave way to the horrendous feeling of warm squishy liquid running down the back of my legs.

I froze and instantaneously squeezed the sphincter and the rest of my body to prevent any further damage.

Too late! The damage was done. I was acutely aware of the brown liquid running further down past the back of my knees. I could also feel it seeping into the fibers of my pants.

I must have been about ten or twelve metres away from my car, frozen on the spot, car keys in hand. Now what? The liquid stopped running but I had to get to the car. Urgently.

"How am I going to sit down in the car without having crap all over the seat?"

"I'm sure there's a towel in the boot I can sit on."

"Don't I have a toilet roll on the back seat? Surely there's some toilet paper somewhere? Then again, is toilet paper going to do anything?"

"Chill out Mark, you're dealing with shitty diapers daily. And vomit! Yes Vomit."

The internal dialogue continued in quick succession.

"I'm not a kid. But I just shat in my pants. Outside the school. What if someone sees me?"

"No one will see you. Get to the car and deal with this. One thing at a time."

With my brain on overdrive and in crisis mode, I plucked up the courage and shuffled forwards one step at the time. The back of the legs of my trousers were now sticking horribly to my skin. The warm wetness was cooling rapidly in the morning air. It felt disgusting.

"Hi Mark!"

Oh fuck no! It was Amanda, one of the other parents. Please don't come towards me or talk to me.

She did come towards me.

"She's coming! She's bee-lining straight for you."

She was all bouncy and bubbly. Just like every morning.

"Shit."

"Shit Shit"

"Double shit."

Amanda approached bright eyed and bush tailed. 'I was wondering if we could arrange a playdate with Luke this weekend. He'd really like it if Sean and Julia could come over this weekend sometime. Are you guys around on Saturday?'

As she approached closer, I sprinted as fast as I could to the car, swung the door open and jumped into the driver's seat. Splat—I felt my cheeks getting covered with poo. Oh sick! I closed the door.

"Ehhm.,..." I grimaced and I opened the window just a tiny little bit, hoping that the tinting on my windows would give me enough cover to conceal everything.

I was trying to act as normal as possible, which was probably too late. I forced a fake smile out of the window trying to fight off and battling the feeling of diarrhea squashing all over my butt crack, all over my legs, my lower back and my undercarriage. It was literally everywhere!

"Hi Amanda." My voice croaked.

"Ehhm eehm, can I get back to you on that? I'm just in the middle of something. And I am late for a meeting as well."

I had never come up with such pathetic excuses in my life before.

"I'll send you a WhatsApp just now. Let me check my diarrhea ... I mean diary!"

And with that I drove off as fast as I could. I wanted to cry. The most putrid smelling shit was now all over my body, all over my clothes and all over my car seat.

By the time I got home, more diarrhea was building up and building up pressure for its imminent escape to the outside world. I jumped straight in the shower, clothes and all, slowly peeling off the clothes and rinsing off the remnants of the horror that had occurred. Luckily there were no chunky bits, so it washed easily down the drain of the shower while I had no control of the next waves of bowel movements that came out in the most horrid fashion.

There were quite a few more of those explosions that day until there was nothing but bile dribbling out and viciously eating the flesh of my sphincter away. My butt was raw from the ordeal and all the wiping of the toilet paper. This was not just a bug or a bit of food poisoning. This was a superbug and it needed intervention. Everything I ate came straight out either at the top, or straight through the bottom. By the end of the day I was weak from it all.

I knew I had some anti diarrhea in the medicine chest. I needed to stop this shit. Literally! I had quite a few over the counter meds built up in the medicine cabinet over the years. And especially with toddlers there was a smorgasbord of medicine in the locked cupboard. I scratched through the pile and found what I was looking for. The label stated:

FOR HAPPY HEALTHY TUMMIES
Scheduling status: 0 Children under 2 years of age: 1
medicine spoon 2 x a day
Children under 12 years of age: 2 medicine spoons 2 x
a day
Adults and children over 12 years of age: Up to 4
medicine spoons every 3 hours or as needed.

Good! 'As needed'. I needed! I needed that a lot. And I needed that urgently. I quickly opened the sealed bottle and took a big swig out of it. Tasted funny, but at least it should help to 'bind' the loose stool in my guts.

Apparently not. Well not yet! Within an hour and a half I was back on the toilet cramping and shitting my guts out. Oh my God. I was sweating. I was praying and asking God where did all this stuff come from? This just wasn't fair. After carefully cleaning and dabbing my raw prolapsed colon back into the space it came from, I got up. I took some more medicine and retired for the night. Retired, where the 'tired' part was being the operative word. I was exhausted, but fate wouldn't have me sleep. I had to get up four or five more times that night.

The next morning I felt like I needed some food. I had no energy in my system and carefully ate some Corn Flakes. Thankfully stayed down. My stomach seemed to have calmed down somewhat, but I didn't want to chance another day like the day before and took some more medicine just to make sure.

Right, much better now. I sat down at my desk and opened the laptop preparing for the day's work ahead. I cautiously made the decision to try a cup of coffee again. I felt like it, and it tasted good. I hoped it wouldn't upset the delicate balance of my intestines, but by ten that morning I was back on the toilet. I really didn't know where on earth all that liquid came from. Clearly this medicine wasn't working. Was I taking enough? I mean, clearly it was more a medicine for kids. Maybe it's too weak. I downed the rest of what was left in the bottle.

I spent the rest of the day on the throne with the occasional ten minute break in between. It was horrid. My guts were in a complete spasm, my body extremely weak and dehydrated. I had never experienced a near death experience, but this must have been it. Early that evening I fell into a deep, deep sleep. I needed to get to a doctor the next morning.

When I woke up late the next morning I felt fresh and rejuvenated! I managed to avoid the toilet the whole night. I suppose there was really nothing left to come out. Although I felt empty and hungry, I also felt extremely light and clear. Well I did probably shit out a toxin or two, while literally losing five kgs in the process.

I needed to eat. My body craved it and my guts were surprisingly calm. Hungry, but calm.

I made a sandwich and sat down at the kitchen table hoping it would all stay inside. I did not want to repeat the previous day's near death experiences. While munching away and sipping on my coffee, the empty bottle of medicine caught my eye. I nonchalantly picked it up and read the contents of it as it didn't really work that well for me.

I read the back instructions and dosages again. I did exactly as 'prescribed'. Ok, admittedly a little bit more when it wasn't working.

I turned the empty bottle around to read the front again.

For healthy, happy tummies.

I nearly choked on my sandwich as I read the words underneath:

Keeps you regular. Assists and relieves constipation.

Forty-nine

My protection order application

I needed to move on and get out of this rut. This divorce and constant monitoring, the false allegations and abuse had to end and I took the bull by the horns finally. No more sitting back being Mr "Nice Guy" on the defense. Selling the house to free up cash was one thing, but that still didn't mean I was rid of her. As she was the applicant in the divorce itself, she could call the shots and stall that process and she was doing a fantastic job at it. I just needed to get her out of my hair and stop her abusive SMS's, emails and general crap. So I filed for a restraining order *pro se* (i.e. on my own steam). Johan didn't believe it would work. He told me:

"Look Mark, there is a chance but it's slim. I'd say you have a thirty percent chance. Remember, she's a female and you're a male. The courts don't easily grant permanent restraining orders against women. I think you're wasting your time."

Even though I wasn't subjected to physical abuse, the courts should take psychological and emotional abuse seriously and I had plenty of evidence collected by now. I let rip in my application and brought out the whole story for the magistrate to read. Isolated incidents have no bearing in court, especially if they're petty, but repeated incidents and harassment on a continuous basis had to be shown and it showed a pattern. I needed to bring the whole story in front of a magistrate. I had nothing to lose and she really needed to be exposed. Without further ado, I went to court and filled in the relevant documentation. It was the first time I had really taken action against her (besides the Rule 43) and it felt good to stand up for my rights. The paperwork supplied did not leave enough space to write the whole story down, so I attached an affidavit (verbatim below—names changed) listing the main events that transpired over the last two years.

> Details of Domestic Violence/Harassment incidents:
>
> I confirm that the Complainant—Mark Le Foncé and the Respondent—Jane de Jager are going through an acrimonious divorce. We have been separated since 31 July 2013.
>
> Since our separation, many incidents of harassment have occurred, of which the main ones being as follows: I have been subjected to a barrage of vexatious litigations by the respondent with the intent to harm me and the minor children financially, mentally and emotionally. Details will become clear below.
>
> The respondent has applied for 3 restraining orders in this court which were all based on lies and she has perjured herself in the numerous statements and in court. I believe this is in order to destroy me and to win her divorce case. The first one she withdrew herself. The second one in 2013 went to trial and was subsequently set aside and the last one, case number XXXX/2014 was also set aside.
> (Annex 1).
>
> I have, to date, not launched any cases against her and only defended myself against her various attacks, except for a Rule 43 which was granted in the High Court of Gauteng in my favour.
> (Annex 2).
>
> In the last interim restraining order (XXXX/2014) she had ordered an arrest for me based on a "violation" for "enlisting the help of an outside party". The reality of the story is that she had seen my parents in the street and construed that as an harassment. (We live in the same suburb). The result of her actions was:

4.1 I was incarcerated for 4 days

4.2 She opposed my bail application the morning of my appearance

4.3 I believe a degree of corruption took place here as:

- Dockets were not opened until Monday morning 8AM and investigating officers were nowhere to be found that weekend. (I was arrested on Friday afternoon at approximately 16:45.)

- de Jager was in possession of a copy of the warrant of arrest and showed me and threatened me with that prior to calling the police.

- Even though the case was set aside in December, warrant officer Chabalala from the Randburg police station contacted my mother to make more statements on this case in March. Police ref # XXX/XX/14. My lawyer has met up with w/o Chabalala and showed him the Form 6. I believe the officer was mislead by the Respondent in order to harass my parents.

5) The respondent was instrumental in me losing my job, which has been vented in various lawyers' correspondences as well as my Rule 43 Application. (Annex 3 para 30.11)

In November, she denied me access (illegally) to my children for a period of nearly 2 weeks. This action was not only in total contravention to the Children's Act, but has caused psychological and neurotic damage to my eldest daughter. Despite my numerous requests to have the children enrolled to a child therapist, this was denied by de Jager. After the Rule 43 was enforced, de Jager appointed a therapist without consultation or consent from me. In order to hide this fact from me and in order to try and manipulate both the minor child and the therapist, the minor was made to believe the therapist was called Michelle and not Marianne. (Annex 4)

Kindly refer to the Child Therapist's report where she refers to splitting.
(Annex 5)

In order to enhance her case for the divorce, I am certain that she planted drugs in my car and tipped off the police. I was subsequently arrested as I had no idea she had done this at the time. As I am not a drug user at all, nor involved in drugs I went immediately for testing to prove the same. The correspondence attached will clarify more on this particular situation. I kindly request the court specifically look at points number 7 and 30 in my responding affidavit for further clarification on this confusing scenario.
(Annex 3)

The respondent has stalked me on a regular basis and will send me SMS's stating the location of my whereabouts or knowledge who is visiting me at my house. She has also driven by my house and taken photo's. When asking her why she is doing this I get answers such as 'evidence'.
(Annex 6)

I repeatedly get SMS's or emails from her insinuating my 'bad parenting' skills, allegations and other frivolous threats, either from herself or her lawyer. As I have been advised to keep communication to an absolute minimum, she'll continue to provoke a reaction out of me. If I do react, that reaction gets turned around and will fabricate or she will use that information against me.
(Annex 7)

When the social worker released her final report last year, the respondent, not happy with the situation, sent pictures of my genitals to her ex husband as well as the social worker. I am not sure who else these went to. The minor children are now told, since I have full custody of them to call the respondent's new boyfriend, Mr Brad H, 'Daddy'. Mr H, in November

also denied me access to my children illegally. The minor children are made to idealize this man as their father whilst the Respondent has access to them. I have not only received the children back from their premises, covered in temporary tattoos (he apparently has many), but I also receive alarming feedback from my daughter such as they all have jacuzzi's together and that she has been subjected to him shaving his genitals!
(Annex)

A report on potential molestation attempts by the respondent has been filed between the attorneys and reported to the Teddy Bear Clinic. Voice recordings to this effect can also be presented to court.
(Annex 8)

Based on various conclusions, I have personally observed, behaviour wise as well as feedback from the ex nanny at the respondents house, I'd like to have to court assist in possible investigation on drug usage.

I have also not received any maintenance support as ordered in the Rule 43, nor any indication that this will be paid. Attempts to recover these moneys by my attorneys, have not been responded to at all and I will have to take this up with the maintenance court in question. The point I wish to make here is that the respondent does not care in the least for the minor children's wellbeing on a financial or emotional level.

The respondent will deliberately manipulate and control the children whilst they are with her during her access periods. Prime examples of this is that she will either block or manipulate telephonic access with feeble excuses, causing emotional distress to both myself and the children. I am able to provide voice recordings of actual telephone calls to this extent to the court.
(Annex 9)

The respondent has harassed both the nursing sister

as well as the school (and various other caretakers) in order to gain control over both me and the kids. She has send derogatory emails about me to the school and made false allegations to the nursing sister in front of the kids.
(Annex 10–11)

The respondent has sneakily moved premises on 3 occasions without providing notice thereof leaving me wondering where the children moved to. Currently telephone conversation between the respondent and the minor children are often based on them moving to 'the bush' house, which I presume is near Polokwane where her new boyfriend works. She should not communicate with the children about their bush 'home' and fake promises about horses, when she has no residency. This only creates confusion for the children.
(Annex 12)

I have further attached a comprehensive report (final) from the social worker, Estelle van der Merwe as well as a drug confirmation test.
(Annex 13–14)

I could have supplied a string of other incidences, but I didn't think it was necessary to go into too much detail and certainly not ramble on like Jane liked to do. The points in the document were serious enough in my mind to have recourse, but as it was, reading it in retrospect, the document was still written from a very emotional standpoint.

Regardless, I was hoping for a positive outcome.

The court called the next day. The interim restraining order was granted and court dates were set! Wow, that was simple. So far, so good. No wonder Jane managed to get these against me so easily. I went and fetched the documents and the police delivered them to her that weekend. I received an SMS from her the same day:

Dear Mark. I have picked up your application for a protection order from the Randburg SAPS, please note ALL Annexures are missing, please provide to myself

and my attorney by 5pm Tuesday 16, June. I note
your lawyer is not on record.

The pretense was extreme. She made out as if she went to the
police station after she was notified via a phone call. The reality is that the police or the sheriff come to your door and deliver
these papers into your hand with the court dates. This is a potential criminal matter. She made it condescendingly sound like
one of those irritating red tape applications at the licensing department to renew your vehicle... 'Sigh, how dare he... what an
inconvenience. And he's got such cheek!'

It must have kept her quite busy for a while. The day before
the actual court hearing, she submitted a reply. It was a bookwork
of note again. A twenty four page affidavit full of lies and stories,
plus a pack, the size of a half ream of paper of so called 'proof and
evidence'. All in all, the responding affidavit ended up being over
two hundred pages.

She was clever though. From the appearance, typeset and
structure of the document and at first glance it looked like it was
written by her lawyer, but as you read through it became clear
it was written by her. She had left her lawyer completely out of
the picture so as not to blow her 'impeccable' façade and cover.
Repeatedly she'd respond on my points and turn the situation
around. For example: it was my fault that she had lost her job in
November. She ended that paragraph with:

> In addition, I had to sell my motor vehicle to pay for
> legal costs, and have been lucky enough to be able to
> borrow my boyfriend's car for transport. The children
> and I have been resident in his house since November
> 2014. I would hate to think where I would be without
> my boyfriend's support whilst I was rendered jobless,
> homeless, without income and transport.

Oh the dramatic damsel in distress. Note the narcissist in this
paragraph. She pretended the children were living with her. She
lied about her car which is not in her boyfriend's name and she
was also lying about not having an income. She was back at work
for over two months at that stage. She also did a sterling job at
playing the victim in this situation. She brought up the drugs

situation again and that I am a druggie. She slammed the social workers report and the credentials of Estelle van der Merwe. She even had Brad do an affidavit wherein he (stupidly) admits that he had shaved his genitals in front of Julia and they do have Jacuzzi parties with the kids! This was extremely worrying for me.

Her response on my paragraph where I question her need to send out a picture of my dick was to attach a photo of my dick enlarged to a full A4 sheet, making it public property in the court file. But the best of all in that affidavit was her last paragraph, which she couldn't resist to add:

> One factor that has not been highlighted in any of Mr Le Foncé's affidavits, is that he is a fully trained actor, starring in numerous roles over the past twelve years, and as such, in the blink of an eye, can act a role, as needed in a particular situation. Of concern here is that Mr Le Foncé specializes in 'acting' psychologically disturbing roles. The propensity to 'act' in a psychological disturbing manner, combined with this history of abusive behaviour, and pending narcotics possession charges, has been hidden from this honourable court repeatedly by Mr Le Foncé himself.

That last paragraph made me laugh. This woman had such a vivid imagination. I was starting to wonder if she actually believed her own bullshit.

As it usually goes in court, and as expected, the case was postponed and a new date was set in order for us to answer her ridiculous (and voluminous) counter affidavit. It was becoming a litigation by paper in its own right!

The weeks that followed were riddled with violations of the interim order. It appeared she wasn't fazed much by the order I had on her at all. She just didn't care! I was bombarded with SMS's, drive-bys and harassment from her. I could have had her arrested a few time on this basis alone, but I didn't want to come across as frivolous or petty. She was escalating, but I was used to it and I shrugged it off until the court date at least. I didn't need to add to the drama and was waiting for the big one as I realised she'd never be able to control herself, with or a without a court order.

Just over a month later the case went to trial. Even though she had mentioned to the magistrate that she would get legal representation, she hadn't. Perhaps she thought that she had proof enough to fight this on her own. Or perhaps she didn't want to expose my affidavit, the true story, to her attorneys to keep her façade clean towards them! Brad, however, was another story. She had him literally by the balls and he was clearly becoming her submissive slave.

She arrived in the court waiting area with Brad in tow. They sat down on the opposite side from me, Johan and my parents who came to give moral support. She had bags and bags of paperwork, files and a laptop with her. They sat down and started frantically paging through her files. It appeared to be organized chaos with mounds of sticky notes and printouts of all sorts. I suppose it was her 'evidence'. Self-made reports, falsified documents and other bits of 'pretend proof'.

Brad apprehensively looked at me frequently, clearly nervous of something. I couldn't help but wonder what picture he had of me in his mind. I just smiled back politely.

We were called into court after waiting a bit. It wasn't the usual restraining order court. They had specially assigned a judge and a court room for our case only. As I walked in I told my mom to watch this circus unfold today! The door behind the bench opened.

"All rise," the clerk announced.

The magistrate walked in. He reminded me of a stern looking Robin Williams with glasses on. He carried our case in a basket and lifted it with both hands to show everyone in court with a mischievous smile. In other words, look at the amount of paperwork!

The mischievous smile didn't last long though. This was serious business and the smile quickly vanished. He asked Jane if she was sure she didn't need legal representation as she had the right. She declined.

He addressed Johan directly.

"As Mrs de Jager doesn't require legal representation, do you mind if I control the cross questioning and participate in the process? I have a lot of questions to ask the parties myself."

Johan didn't object. Courts still had to be fair.

Both Jane and myself had to stand in front of the magistrate and were sworn in under oath to tell the truth, the whole truth and nothing but the truth. Yeah right... with her, nothing was truthful and gosh this was now becoming repetitive. Another day in court. I had probably been in court rooms over forty times by now over the last two years. Although taxing, I wasn't even nervous any more. As Johan was representing me, I sat down again and started monitoring Jane's behaviour. She was clearly nervous, as her crossed leg was bopping up and down and her eyes were not making much eye contact with the magistrate at all. After exchanging some formalities and some incomprehensible legal speak with Johan, the magistrate turned to Jane.

"Mrs de Jager, I have some questions for you."

"Okay."

"Please stand up when I address you and speak into the microphone for the court records. And remember you are under oath." The magistrate's voice sounded stern.

"Okay."

"Now under point number five in the applicants' founding affidavit, it is alleged you were instrumental in him losing his job at the company he worked for based on the correspondence you had sent to his employer. I would like to know from you why you sent these documents and for what purpose."

"Well sir, eehhhmm your worship, as you can see from my responding papers I was not instrumental in him losing his job. That was his employers' decision."

"Yes, but you sent the fax to his employer making allegations that he was moonlighting. Not only that, but had also threatened the applicant that you would send this fax approximately two weeks prior. What were you trying to achieve by doing that?"

"There was a medical aid issue outstanding that still... "

"What on earth does the medical aid have to do with this?" the magistrate's voice bellowed through the court.

Jane clearly had no clue as to what the magistrate was saying and carried on more about the medical aid and other irrelevant stuff and clearly couldn't answer the question. After a few minutes of allegations and rambling on, the magistrate stopped her.

"We'll leave it at that then."

Johan took over and went through some more points where she clearly had contradicted herself on paper and various other paragraphs were struck out altogether.

The point of my (now famous) genitals came up. The magistrate read the paragraph where I alleged that she had sent this out via email to various people.

He stopped on the actual picture of my knob and lingered on the photograph. He raised his head slowly and looked up over his glasses at Jane. He gazed at her uncomfortably for a while, sighed and slowly began:

"Madam,..." a pause of silence.

"I have in front of me a picture of a penis."

The court was dead silent.

"Yes" she pointed at me and responded, eager to talk about it.

"It's his!"

The magistrate raised his hand and stopped her midsentence. He looked sternly over the rim of his glasses.

"How do you know this is his penis?"

"Well... Uhhm... I recognize it!" she blurted out.

That mischievous smile came over the magistrate's face again as he glanced through the public benches of the court room. He removed his glasses from his nose and addressed the entire court.

"Could all the men please stand up and drop their trousers? Perhaps an identity parade might resolve this mysterious penis issue then?"

The court cracked up, save for her and Brad. The sniggering continued for a while, but matters soon returned back to business. The cross examination was complete and the magistrate asked if she wanted to add anything. Surely she did.

A string of allegations which were not mentioned before came out, but were quickly set aside as irrelevant, not previously mentioned or clearly made out as lies.

The court was adjourned until the following Monday for judgment. The day was long and draining, especially for the opposing party. Jane remained cool as a cucumber and thought she had the case well under control and wrapped up. Brad, who had been getting greyer and greyer in the face as the day went on, packed up her numerous bags for her and carried them out. Maybe she felt powerful now and believed she was a lawyer, with him as her assistant!

They walked out. Brad seemed worried, but her, never! She was triumphant in all her delusional glory. I couldn't help shaking my head.

I believe, that day Brad was exposed to some things he didn't have a clue about. She must have truly kept him in the dark in the year since she met him and kept on brainwashing him to believe how bad I was. That day, surely, some things must have come to light for him. Perhaps that was why his hair was going greyer. On the flip side he must have been really stupid for believing her lies for so long. Then again, to give him credit, how much came to light for me only when I realised something was wrong with her. It did take me two years as well before I saw her truly for what she was. She had kept me busy with babies and pregnancies during our marriage and yes, although she was always fighting with someone, somewhere, she kept me pre-occupied and very much in the dark about her past, her exes and her family!

The magistrate wanted to see us on Monday for the verdict. That Monday, however was also booked with the family advocate. Again! He allowed us to come in later on the Monday, when we were back from downtown. It was chaos. The one meeting and court case after the next. Cops, court cases, allegations, lawyers letters, phone calls, SMS's. It seemed never to end.

Fifty

The Family Advocate

The family advocate's meeting was set for nine am at the Schreiner Building in downtown Johannesburg. I asked Caroline to come with me as the kids needed to be in attendance as well, but they requested we bring a baby sitter while the parents were in the meeting. Downtown traffic was chaos and because I had taken a wrong turn, I got lost in the process. The one way streets and traffic jams didn't help either. So at five to nine I phoned the offices of the family advocate telling them that we would be a few minutes late.

"No problem," they said.

"We'll wait for you—don't rush."

Stressing we left up to Jane. Shortly after nine I received an SMS.

"The family advocate and I are waiting for you and the children. The appointment was for nine o'clock."

I knew the offices there from the previous meeting of course, and I also knew that she was sitting in the waiting room with all the other parents in dispute. She wasn't sitting with the advocate as she pretended. Every time she behaved like that, I had to laugh. But I also couldn't help but wonder what she was smoking.

Caroline, the kids and I walked into the offices shortly after nine. Although the kids greeted her, there were no hugs and kisses and they immediately got pre-occupied with the toys in the playroom. Caroline frowned at me and whispered:

"Did you see how the kids basically ignored her and walked past her?"

Of course I did, but I knew the dynamics well by now. Jane tried some feeble interaction with the kids by handing them an iPad to play on, which was the wrong move from a parenting perspective. Also this ensured the kids were now competing over who would go first on the iPad. I had other matters to attend to though, because Sean had a stinker of a nappy all of a sudden which now needed attention.

I had packed a bag with wet wipes, nappies and clean clothes (as any parent would) but, due to lack of changing facilities, I had to change Sean right there on the spot, in the corner of the playroom.

As luck would have it, the family advocate and the social worker came into the room to call us into the meeting right in the middle of the nappy change. It must have been funny to see me changing a two year old, whilst Caroline had Julia on her lap and mom... well... mom was in attendance but uninvolved!

I had done some preparation for the meeting. I needed to, because like the restraining order application I felt that the family advocate needed to be briefed properly in this confusing mess of a divorce. The night before I had spent a couple of hours prepping a time line and what had transpired and at what point. It would just give clarity to the whole picture. For me it was confusing enough already to recall the events correctly, so you can just imagine how an outsider must see things. I also knew that confusion is a narcissist's tactic. Confuse the target, deviate from the topic at hand, and then go in for the kill with shock tactics. I wasn't prepared for the shocker she had in store for me though.

The meeting proceeded normally with a review of the issues at hand from the previous year. They let us talk individually and they don't allow you to butt in when the other party talks. My approach was to let Jane talk as much as possible because the more she talked, the more she would hang herself. The more she spoke, the better it was for me. After about half an hour of various issues that were aired on the table I handed them my timeline and events schedule. I prepared an excel spreadsheet with all the court cases she opened against me and all the major events that had happened thus far. I put that in a timeline so it was easy to comprehend. We went through the document. The social worker remarked:

"I am shocked at level of fighting that is going on between you two. And all the litigation? That money should have all been spent on the wellbeing of the children!"

To me she was singing to the choir. I couldn't agree more. But, as mentioned before, Jane had prepared the 'shocker'. Whilst we were being lectured about parenting and behaviour, Jane pulled out papers from her briefcase with pictures of Sean. High gloss pictures. It was not just Sean. It was Sean lying on his back with his legs held wide open, anus and genitals showing and some kind of blister mark on his inner thigh which I had never seen before! Underneath that a picture of Julia who, at one stage had a dummy rash around her mouth, but this particular picture looked so horrible, I had no words for it. She had obviously photoshopped the pictures and coloured them in. She is, after all, a graphic designer and knows her way around these editing programs.

I was flummoxed, but thank God I wasn't the only one. Mrs Patel, in the middle of her sentence turned around to Jane and said:

"Madam, what have you just put on the table?"

Jane slid the pictures with a majestic gesture across the table. She handed me a set as well. She had copies for everyone and dished them out with a smirk on her face. I wanted to vomit and couldn't look at it.

Mrs Patel raised her voice

"I have a SEVERE problem with parents who come up with these sorts of things."

She handed the photos to Advocate Johnson and got up.

"When were these pictures taken?"

"Last year" Jane replied.

"And you now want to bring in these pictures of a nappy rash and a dummy rash a year later? Did you take them to the doctor? Did you do anything about it?"

Jane responded "No."

"Disgusting!" Patel said. "Bring the children in!"

She was visibly upset and our meeting was abruptly ended on that distressing note.

The kids came in, milled about and I left the room to get my bag. Julia followed me of course, but Sean stayed behind with mom. Or rather, Sean stayed behind in the office with the social worker playing cars under the table. No physical interaction between Sean and Mom at all. When I returned, I sat down. Julia climbed on my lap. The social worker must have noticed the dynamics from that angle as well.

"Mrs de Jager? When last did you see your children?"

Jane remarked nonchalantly whilst chewing gum frantically:

"Oh about a week ago hey!" as if it was a normal standard questions which needed a stock standard answer.

In the meeting Jane had severely opposed my upcoming relocation move, but the family advocate made it clear that I could do so as I had the court order in place and there was nothing they would do to interfere.

They requested a full copy of the restraining order outcome that was to be issued later that day. The parties also agreed to have a full forensic assessment done as soon as possible to establish where the kids should reside. I had requested a full forensic psych report already from day one, but that had conveniently been side tracked and made redundant up to that point. The family advocate would wait for these two documents and make a final recommendation to the high court as a matter of urgency. They could not understand why the actual divorce was delayed in January without applying for a new date. Well let's be honest, neither did anyone else.

The meeting ended. Jane said bye to the kids who waved her bye back, again without hugs or kisses. I couldn't help but wonder what the family advocate was thinking about our 'family' dynamic.

Fifty-one

The PO verdict

I met up with Johan that afternoon at the court building to hear the outcome of my protection order application. My mom, now so engrossed in my divorce was also present purely out of curiosity and albeit nerve wrecking, it was an interesting process to witness as none of my family had even been in court before. But my mom's main reason, of course, was for support. We had no idea what the verdict would be like:

"A no you've got, a yes you could get".

We were called into the court at two pm just after lunch. Again the magistrate arrived with an "all rise". The Robin Williams look alike magistrate arrived with a serious demeanour. We all sat down and an uncomfortable silence prevailed in the court. You could hear a pin drop. The only noise audible was Jane's crossed leg, nervously bopping up and down.

Bop... Bop... Bop...

The magistrate cleared his throat and started reading his verdict and findings into the record. He covered topics from me losing my job, my genitals being displayed, the driveby's, the photos she randomly took of me and the house, the harassment and the drug planting.

On the drug planting he mentioned that although this particular court was not a criminal court, and he did not have access to the docket, it was clear to him that she had a very vested interest in this case and he made it abundantly clear that he firmly believed she planted the drugs.

His judgment reading lasted twenty minutes. He looked up at Johan who was frantically writing things down. The magistrate issued the following court order.

"The court orders that the interim order is granted and made permanent" (I had asked for three things.)

He continued,

"And is amended as follows"

In a slow meticulous manner the magistrate carried on.

"The respondent is prohibited from: Following him, Publishing information or opinion about, Making defamatory statements about the applicant, Entering or loitering outside the applicant's premises at 27 Monument Drive, or taking photographs thereof, Entering or making physical contact with the applicant's motor vehicle."

The magistrate read these out slowly. Johan in between writing these items down looked up at the magistrate. The magistrate looked back at him with a look as if to say 'keep writing, there's more'.

"Allowing the minor children to be exposed to nudity, Restricting the applicant's access to his minor children Sean and Julia, Removing the minor children from the province of Gauteng, Moving her place of residence where the children will be when they visit her without prior notification to the applicant, Enlisting the help of anyone else to do the above."

"That will be all. Court is adjourned".

Jane had not made eye contact with the magistrate at all during this session. She slowly packed her bags and walked out.

Johan turned around all smiles. The magistrate, still on the bench packing up exchanged some pleasantries with Johan and the clerk. He was also smiling whilst picking up his basket of papers and made a joke about volume of paperwork he had had to go through in this matter. He left through the back door behind the bench greeting everyone that was still left in the court.

Johan approached me.

"Oh my God.... Mark...! This is the biggest restraining order I've ever heard of issued against a woman. Congratulations!

Well done!"

"No Johan, it was you who represented me in court! Well done to you."

"You were the one who issued the founding affidavit without my help!" he said. "I'm going to use your template from now on!"

"Sure." I laughed. "I'll charge you a copyright fee!"

Apparently it was a tough restraining order I had won over. I asked for three items. Pretty much to leave me alone and not to harass me. The magistrate out of his own steam added another eleven points.

My mom was nearly in tears with emotion.

"I wanted to kiss and hug that magistrate so much" she said.

"Me too," I said. "finally someone really saw the situation for what it is."

I couldn't help feeling sorry for Jane though. I don't know why I sometimes do it, but when I saw her walk out of that parking lot to her car, I had to wonder what was going through her mind. Sure, she had brought it upon herself, but I still wasn't the conflictual type and perhaps even too sensitive or empathic for this world. I had to stop doing that empathy thing!

Johan told our advocate about the order on speaker phone. We all listened in. As he listed the points to the advocate, you just heard chuckling on the other side of the line.

Fifty-two

Sad Brad goes mad

We have to rewind the story back a couple of weeks here. When I took out the interim restraining order on Jane, she didn't like it and had to have the upper hand. A narcissist cannot be beaten at their game. Because she had attempted to get a restraining order out on me on numerous occasions under false pretenses, she realised that that wasn't going to work on me. So within a week after my interim order was delivered, there was yet another surprise.

I got home late in the afternoon from a meeting. Sophie was looking after the kids most of that day while I was on the road and working. I wasn't even through the front door yet and Julia came running to me.

"Daddy... daddy..." she jumped into my arms "why was the police here?"

Oh no, not again, I thought to myself.

"I don't know my baby, what happened?"

Julia mumbled some incomprehensible toddler speak. I greeted Sophie.

"So? Now what happened?" I asked her. "Were the cops here again?"

"Yes sir, she answered, I asked them what they wanted, but all they could say was that they had papers for the court."

"Was it the police or the sheriff of the court?"

"The police in a police car."

"Where are those papers?" I asked.

"They didn't give them to me. The policeman did leave a number to call though."

All the while Julia was pulling on my trouser leg demanding my attention. She was clearly worried that her daddy was going to get arrested again.

I called the number they left for me at once, but that number was disconnected. I tried numerous more times, but no luck. The nerves got to me again, because I wanted to know what kind of documents the cops were delivering now. I had had enough stunts from my ex already, and I really didn't need any additional drama in my life.

I went to the police station the next morning to meet up with the constable that left his number. I tracked him down on the first floor. He was a young, friendly chap and I was lucky to catch him at the office. He gave me the papers and I quickly glanced over them.

A harassment order!

But this time it was taken out by Brad out of all people! A person I had no contact with and I had nothing to do with him.

Not only that, I was summonsed to appear in Polokwane out of all places! That's more than four hundred kilometres up north from where I stayed!

This didn't make sense at all. It was the wrong jurisdiction, and the reasons for taking out the harassment order were even more bizarre.

Besides a few differences, a harassment order and a protection (restraining) order, are pretty much the same, save for a harassment order can be taken out on a stranger who is not related or in a relationship with you. He claimed that I had threatened him in November. It was now almost a year later. I had looked at his car in February at the petrol station during a handover of the children. (Wow. Imagine that? That's totally criminal—apparently!) And then I had also accused him in my court papers—my restraining order against Jane—that he had shaved his knob in front of my three year old daughter. Not only was that true, he even admitted this in his own affidavit in Jane's court case! I mean seriously? How much more bizarre could this situation get!

Whilst I was still at the cop shop, I approached my contact Captain du Plessis at his office and showed him the documents I had just received. He just shook his head in disbelief.

Although it was Brad taking out the case against me, Jane had made absolutely sure that her name was plastered all over it and requested protection in that very same document. The affidavit and the application were clearly her work. This was her writing style through and through. Brad had just basically signed it off. This woman certainly had a full grip and power over him. And he was clearly super stupid!

The captain looked up at me:

"This woman is actually truly dangerous!" he said to me. "I am going to see if I can take this further, but if I can give you a bit of advice, I think you need to move house and get out of the area."

"I am," I told him, "I'm moving sixty kilometres up north to get away from it all. Not only that, but I need to sell my house, because I can't cope with the legal bills anymore."

"It'll be better," he continued, "It'll be better for you and the kids. I've seen these kinds of things before, maybe not all as bad as yours, but some crazy stuff happens to people in divorces. Just don't let it get to you. Keep sane and do me one favour. Don't get paranoid."

He seemed to have quite a clear picture in his head about all this. I had indeed caught myself out with bizarre and paranoid thoughts from time to time.

Since November, after she planted the drugs, I would regularly check my car and property to see if there were any more drugs planted. Almost every time I got home, before I opened my front door, I'd first look to see if she wasn't driving past, standing in the street or photographing something. Every weekend when she had visitation rights I was extremely worried for the kids, but ecstatic to have them back in one piece instead of being kidnapped or hurt. Paranoia? For sure, but then again, I suppose I had enough reason for it. I might have been suffering from PTSD. Captain du Plessis asked me for her and Brad's IDs, car number plates and some other information to check records and pull files where necessary. He couldn't find any more cases open on me besides the drugs charges which were still pending and a case that was re-opened by someone recently. Guess who?

Bleep Bleep... my phone gave me an SMS notification. It was an SMS from Jane:

> Mark, I've just noted that you drove past my house on 5 Mountainlake Drive. I am feeling stalked and harassed.

I showed the captain who started laughing.

"She's totally nuts!" he said.

"Yup, told you. And clearly paranoid as well! And delusional!"

I responded to her message:

> Well that's paranoia for you. Just ask Captain du Plessis from the Randburg police station where I am right now this minute.

She replied:

> Please provide his number

Me:

> You can call the Randburg Police station.

Obviously she never bothered to call the station or the captain.

The war wasn't nearly over though. My protection order application was due in court in three weeks and now I had to deal with Brad's harassment order in Polokwane as well. The rescission application on the Rule 43 was still hovering in high court and scheduled for October, and I had also secured a garnishee order out on Jane's employer that month which was approved in the kids' favour as well. Four cases all happening at the same time.

The only problem with the garnishee order I obtained was that she resigned the same week the sheriff had delivered the order on her employer. She clearly had no intention of looking after or contributing towards the kids' wellbeing in any way whatsoever. Money and power was a bizarre obsession she had.

I had some questions for the court in Polokwane as the jurisdiction was incorrect as well as some other irregularities. Despite my attempts to get hold of the magistrate there, I could only get hold of the clerk, trying to find out what the heck was going on. I needed to know if anyone had even looked at the matter and its merits in the first place!

All the clerk could tell me was that Brad visited the court sometimes with a woman, and he kept on adding more and more papers and affidavits to the court file and he kept asking them if I had been arrested yet. Cleary he had a 'bone' to pick with me.

The magistrate hadn't even issued a warrant against me, and based on an interim order which hadn't been in court yet, it wasn't going to happen either. He was now smoking from the same delusional narcissistic pipe as my ex. She had a complete control over him. He was façade she could hide behing. This was triangulation at its best.

Fifty-three

The Polokwane Trip

It was irking me, this Polokwane story. I knew there was no case of harassment at all. What was irking me more was that I had always thought that Brad was still a decent guy. At least the kids seemed to like him. But, having seen him now in the court with Jane and with his action of taking me on with a harassment order on her behalf, this very quickly changed my outlook on him.

It was obvious from the writing style that she had prepped all the documents. She wasn't stupid and by now she had a lot of experience and exposure to the legal system. He just blindly signed the documents off, but my question remained why? Were her blowjobs that good? I certainly couldn't recall that bit of detail from my time with her!

I also couldn't understand how a magistrate would just approve an interim order like that. The merits of the case all seemed too bizarre. So I wasn't really worried about the actual case, but I could not understand how they managed to get away with even an interim order in a town I never set foot in in my life!

I suppose a small town like Polokwane was very excited to have some drama and another case on their books. I mean, it was case number twelve of 2015 after all! And we were in August already! That gives you an average of one and a half cases per month they were dealing with! My imaginative and creative mind started drawing up scenarios already. Imagining the local press in front of the court and headlines that read: 'Jo'burg guys in court action!' My mom was getting paranoid though. We all couldn't understand this process and the fact that there was potential bribery and corruption going on with the Randburg police didn't put her mind at ease.

She kept on Whatsapping me and calling me days in advance insisting that this was a trap in a one horse town and some corrupt cops were going to pull me over in a roadblock and I would disappear forever. I had to put in some serious pep talk to calm her down. I arranged with my cousin Marcel, to come for the drive with me. Not only was he young and loved driving, he was also built like a brick shithouse and knew the area well as his gran lived in that region. I took him with me for company, chaperone, body guard, witness and a driving companion.

The trip was there was truly beautiful for me and the scenery splendid. As we headed further up north, civilization became scarcer and scarcer and wildlife increased. Driving early in the morning we saw loads of buck, animals and birdlife. The roads were empty and we made it early to Polokwane well before the court appearance.

Johan had called Brad the week before asking him who his legal representative was, but he didn't have any. Two days before the matter was to appear in court though, he changed his mind and got a lawyer, Rossouw attorneys. Mr Rossouw called Johan the same day and he made it quite clear in the 'collegial sense' he was pissed off with his new client. He was annoyed with the ridiculousness of the case and the paperwork that Brad (well Jane actually) had produced for this matter. It had no merit, as we all knew, but they were trying. The paperwork was there just to confuse everyone. I already 'liked' this Rossouw. He seemed straight forward.

Johan had other commitments on the actual court day and he told me to handle the matter myself. It would also be a very costly bill to me, for him to travel all that way up. After my protection order success, he fully trusted me. The matter itself wasn't complicated and I could call him any time in case I needed assistance.

I walked into the court building fifteen minutes before the requested time at half past eight. The place was pretty empty except for six security guards taking their jobs very seriously. Because there was no public, the security guards made certain that both Marcel and I were 'secure'. I've never seen security as tight as this, but then again, if there are only one and a half cases to be handled every month, I suppose they enjoy having something to do at least. Surprisingly the building itself was a maze of corridors, offices and courts! I wasn't sure where to go so I wandered through the corridors following signposts that didn't make sense.

And there she was. An enigma! Walking directly towards me came the perfect specimen of stereotypical Afrikaans middle aged woman. A real 'tannie' as we call it in South Africa. Her hair was meticulously highlighted in multicoloured facets with hues of orange blue and pink. It was teased in an eighties style, sprayed stiff with hairspray stronger than superglue, leaving holes in the ozone layer larger than South Africa itself. This was most likely done the day before by her hairdresser. The nails were long and a work of art in its own right. Her skirt straining and battling against her middle aged cellulite, which was truly well concealed. A silk blouse revealed just enough cleavage from the wonderbra without appearing too crass. She went to town in getting ready for the day's proceedings and needed to leave an impression.

She aimed straight for me with long strides in the endless corridor with military precision. Her heels slightly off balance, like a drag queen on a modeling ramp. In my head this all became a slow motion movie with the tune of Chariots of Fire playing in the background. Her heavily made up eyes pierced straight into mine, never breaking contact on her approach.

"Mr le Foncé?" she announced with a big smile as she got close.

Dumbfounded and caught off guard I managed to squeak out: "Yes that's me."

"Come with me. We've been expecting you. It's a pleasure to meet you. I am magistrate Sanette van Jaarsveld." Marcel and I followed her through the maze of corridors flowing from one section to the next. We arrived at some sort of waiting area.

"You can just sit here and wait, okay? I'll be with you now now." She pointed to a wooden bench and disappeared through a guarded and alarmed door.

I looked at Marcel.

"Dude. This is perfect." I exclaimed.

I get along well with the Afrikaans middle aged and older 'tannies'. They seem to like me and I could already sense a connection just by the way she looked at me.

There was no sign yet of Brad, nor his lawyer.

The alarmed door screeched and opened again. Sanette came and stood casually leaning against a pillar close to the wooden bench where I was sitting. She probably had to put a couple of hairs straight in her office and redo her lipstick before she could talk to me! The way she was leaning against that pillar though, made me feel a bit uneasy. In a sort of husky voice she addressed me.

"So tell me Mr le Foncé, what is now actually going on between you and Jane and the divorce? Are things better now?"

Her English was far from perfect and heavily accented with Afrikaans undertones. She was hard to understand.

"Yea, well no.... I mean, her boyfriend is busy taking out harassment orders against me. And I mean firstly I've never been to Polokwane in my life before and neither do I have anything to do with this guy. At all! I wouldn't consider that things have calmed down as yet."

As I finished the sentence Brad and his lawyer Rossouw walked around the corner. Jane was trailing just behind them. She had to be there of course to manage the situation she had created. Her presence was no surprise to me. Magistrate Sanette regained her composure quickly and mumbled a few words in Afrikaans to Rossouw. They obviously knew each other well. I mean, how many lawyers and judges does a town like this have? Really.

They both disappeared through the alarmed door. Ten awkward silent minutes followed in the waiting room. Brad kept on looking at me with downcast eyes, whilst Jane was frantically busy on her mobile phone trying to look important. Needless to say she had her three large bags of paperwork and her self-created 'evidence' with her again. In the silence I was wondering what was really going through her mind and also what was going through his mind. Dumb fool!

The silence was broken by the alarmed door again. Rossouw stepped out and Magistrate Sanette beckoned for me to come in through the door.

The scenario was all a bit strange to me. I was expecting to stand in front of a bench in a courtroom, instead I am invited in alone by a magistrate through an alarmed door. Things were getting surreal.

We stepped into her chambers.

"Please take a seat." She said pointing at two massive leather visitors chairs at the end of her desk.

"Would you like some coffee?"

I was flummoxed. Now I heard it all. I love my coffee and I would never say no, but this came as a total surprise.

"No. No thank you your worship."

I didn't know how to address her, but I thought that would be the right form of address. It appears it was.

She started off with the application from Brad and that she hadn't issued a warrant for my arrest because she didn't 'like the feel of the story'.

We had a long discussion on the relationship between me and Jane and how Brad fitted in. She wanted to know about the kids, how they were doing and she took a great interest in finding out how they came to live with me. I gave her a brief rundown on the divorce happenings and a copy of the restraining order that was issued the week before against Jane.

She just shook her head and was quite taken aback by the information I provided her. I believe she was also not impressed with both Jane and Brad for co-habiting whilst Jane was still in the process of divorce. In Christian towns like this, that is quite a sin.

She gave me a lecture about looking after, and not fighting with Jane in front of the kids. The conversation was more like a life coaching session and got so casual towards the end that I told her straight:

"Your worship, you are singing to the choir."

She smiled at me and regained composure. Our chat was at least half an hour long. In a very stern and professional voice she announced:

"I will now call in the other party okay? Wait here."

She left me alone in the office to fetch the 'other party'.

Make that 'parties' rather. The three of them walked into the office behind the magistrate. I was still seated in the massive leather chair. Rossouw took up the other chair whilst Brad and Jane had to stand behind us.

Magistrate Sanette started lecturing. She rambled on about the divorce and that Brad should not interfere. Due to Afrikaans being her first language, she battled from time to time to express herself in English. As she stammered on some more complicated sentences, Rossouw asked for permission to address his client. She allowed it. He turned around in his chair facing Brad.

"Brad, what the magistrate is saying to you is that you, as an outsider, should not add fuel to the fire here. The divorce situation is already volatile enough and it is not for you to make it worse. You should be calming the situation down and be the proverbial water on the fire instead of the fuel."

Now I heard it all!

There is his own lawyer shitting him out from a dizzy height. This guy is on Brad's payroll but all Brad is getting, is lectures!

This was like watching a bad soap opera. Days of our lives! I think Brad was just as dumbfounded. The magistrate addressed Jane and immediately amended the order by taking her name out completely. This was clearly not Jane's case, but rather Brad against me. The matter would be enrolled for a later date if Brad so wished to proceed. She asked him twice to make sure he wanted to continue the matter. A new date was set for trial some two months later. The 'party' left the office but magistrate Sanette told me to stay behind. She wanted to give me an amended order with Jane's name omitted.

Marcel, still waiting for me to come out, overheard a heated debate in the corridor. Apparently Rossouw advised Brad to withdraw the case at once. When we walked out of the court building, I saw them in the distance standing by their car, arms frantically waving and in a heated debate. Clearly it was not their day today.

Marcel and I explored the town and had an early lunch. I made it back just in time for dinner with the kids that night. My parents had looked after them. Since I already left at four am that morning, we hadn't seen each other at all that day. Needless to say, they were elated to see daddy back home again and jumped around my neck.

Fifty-four

The emotional bomb

I had an offer on my house and my sister's house was available to live in. So the kids and I moved. We moved close to their grandparents which helped, and the kids could move straight from one school into the next. They weren't at legal school going age yet, but they needed the interaction and learning environment of the pre-school.

Julia and Sean had seen the new house a couple of times before in the planning stage, and were overly excited. I think in their little minds they had had enough of the dramas at the old place and we were all hankering for a fresh start. Although the house was not even half the size of what I had in Johannesburg, it was situated in a beautiful estate right on the water and surrounded by mountains. In the estate we had a clubhouse, pools, tennis courts, jungle gyms for the kids, biking and hiking trails and a boat jetty. It's a bush estate, so there was also plenty of wildlife roaming around freely, from bucks to monkeys, birds, bushbabies, jackal and hyena. A lion breeding facility some two kilometres up the road ensured we could hear lions roaring every night, right from the safety of our beds.

This was bliss. It was like living permanently in a holiday resort. The move would do all of us good.

The kids settled in very quickly. They were enrolled in a little 'farm' school and the distance we had now from our stalker, created some peace at home. It didn't stop Jane from harassing me though, but the restraining order did minimize it slightly. I believe it had some impact for a while.

Johan received some protesting letters from the opposing attorneys MNM about the move, but Johan found out that MNM hadn't even been informed about the restraining order I won against Jane.

She had represented herself in that matter and kept it under wraps from everyone in order to save embarrassment I presume. Johan sent a copy of the order to MNM for filing purposes and three weeks later, MNM attorneys had officially withdrawn from the matter.

An email came from Johan. The header read:

"Another one bites the dust!"

She was now changing lawyers as fast as you'd change your underwear.

Just prior to them withdrawing from the case, both parties agreed that we would appoint a forensic psychiatrist to issue a report on us, the parents, pertaining to the best interest of the children.

It would be an in-depth psycho/legal investigation and it came with a hefty price tag that needed to be pre-paid upfront. I didn't really have the money for it but it was crucial in my mind that we do this, because I believed she would really fall through the cracks as a narcissist, a sociopath, a borderline or worse (if worse exists). Something was certainly not right with this woman and I loathed the fact that she used the children as pawns in our divorce. It was time for the heavies to come out. We agreed, after some reference checking on a psychologist named Madelein O'Connor.

Her contract came in via email and I read it. Holy shit! I felt quite elated as I read the document. It was almost written with Jane in mind. A watertight piece of document that gave no-one any leeway. A dodgy narcissist's nightmare in other words.

Thanks to my sister, I managed to get the funds together to pay the psychologist and the process started a week later. Madelein was going to conduct interviews, tests, home visits and she had the right to ask anyone any questions and ask for further tests where necessary.

My first appointment was on the following Tuesday. She spent some time going over the various aspects with me and what processes and procedures she was going to follow and employ. I liked her presence. I liked the way she worked. She was thorough, but friendly, soft spoken, nonjudgmental and yet, to the point.

Our first meeting was a chat really. I gave her some background about myself, my family and my youth. Almost like a personal CV if you will. She let me talk generally and occasionally confirmed something with me to set the record straight. I went on to how I met Jane and what featured in our relatively short relationship. I had a lot to say about that, because so much had happened.

"OK, time is up." She announced.

"What? That was quick?" It felt like only fifteen minutes had passed by.

"I need to see you again as soon as possible to finish your story. Can you come and see me on Thursday for two hours again to finish your side?"

"Okay," I responded.

I was also booked with her for Friday to do psychometric testing. This would be a three hour test to see if there were any pathologies present.

That Thursday, I barely managed to finish my story with Madelein within the allocated time slots. I told her more about what had transpired in the last two years. My near bankruptcy, my arrests, the denial of access to the kids, jail time, the harassment, some legal stuff, restraining order attempts and so on. I told it all and it still took me hours to complete. She wanted even more time with me which was booked for the week after. By the time I walked out of there, I was shattered beyond comprehension. All in all I had spoken about my divorce issues for over four hours that week. My emotional brain was in overdrive. It was like someone had poked, prodded and trampled all over my mind with a hot poker and heavy duty safety boots. My mind literally felt bruised.

I left Madelein's premises, got in my car and started driving. Everything was on autopilot. My brain felt dull, like it was stuffed full of cotton wool. There was this grey cloud taking over and muffling any thoughts that tried to penetrate my conscience. I drove around for a while in that weird state of mind. I had no sense of time. My phone rang.

"Hi Mark."

It was my mom.

"Hi mom."

"How did it go with Madelein today?"

"Fine."

"Are you okay?"

"Yea I'm fine." That was an outright lie!

"Can you talk now? Do you want to even talk about it?"

"No not really. I'm driving as well. I'll call you when I get home."

"Okay." Silence. "Are you sure you're OK?"

"Yes mom, I'm OK. I'll chat to you a little later. Love you."

"Love you too."

Whilst talking to her an overwhelming feeling came over me. Something burst in my mind like an emotional pimple that erupted under the pressure of all the years of stress. Snapshot imagery of the last few years attacked my senses and I felt very sad. Very sad for myself! Although the main feeling was pity for what I had been through, there were other emotions playing around too. It attacked my body, mind and spirit without any warning and I started sobbing. The tears were streaming down my face and I found a parking spot in a busy shopping street in Parkhurst. I was totally unaware of my surroundings. I didn't care if someone saw me. I didn't care if I looked silly, stupid or like a sissy. The crying turned to howling for a brief moment followed by uncontrollable sobs but I had no desire to recompose. For the first time in my life I enjoyed the pain. It was a pain that came with pleasure. It needed to come out and I wanted it out and I let it out. It was a release, just like the pus oozing out of a pimple that overstayed its welcome. It felt so terrible and so good at the same time. It only lasted for a few minutes. Some passing pedestrians gave me strange looks. I didn't care. I just sat there. I sat with the pain. The emotional pain. The spiritual pain. The physical pain. I owned it now!

As quickly as it arrived, it was gone. I felt a lot lighter. My thoughts were clear, but without the underlying stress and tension. I dried my eyes on my shirt, because, Murphy's law, when you need a tissue in the car, there wasn't one to be found. The kids had used those up on snotty noses! I drove off leaving all that

emotional mess on the pavement in the suburb of Parkhurst. I
didn't understand what had happened, but what a relief! I so
needed that!

Fifty-five

A Hair Affair

Madelein's investigation were to be completed as quickly as possible and it was estimated to take a total of around six to eight weeks. We both had our initial interviews with her and did the psychometric tests which were obviously stressful by themselves. Three hours of multiple choice questions. More than fifteen hundred questions in all. Some were just yes/no answers and some tests were the multiple choice type of True/Mainly True/Sometime True/Not True/Not applicable—type of questions.

After we had completed the first week of grueling psycho analysistand digging, an email arrived that Friday evening. It was addressed to both Jane and myself with copy readers, the lawyers, and a psych professor who was monitoring and overseeing the investigations from a distance.

Madelein had mentioned from the beginning she wanted open communication with everyone involved. She wasn't kidding about that.

Everyone was informed of the progress of the investigation thus far and what had been completed that week. She also then addressed both of us individually in that same email:

Jane and Mark

Please contact Zelda at the University of Pretoria on Monday to book for a hair follicle drug test. Let me

know when you've done it, because the results can take
up to four weeks to complete.

She supplied us with the university laboratory numbers, and
the address where to go to.

Shit! Another big expense. I still believed Jane was somehow
using drugs which added to her unstable mental behaviour, so I
was glad with the order and was happy to comply swiftly on my
part.

On Monday I called the University of Pretoria and got connected to the relevant faculty.

The phone rang a number of times.

"Hi can I please speak to Zelda?"

"It's her that is speaking!" answered a bouncy upbeat jovial
voice on the other side.

"Hi Zelda, its Mark le Foncé. I need to book a hair follicle
drug test with you.

"Okay. Hold on a seccie, let me get the diary. How does
Thursday sound to you?"

Her jovial voice had a positive effect on me and lifted my mood.

"Sounds fine with me. What time?"

"Would ten in the morning suit you?"

"Yea okay. No problem. Can you please email me a map of
how to get there? I have no clue where you are and I don't know
Pretoria that well. I don't want to get lost."

"Will do."

She sent the email almost instantly.

I put the phone down and I thought about it for a while. Sigh.
This was again an absolutely ridiculous scenario. I'm not a drug
user at all—besides my ciggies and caffeine which are my only
vices.

I was now ordered to go for hair follicle drug tests at a scientific
facility! How insane was all this?

An email arrived that day from Madelein. This drug test
didn't sit well with Jane and she apparently had different ideas.
She had emailed Madelein directly without copying me or any
other parties in. This was despite instructions not to try and
manipulate the process or make direct communication without
copying everyone.

Madelein responded to Jane's email and copied in everyone for transparency purposes. I read the mail:

Hi Jane,

I do understand that the cost is high and that it all adds up. However, I need to ensure that my assessment is thorough and drug use could definitely impact what is in the best interest of your children. In our interview you said that a concern you have is that Mark may be using drugs; also, in Mark's interview he said he believed you planted the drugs. It would be a huge oversight not to rule this out and as such I need you both to be tested to ensure neither of you have used drugs habitually.

Wednesday is 100%, I'll see you at 4pm.

Many thanks

Madelein

What was this all about? The email Jane had sent to Madelein was below Madelein's response.

Dear Madelein

Thank you, I was about to email you as I spoke with the lab office after SMS-ing Zelda.

I am trying to get the R 2,600.00 together for this test, as you are aware I am unemployed, and need to find the additional funds from somewhere, as this is more costs on top of paying for yourself and my legal fees, I am indebted up to my eyeballs already. Before I go begging for the funds from somewhere, Brad has already said he does not see the point of the test and the additional money, on top of what he has already lent me. Is the cash outlay absolutely necessary, as I have already voluntarily done 2 x urine screens, last November (which Mark insisted I do and he promised to repay me, and never did) and this past July. This has already been an outlay of over R1,000 in the process for drug screenings.

In addition the validity of this test is the last 90 days and not the dates around when Mark was arrested?

Should you definitely require this test, for the purposes of your report, I will do what I can to get the funds together, and attend to the test as soon as possible.

Can we confirm you will be seeing me and Julia and Sean on Wednesday afternoon at 4pm?

I am then out of town, for a week, as I am going up to Polokwane until September 16.

Kind Regards

Jane

What a lying, sneaky con artist. Now it was clear! I forwarded the mail to her ex-husband, Michael, immediately and I also told my family about it. She just cooked herself big time. A druggie? Oh my God! I felt stupid for giving her the benefit of the doubt for so long. And the way she spoke in her email again. As if she's the queen herself! Where were her priorities right now? Certainly not in the best interest of her children! She preferred to be with her boyfriend up north for the week instead of speeding up the forensic investigations so we can finalise the divorce! I had a brief moment of jubilation and the offers came rolling in from everyone, including my family to pay for HER tests, because it was clear she was guilty of drug use, but again, in court nothing was set in stone unless you have the proof, which we technically didn't have as yet.

I went for the test that same Thursday. The lab people were all friendly and nice and explained the process to me. A young student beckoned for me to sit down and ruffled my hair.

"We're going to take some of your hair from the back of your head on top."

"Okay."

We need quite a bit, but don't worry, we use a thinning scissors. And you won't see a thing.

"Well duh...I definitely won't see it because it's at the back of my head!"

The assistant laughed.

"Don't worry, you really won't see it. You can't."

"I hope you are right."

"Do you use bleach or colouring in your hair?"

"Does it look like it?"

"Haha. The answer is obviously not!"

She jotted down her findings, filled out some paperwork, ticked some boxes and got up. She picked up the scissors and walked behind me.

I didn't like it.

Crunch...crunch...crunch.

Every time she cut her hands would ruffle up the remaining hair on my scalp. Her hands had an electrifying feeling to them. Like some kind of magic was happening in my head. It really relaxed me. Her touch, but also her presence. She had something about her. Must have been her energy. I saw chunks of hair going into a plastic vial. It felt like half the back of my head was cut off. She ruffled my hair again. Shivers went down my spine.

"So how does this all work? I asked."

"Your hair gets washed first in a special solution of ours to avoid any contamination from outside."

Crunch...crunch. The scissors were going ever so slowly. Followed by the touch of that hand. I wanted that hand again. It felt good.

There it was. Electricity buzzing on my head. My legs going jelly. What on earth was happening to me?

"Okay" I managed to squeeze a frog like croak out of my throat.

"Then we chop it into small pieces and it goes into a solution that dissolves it."

My imagination took over. I could picture these lab assistants stirring up pots of hair like witches in the laboratory. Bubbling kettles, snakes, frogs, lotions and potions everywhere. My body felt limp, my skin buzzing and the visuals started getting vivid. The lab assistants, now turned into skyclad witches. My thoughts were turning weird. I imagined them like nerdy librarians and professional legal secretaries. The type that take off their glasses, loosen their hair buns and shake out the hair. I imagined them like witches, stirring pots of my hair smiling at me while boiling their brew half naked.

"Stop it Mark."

I caught myself daydreaming, while 'miss sexy' was filling out more paperwork and talking to me about the process. I must have been daydreaming.

There was her hand again.

"Mhhhhh. And then?" I asked her. I could hear my own voice quivering.

She was writing on the vials and her clipboard.

"Well, like I was saying the mass spectrometer and gas chromatographer measures every single molecule in the solution. And even by the shape of the molecule we can see what kind of drugs it came from. So if you had taken an over the counter pseudoephedrine for instance we can even sometimes allocate which brand it was."

Mhhh her voice sounded very sexy with all that lab talk which didn't make any sense to me. I had to remind myself that I was here for a serious drug test and not to get aroused over some lab assistants. I recomposed myself for the second time and focused on the topic at hand.

"What? Oh really? Wow. So you can pick all that up?"

"Every single molecule." She replied.

Despite trying my absolute best to block out any inappropriate thoughts, her voice remained husky and ever so sexy. It sounded like a lot of work, counting and complicated mathematics.

"Okay... We're done." The words snapped me back from my daydream.

"Mark, the back of your head is looking just fine. No one will notice. Please sign here on the seal and we're ready to go. The electron spectrometer is running tomorrow so your hair can run with this batch. You'll have the results by next week."

The imagery of the hair batch and sexy witches and cauldrons flashed in my mind again.

"Stop it Mark... Stop it!"

I signed the seal on the envelope, recomposed myself, said my goodbyes and walked into the corridor. Another friendly (and rather sexy) blonde lab assistant crossed me in the corridor. Gee whizz, they really were everywhere! Maybe it was just my testosterone going into overdrive. Maybe it was time to start looking for a girlfriend.

I left the building as quickly as I could. Back to reality. I got into my car which was parked in the sun. It was a scorcher of a spring day. My car was cooking and my air conditioner wasn't running optimally. The gas needed to be topped up. It was a long way to drive home.

In silent sweaty conditions I reviewed the topic I had just discussed with the lab assistant. I was clearly focused on other things whilst in the lab supplying them my hair donation, but at least I remembered most of what was explained.

"Every single molecule we can pick up...

Every single one..."

Mhhh.

My pensive mind kept the vehicle on the road whilst internal dialogue kicked in. I started getting paranoid. This is like going for an HIV test. You know there's no way you can have it, but once you've donated your blood you start wondering about the what if's.

"Every single molecule..."

Shit. I knew hadn't taken any drugs, but what if I touched a banknote with cocaine on it? Or I sat on a toilet which still had powder on and somehow some cocaine molecules crawled up my butt? Oh my God.

Naaahhh surely they know.

Would there be traces of crack in cigarettes? Whose cigarettes did you smoke?

Naaaaahhh surely they know these things.

"Every single molecule."

Holy crap, I took Sinuclear a month ago when I had a cold. Would that contain pseudoephedrine?

I didn't like the sweaty drive back. Too many thoughts and worries and 'what ifs'. I resigned myself to the fact that if they can see every single molecule, then surely they also know what they are doing!

I was just being paranoid.

Jane ducked out of town for that week. She was clearly running from the drug tests that were ordered. She never went out of town before. No one heard anything from her. It was eerily quiet. No accusatory emails, no SMS's. Even her ex-husband in Yemen noticed the radio silence.

The silence didn't last though and that week went past fast. The narcissist reared her ugly head again soon after her return to town. Emails were sent ad nauseum behind my back to Madelein with all sorts of accusations about me, my behaviour and about how I abused the kids. If she'd seen one of the kids with a mosquito bite, she would make a massive medical drama about it. If they had a scrape on their knee because they bumped it somewhere, the emails would go flying again accusing me of being a bad parent and requesting medical intervention.

The topper came when Madelein did her house visit at my place. Jane, fully aware that Madelein was going to visit me that Sunday morning for two hours, sent me an SMS the night before.

Unfortunately I cannot get through to the kids tonight.
I will phone them in the morning.

Interesting! In the last two years she had phone access, on her own version exactly at six pm every night. She had her alarm set and literally every night without fail she would call at that time. On the dot! Generally the kids still didn't want to speak to her despite my insistence to say hi to mom quickly. Every night, Jane would monologue with the kids on speaker phone for around ten minutes. Even though the kids were distracted, uninterested or they would push the red button on the phone to cut her off. I tried my best, but they wouldn't have it.

I didn't respond to Jane's SMS. I knew it was a ploy to try and show what a 'dedicated' mother she was in front of Madelein. I just left it.

She SMSed again at nine thirty in the morning.

Is it OK if I call the kids at 10am?

Because Madelein was already doing her home inspection at my place, I wanted to talk to her about this odd behaviour from Jane, but Madelein was busy with the kids. I didn't have the chance. Neither did I want to discuss this matter with her in front of the kids, because those little ears were picking up far too much already.

The phone rang at ten am sharp. I saw Jane's name on the screen. Madelein looked up and I showed her my screen and indicated that Jane was calling. Madelein told me to take the call.

"Sean... Julia... Its mom on the phone. I told the kids and answered the call and put it on speaker."

Jane's shrill voice came though the speaker.

Hello... Hello...? Julia ran for cover on her beanbag by the TV on the other side of the house.

"I don't want to talk to mom!"

She covered herself and hid underneath her favourite blanket which was her safety net.

Sean started yelling

"Julie talk first... Julie talk first..."

The shrill voice continued.

"Hello Sean, how are you doing?"

"Julia first.... Julia first..."

I followed Sean who ran outside with the phone in my hand. Jane was yackking away in her usual high volume and high pitch monologue.

"Don't be rude guys. Please talk to mom quickly." I remarked.

This was the usual daily scenario. But I couldn't do anything. I already found it bizarre that they didn't want to talk to mom, but I could not get it into them that they shouldn't be rude either.

I walked back inside the house. Julia was lying on her beanbag hiding under her blanket still.

"Julia, please just say 'hi' to mom quickly."

She came out from her hiding place under the covers and grabbed the phone from my hand.

"Mom. Why are you phoning now? At this time?"

"Oh... it's because I can't phone you tonight..."

Before mom could finish her sentence Julia had cut the call and handed me the phone.

Madelein, even though I'm sure she had seen some things in her life before, sat there wide eyed. She recomposed herself and addressed me in her best non-emotive psychologist voice. She grabbed a clipboard and started writing.

"Does Jane ever phone at this time?"

"Ehhhm no. Never. This is the first time."

"And her nightly phone calls. Are they always like this?"

"Yes. Well usually this is the extent of the conversation they have." I responded.

"OK" she said. She focused on her notepad again. Some frantic scribbles followed. The kids resumed playing with their toys as if nothing had happened.

The rest of her home visit and inspection was rather uneventful. The kids showed her the house, their bedrooms, my bedroom and the bathroom. Madelein watched me change Sean's stinker of a nappy as well. It was definitely a gag worthy one. The kids played a bit on the street with their bikes and Madelein remarked.

"It is truly peaceful and safe out here! I can see why you moved here."

I took it as a compliment and responded:

"It's a great environment for kids to grow up in."

Jane's slagging email campaign continued in the weeks that followed. I had to stick to the court order and give her access on the Wednesday afternoons and the alternate weekends. I wasn't happy with it, because the kids were being manipulated and were returned to me in a frazzled state of mind and often aggressive. I felt sorry for them and I worried when they were with her. But I got to a point though that because there was nothing I could do about that, I resigned myself to the fact that although abused mentally by her, they would be OK. I, as a parent, had to ensure their wellbeing and health and that is all I could do. I also noticed that the more I worried, the more aggravated the kids became. Whenever there were issues between Jane and me, and I was agitated, they'd pick up on that energy and became difficult to handle as well. All of our strings were being played. Our energies and emotions were at wits end. Everyone was involved. I spent hours and hours discussing the divorce and Jane's antics with my cousin Caroline, my parents, her ex-husband Michael and it consumed our lives. How one person has that power to pull this off, is still beyond comprehension to me.

Internally I was starting to feel better though. I started ignoring her more and more. I didn't let the SMS's and emails affect me. I didn't want to let her mind become a virus in mine. I realised that the courts, lawyers, social workers and shrinks saw right through her despite her accusations and frantic accusatorial behaviour and fabricated evidence. So I started taking time out for myself. I started relaxing on the weekends when I didn't have the kids with me. There was no point in worrying about them.

I had to accept and believe that they'd be fine. I needed to look after me as well. I needed more income, to stand up for myself in the right way against her. She caused me hundreds of thousands in debt. She owed the kids tens of thousands in maintenance, but I knew it would come somehow. The kids had their own little "wallets" and we would be OK. They were happy at the new farm school surrounded by horses, lakes and mountains. I started sending Julia to horse riding lessons from time to time when I had some money. The kids had made some new friends in our complex and they had regular play dates. I was practicing my music again and did some jamming with another guy on the weekends. We were doing sessions at the local clubhouse and although making total fools of ourselves, we had lots of fun. The locals also enjoyed us playing live. Things and life started to ease up on some levels.

There was no more looking out of the gate to see if Jane was stalking or driving past. No more worrying about accusatorial SMS's and emails because she'd be in violation of her restraining order. Despite the restraining order confirmation, she still kept on violating it on quite a regular basis. I didn't want to get her arrested for something frivolous though, with more unnecessary stressful court appearances, even though I could have. I did keep a record of each and every incident that occurred, for a possible serious violation at a later date and my lawyer officially warned her on a couple of occasions that she was in breach of the court order.

Summer came early that year. By August 2015 we were swimming already and it was hot. Dry and hot. Madelein continued with her investigations. She kept asking me if there was anything else I wanted to discuss with her or expose.

"Madelein" I looked at her in all earnesty.

"I can supply you with tons and tons of weird behaviour. Pages and pages of evidence. Bookworks about how worried I am for the kids. I am aware that you are a psychologist, professional and with experience. I am also aware that you have picked up on stuff already. I don't believe that I need to bombard you with more things that you need to investigate. I am convinced that you, as a forensic person, have seen already what is going on. I am aware that I cannot be the perfect parent. I have my quirks and moments. We all have. I am not trying to be perfect. I put my full faith in you to act in the best interests of the kids. I am tired and so are the kids. This needs to end."

"You're right" she said.

"It is my job to see what's true and not. I am aware."

That's all I needed to hear. I hoped she had seen it. Now it was just waiting on her report.

An email from the forensic and biological laboratory came through within two weeks. As expected the email from the lab indicated no drug usage on my part. Well I knew that and my overactive imagination and paranoia were just toying with cocaine molecules crawling up my butt from the public toilets which had just been snorted upon.

The report stated clearly that I am not a druggie. Even though I knew that, I still felt like driving back all the way to the lab to hug that assistant and giving her a big smooch on the lips.

Jane was procrastinating the hair test though. She had sent an email to Madelein and told her that she had been to the lab the week before which was a lie. Two days later she told Madelein in an email that the lab was taking very long (over two weeks now) and that she'll follow up herself. I had a feeling that she hadn't been at all and was just buying time. I knew her tactics. I was convinced that the lab would mysteriously lose her hair or her file or something like that. I knew that was the way she operated. Not only that, but all of a sudden her hair was shaved off! From long hair, she all of a sudden had Sinead O'Connor hair! Wow, if that was not a dead give-away, I don't know.

In the interim I was also in court again. The state still had the case open against me for drug possession which they found in my car and clearly the flow of documentation was being tampered with. I had already been to court ten times for this procedure and I was ready to defend myself.

This wasn't necessary though. After the drug planting was vented in the restraining order court against Jane, the DPA (Directorate of Public Prosecutions) was informed by the magistrate that handled my restraining order what had come to light in our restraining order matter. They had a meeting together with Johan in their offices and the case was exposed. The Robin Williams look alike judge had advised the Public Prosecutor that there was no *prima facie* case and that the state should drop their charges.

They did. It took three more futile appearances in the criminal court because the docket or the charge sheet was missing, but eventually the magistrate declared the case closed. Someone had certainly been tampering with documents!

I wasn't worried about the case as such, but the relief of having that out of my way was immense. The Damocles sword had been removed officially and now I was no longer a potential criminal! Yay! Jane could now also not paint me as a drug dealer or user to anyone anymore. Another step in the right direction. Things were moving swiftly. And it was about time too.

Well swiftly... no not really. It would still be another year before the divorce itself would go to trial.

Fifty-six

A Rule 43 rescission application

Two weeks later an email arrived from Johan. It was titled 'Another one bites the dust' with an attachment. I opened it and it was an official notice filed in high court that MNM Attorneys would not be representing their client any more with immediate effect. Wow! I wonder whether that was money related or because of the fact that they realised they had no case? Probably a bit of both, because via the grapevine I also heard that the sheriff was chasing her for five weeks on end trying to deliver her notices and default judgments. She refused to come out of the house and stayed in hiding while he tried to serve her. One time when he chased her in the car she ended up running red robots, while the kids were inside the car! She was endangering their lives again! That information was passed to Johan by the sheriff himself. Oh my God, she was really in troubled water now.

It didn't take long for her to appoint a new lawyer. It was a lady by the name of Jessica Summers. A quick Google search revealed to me that she was more specialized in property matters, than divorce, but OK, as long as she could do the job. She was on board and handled matters with a vengeance. New brooms sweep clean I suppose. A few emails and some correspondence (with the necessary allegations from Jane that filtered in) was done by the lawyers in question and within three weeks, we were in high court again.

After nearly a year of protests, delays, futile court dates and

other technicalities, finally Jane's rescission application on the
Rule 43 was going to be heard. I attended court more out of
curiosity and for learning purposes than anything else. There was
no real need for me to be there though. Jane wasn't there, but
Jessica, her new lawyer, was. The advocates and lawyers were
frantically in and out of the court room waiting for the judge to
appear. Johan called me outside of the courtroom.

"Richard (my advocate) wants to see you. We need to talk."

"Shit, I hope it isn't bad" I said.

"No don't worry."

We went outside to the corridors. Richard pulled me aside and
in a serious, stern manner addressed me out of earshot from the
other lawyers.

"Mark, we're going to settle."

"Huh? What do you mean?"

"Jessica is proposing that the rescission will be accepted and
that the conditions of the existing Rule 43 are met by voluntary
agreement."

"OK, what does that mean?"

"Well technically nothing changes, except that the following is
going to be added."

He pulled out some papers and showed me the points in question.

> - Each party shall, within 10 court days, after
>   receipt of Madelein O'Connor's Report, advise
>   the other in writing whether he or she accepts
>   or rejects the said Report. In the event that the
>   parties, or one of them, reject the Report, the
>   parties shall within 10 court days of receipt of
>   such advices, jointly approach the Deputy Judge
>   President for the appointment of a Judge as
>   Case Manager to assist the parties in resolving
>   the issue of the minor children's residence and
>   contact.
>
> - The recommendations made by the appointed
>   Judge shall not be binding upon the parties and
>   either party may launch an Application to the
>   Court for the relief required by him/her.

I read it. It was Hocus Pocus to me. I addressed Johan and Richard again.

"So what does all this mean?"

Johan came closer and whispered in my ear.

"She's blown her divorce case, if they accept. In other words, she's stuffed!"

I had to accept and trust the guys. They were my lawyer and advocate after all. Like I've mentioned earlier, High Court matters are a totally different kettle of fish compared to Magistrate's Courts. Law applies here, and not what we think makes common sense.

The legal guys chatted to each other out of earshot again and papers were being drawn up and printed in the Court Building's admin department. With the relevant paperwork we moved back into the courtroom.

Jessica was all chatty and approached me with a fake smile.

"Oh well, better an agreed settlement than a court order no one likes hey?"

I just frowned at her. I had no clue what she was trying to imply with that statement.

"All rise."

The judge walked in and beckoned everyone to sit.

She handled another matter quickly and our case came up.

"I believe the parties have settled?"

Richard and Jessica approached the bench and supplied paperwork to the clerk.

The judge glanced over the paperwork and announced:

"So the Rule 43 is set aside and this agreement is now an order of the court."

She sat back in her chair and glanced at everyone. Our party and Jessica were the only ones in court.

"I have to add," she continued "that I've glanced through the divorce file."

She paused. "I have never in my life seen a case like this before! This story makes a better script than Days of our Lives!"

She was, ironically, a hundred percent correct and it dawned on me that I was truly living in a soap opera that was imposed on me.

Fifty-seven

Madelein's recommendations

Madelein's report came out a few weeks later. An email came through and I opened it on my phone. I ceased work immediately and opened the document. Holy crap! The document was huge! A total of one hundred and sixty five pages of psycho legal report. I wasn't near my computer, but I wasn't going to wait to read it either. I felt quite nervous about it. It was like opening up your high school final year end results not knowing what subjects you passed.

I read through the index and at the end it stated recommendations. Needless to say I went straight to that page.

In summary, the results were pretty much the same as what the social worker recommended more than a year earlier. The children should stay with me. Madelein did pick up that there were quite severe attachment issues between the kids and their mom. This was something I knew already, but the word 'insecure attachment syndrome' were new to me. However, she recommended that the kids should spend more time with their mom in order to try and heal that imbalance. I was pissed off reading those words. What the heck! My heart sank, but when I continued reading, I noticed that she had put a clause on her recommendation. Or rather, a proviso which read:

> The above contact and residency recommendations should be based on the following provisos:

Mrs de Jager should attend therapy, which focuses specifically on becoming more attuned to Julia's needs and developing a more secure attachment. Increasing Mrs de Jager's contact with Julia and Sean is beneficial to building her attachment relationships (especially with Julia), however, without therapeutic intervention and with no change from Mrs de Jager's side increased contact may be more destructive rather than constructive.

Madelein also insisted a case manager to be appointed. She stated that that was imperative.

The case manager was already made an order of the high court in order to sort out our communication issues and to speed up the divorce, so her recommendation was not a surprise.

The rest of that day I spent reading the report. Twice. But before I had a chance to finish it, Johan called me.

"Congratulations," he said.

"Did you read the report already?"

"I have."

"Wow, you read fast!"

"It took me an hour and half. But I wanted to phone you to tell you that you've done well."

"You think?" I asked him.

"Yep, it's a good report. From a legal perspective certainly."

"I thought the recommendations are rather weak."

"You went straight to the recommendations section, didn't you?" he said.

"Yea, the juicy bits first!"

"Don't. Read the report and read it again. There's a lot that is being said. It's well written from a legal point of view, but read it in full, let it sink in, and read it again in a couple of days."

The report was extremely detailed. Not only on Jane, but on me as well. Of course I wanted to know all the slander on her first. I wanted to know how bad of a mother she really was. And how mad—from a psychologist's point of view of course. I was hoping on a full on and simplified diagnosis that said—'Mrs de Jager is fucked up in the head', but of course that wouldn't have been the most professional sentence! I read and read and read. Bits and pieces at first, and eventually the whole report. I didn't know what to expect and of course my parents wanted to read it too. That was pretty scary, because I was also being exposed mentally in the report. And I didn't like some of the stuff that referred to me. I didn't want my parents to read that, but hey, I suppose they knew me better than anyone else. It took me over four hours to go through the entire document and I still didn't understand everything. I wasn't used to that kind of technical psycho-babble.

I didn't agree with everything that was said, but then again sometimes you don't acknowledge things about yourself, that you really should. I learned a lot about myself. Stuff I needed to acknowledge and work on. Personality characteristics that are not so nice and some things you really don't want to see in yourself. But these are items you need to acknowledge for what they are and not avoid, like we all have a tendency to do.

Apparently I am fairly hedonistic and non-conformist. (OK I admit, I did know that part about myself). But one of the things I didn't know about myself was that I can have anger issues that needed to be controlled and worked with. I still don't know if that part was a misjudgment or if it's true, but the nice thing is that I now had the opportunity to explore it and work with it.

Jane's part of the report came back quite different though. Not surprisingly, she had pathological and clinical issues that came forward and out of the tests. Anxiety disorders, addictive disorders, delusions, uncontrolled thinking patterns and a host of other things.

The bottom line was that the kids should remain with me as the primary caregiver, however, Madelein did make a recommendation that a case manager should be appointed and that, with therapeutic intervention, Jane should be afforded the opportunity to see the kids more in order to build up her relationship with the kids and work on the attachment disorders. Clearly I wasn't in agreement with this part of the recommendation, but keeping the best interest of the kids at heart, I reluctantly accepted that that might be the best. As long as it was monitored by the case manager and a clinical psychologist.

We had ten days to either accept or reject the report via the lawyers and also as per the agreed court order that was issued just recently. From my side we advised within a couple of days that we accepted the report. Johan thought that that would be the best option. Her lawyer came back with a different response though. They were neither accepting, not rejecting the report as they were not in agreement with some of Madelein's recommendations. In other words, they wanted to cherry pick the best parts out of it.

I don't know what transpired with her newly found lawyer Jessica, but something clearly happened. She withdrew from the case a few days later. Either she'd seen the light or just didn't see the point of continuing. That, of course left Jane stranded yet again with no legal representation and she advised Johan that she'd be representing herself from there on. Big mistake, but she felt she could do it and carried on pretending to be on top of her game.

Immediately the onslaught of emails and accusations against me started again. Now she was harassing Johan directly, clearly to waste time and rake up unnecessary costs on my behalf. Johan did warn her though that she should get legal representation as soon as possible, even if it was in the form of state supported representation such as legal aid. He limited her to one email a week, and it had to be relevant to the case or the children. That fell on deaf ears of course. She also would not admit that she had now run out of funds. To admit that was totally beneath her.

To top it all off, we knew she left behind a trail of debt with her previous legal representatives, which she denied. She obviously didn't want to lose face and continued pretending to be her 'confident' self. I couldn't help but wonder who, and when lawyer number four would come on board.

Fifty-eight

Christmas antics

Jane's antics hadn't worked for her. I wasn't jailed, her rescission application had worked, but that didn't pan out the way she wanted it to. She ran out of steam, the psycho legal report was pretty damning against her and overall her plans didn't work out the way she wanted them to. She somewhat withdrew and needed time to compose herself and plot the next scheme.

Christmas was dawning, and I knew from history, that this was a difficult time for her. She had to be in 'control' of the holiday schedule of course and on advice from Johan, I kept on being amicable with her requests on when she could have the kids. Although emotionally I was tempted to punish her and wanted to resist all her requests, he advised me to not be resistant, stick to the court order and most of all, to keep my hands totally clean. He knew I was getting frustrated, but he kept on advising me to remain calm and amicable. No knee jerk reactions and I was not to engage in conversation with her, unless it was an emergency pertaining to the kids.

The kids went to her for a two week period in December and I would get them back on Christmas Day at noon.

My telephonic access to the kids was a disaster and I recorded every single one on my ipad, just in case. Within a day, the kids were manipulated into not talking to me, but then all of a sudden after day five they were all cheerful and happy to speak to me again. I wondered if Brad had told her to behave, or if by chance,

314

she had some clarity and actually tried to comply with the court order. I had realised by now that although she manipulated the kids with bullshit stories about me, her aim and target was to hurt me. I didn't want to go into that with the kids as they were far too young to discuss these matters, but what was clear, was that the underhanded brain washing and manipulation was extreme.

Michael had also phoned me a couple of times from overseas. His son Steven, was up from the coast at his mom's house to celebrate Christmas with her and Brad. Michael was also frustrated with getting access on the phone and most days he just could not get through, or his calls and messages were ignored. Since Steven's move down to the coast, he had never had such issues, because the grandparents (where Steven now lived) allowed him normal access. Now that Steven was with him mom again, his phone had probably been taken away and calls were being recorded, on the very odd occasion that he did manage to get through.

I was extremely worried about the kids, while they were under her care, but tried to remain calm under the circumstances, hoping they'd be fine. I also needed a much deserved break, but I had no money to leave town for a holiday. I tried to make the best of it at home doing small things that needed to be done. Raising small kids on your own while stressing about courts, a psycho ex, not having enough income and being reliant on family was not a joke. My stress levels were again at an all-time high, and I wanted to make the most of my 'alone' time to reflect and rest. I did manage to do that somewhat, but my anxiety levels peaked again from the moment I picked up the kids from mom on Christmas morning.

Besides being inappropriately underdressed and unkempt, a common occurrence and more of an irritation than anything else, the kids were covered in bites and welts on their skin. I was shocked to say the least, and within a minute of having them handed back to me at the petrol station, an email came in from Jane on my phone. She had obviously prepped it beforehand and it was ready to press 'send' the moment they were handed over. Which she did, from her phone within two minutes of the handover time itself.

Dear Mark,

Prior to the 12 noon handover.

1. Both Julia and Sean have not been using diapers at night, and both have been dry throughout, which is a massive leap forward for Julia.

2. Both have dropped their midday nap, with them getting tired around 5pm, which means they have both been asleep by 7.30pm nightly.

3. Both of them arrived with snotty noses and coughs, which have all but cleared up.

4. They are only using dummies at night when going to bed.

5. We have worked hard with both of them to reduce the jealousy and aggression that appeared between them over the last 6 months.

6. Julia has a some mozzie bites on her arm from been outside on the grass during the xmas eve party last night. We treated last night.

7. They both need a haircut, please advise if you will take care of.

Regards

And the 'mother of the year award goes to...' thunderous applause please!

Both kids had already stopped diapers two months prior, but she obviously felt the need to make out to the copy readers as if it was her doing. The midday nap story was far too early because, also at school they were napping still. She just felt it rational and necessary to make that change, making her feel in control (typical of a narcissist to try and blow their own trumpet whilst not thinking of the true wellbeing of the kids.) The jealousy and aggression story, I don't know what she achieved or what she was trying to imply with that. It was clearly a shot at her own perceived fantastic mothering skills. Besides chopping Julia's hair off radically herself in the April holidays earlier that year (and under great protest from her daughter who cried crocodile tears because she now looked like a boy), she never bothered to do anything about their grooming whatsoever.

In respect of the so called mozzie bites she mentioned, both kids were covered in bites and welts. When I inspected Julia after she complained about her arm, I nearly had a heart attack. I stopped the car when she showed me and lifted her sleeve. Her mother had dressed her in a long sleeve top despite the sweltering December heat clearly to cover the damage.

Julia's forearm was swollen to twice that the normal size. It was covered in bites—not mosquitoes either—and it was red and inflamed. The skin on her arm was stretched so tight that it was about to crack open. It was red and sore. I phoned my cousin Caroline who was going to meet us for Christmas lunch. I tried to remain calm in front of the kids, but Caroline heard the panic in my voice.

"Whats up? Have you got the kids?"

"Yea, meet me at the hospital in Fourways asap." I said.

"OMG, what's going on?" Now she panicked.

"It's OK, I need to take Julia to a nurse or a doctor, her whole arm is swollen."

"Shit Mark. What is it?"

"I don't know. They need to look at it now."

"OK I'll see you there. Please drive safely."

"Will do."

I tried to keep my composure with the kids and make out as if it was nothing. The kids were calm and appeared to be ok, although they didn't say much. I was more worried about that arm than anything else.

Caroline and I arrived at the hospital at the same time. It was perfect timing. The hospital was ill attended because of Christmas and we ran to see if we could find a nurse or doctor somewhere. Most of the doctors and other staff were on holiday and they were operating on skeleton staff only. Instead of waiting, I ran into the pharmacy and asked the pharmacist for assistance. She had a look at Julia's arm.

"Mhhh" she said.

"It looks like your daughter is having an allergic reaction to what looks like either flea bites or bedbug bites. I'll give you some cortisone cream and an oral antihistamine to reduce the swelling and the reaction. It's not serious but it does need to be attended to. If the swelling hasn't subsided by tomorrow, please see a doctor."

Not serious? For me it was serious enough! My kids come back covered in scratches and itchy bites and the frigging pharmacist tells me it wasn't serious?! My poor babies! I had to take a deep breath and get control over my emotions. Fuck...I thought to myself. Nice start to Christmas. I mentally cursed her and swore at her internally.

I immediately applied the cream and gave Julia the antihistamine. I also applied some cream to Sean's bites right there in the pharmacy and tried to remain calm and composed in front of them. Shortly thereafter we were on a merry way to home to do Christmas presents and lunch at my sister's house. What a morning so far.

The lunch went well and of course Santa had brought heaps of presents for the kids and cousins. It was excitement all around and the kids forgot about their bites. The family, on the other hand, were gob smacked about the flea/bedbug bites and of course that was topic of conversation. Everyone had to chip in their two cents worth. I tried to relax, but it was difficult. I was watching the kids play with their new toys, but I was concerned by their 'offish' behaviour. They tripped over their feet a couple of times, bumped into things and they were clumsy in general. I reasoned that they'd probably been through a lot the last two weeks with mom and they were just adjusting.

Caroline was going to stay at our place that night, and we left my sister's house after our late lunch. Just in time to put the kids in the bath give them a light supper and let them settle in at home for the night.

The kids settled in, had their bath and dinner and at story time, Julia walked into the room. Out of the blue she tripped and fell again. I managed to catch her in the nick of time.

"What's wrong baby? Why are you falling down so much today?"

"I don't know."

"Are you feeling okay?"

No answer.

My mind was racing. Did her mom give her medicine I didn't know about? Was it the antihistamine from the pharmacy that made her clumsy and dizzy? I asked her:

"Did mom give you medicine?"

"I don't know."

I left it at that, because I knew she wasn't allowed to talk about anything that happened at mom's house and I didn't want to push the issue too hard. Maybe I was over reacting. I read them their bedtime story and they snuggled up. They were happy to be home again. I tucked them in and they went to sleep quickly.

Caroline and I sat outside going over the day. She knew everything about the kids and my divorce and was involved on a daily basis. She was like a second mother to the kids and she was my confidant and support through all this drama.

"Glass of wine?" she asked.

"Make that a bottle please. I need it." I joked.

The rest of the evening was spent analyzing and discussing the divorce again. Jeez, my ex was really a negative energy on her own. Almost every discussion was about the divorce and her. I so desperately wanted to have a normal life without having to discuss her, without thinking about her, the divorce and her psycho antics. I was sick of it. I wanted to pick up the pieces of my life and carry on like a normal human being. Have some money to spend on myself and the kids instead of lawyers and crap. Being able to go to work every day and focus, mingle with other people, get laid again, fall in love. You know... all the normal stuff.

My life was riddled with an obsessive ex and despite my best efforts to eradicate her from my life and mind, she still managed to stick in my brain like a worm eating through an apple. She was all over and it needed to stop. Restraining orders didn't help. Court orders were laughed at and lawyers, shrinks and other professionals were being played like marionette puppets on her strings. I had achieved so much but it felt like this was going nowhere. My biggest constant fear was that she was damaging the kids psychologically and that she would do something physical to harm them if things didn't go her way.

That night I went to bed early after my glass of wine. Caroline was also tired after the emotional day and we got ready for bed. I checked on the kids and tucked them into their blankets. Earlier on I heard them tossing and turning in their beds. They were very restless and obviously had some bad dreams or things to process in their minds. I was happy to have them back though, snuggled up to them and kissed them goodnight while they were sleeping. It was somewhat back to our relative normality again. With that positive thought I went to bed.

Julia woke me up from a deep sleep. She was in my bedroom, crying.

"Daddy, I fell out of my bed."

"I'm sorry baby, are you OK?"

"Yes, I bumped my head."

In the faint light shimmering through the curtains from outside, I kissed her head and she then cuddled up to me in the bed.

Caroline had woken up from the commotion as well and stuck her head into my bedroom.

"Is everything alright?"

"I think so. She fell out of her bed and bumped her head." I whispered.

"Shame. Something is up with her hey?"

"Yea, they're both very restless. Even in their sleep."

"I'm sure they'll be fine tomorrow morning. Night-night."

"Night."

Julia was quiet again and already fast asleep next to me. As I dropped off, it must have been half an hour or so, I woke up from a loud thud.

"Whaaaaahhhh...."

This time it was Sean falling out of his bed! I rushed into his room and picked him up.

"Daaaaaddy.... I fell down" he cried.

"Yes my boy, Oh no. I'm sorry. I know, I know! Are you ok?"

He calmed down quickly. It was more of a fright than anything else I suppose.

I took him into my bed as well and he snuggled upto me fast asleep in no time. I spent the rest of the night half asleep, half-awake pondering why they were falling out of their beds while being kicked by restless sleeping kids. When morning came, I scraped myself out of bed. Sean was already up and playing with his aunty. I needed coffee after last night. Lots of it.

"Morning Daddy!"

I was greeted by two cheerful faces of Caroline and Sean. Julia was still in my bed sleeping.

"What a night hey?" Caroline said.

"What is it with them falling out of their bed? They never do that!"

"I don't know. I just hope today is going to be better than yesterday and last night. All this is a bit much for me."

I poured a coffee and sat outside on the patio. I needed some un-interrupted waking up time, which was not possible, because Sean was clambering all over me showing off his Christmas present received the day before.

I heard shuffling in the bedroom and knew that Julia was awake now too. She jumped on my lap with her blankie in hand.

"Daddy, I have a headache" was the first thing she said and turned her face to me.

"OH MY GOD...OH MY GOD...CAROLINE COME AND LOOK HERE..."

Caroline came running.

"What? What?"

"Julie, are you OK? What happened?"

"I don't know." Julia replied.

"Jeezus Christ! Oh my God...." Caroline joined me in the panic.

"Julia, what happened?"

The right side of her face was covered in blood. Dried blood. I ran to the bathroom to get a cloth and see where it came from.

"Caroline, call the doctor. There's an emergency number on the fridge."

My daughter stood there, confused by the commotion and mayhem unfolding in front of her. She looked like she'd stepped straight of a horror movie covered in blood. I frantically washed the dried blood of her trying to establish where it came from. The hair of her fringe was covered in blood too, caked to her face. I wet it and carefully pried it away. She had a small cut on corner of her eyebrow that was the culprit. When she had fallen out of her bed in the middle of the night she must have hit the corner of the wooden box next to her bed and cut herself.

"Mark, I have Dr Wilson on the phone, he wants to speak to you."

"Hi doc."

"Hi Mark, what seems to be the problem?"

He knew me and the kids well, we had visited him a couple of times before.

"I don't really know, Julia has a gash on her eyebrow and its split open. I recon it needs stitches. It's not bleeding now, but it must have happened in the night."

"Do you think I can do stitches in my rooms?" he asked.

"I don't know, let me come through and you have a look at it. If need be I'll drive through to the hospital."

"OK come in immediately. I'm on emergency standby in my rooms."

I got myself and Julia dressed as quickly as possible and raced through to the doctors' rooms. Caroline would stay behind at my house and look after Sean.

Dr Wilson was a very kind and compassionate man. He was very good with the kids, they always liked him a lot. I knew he also had a daughter the same age as Julia, which also helped.

Julia needed four stitches. The eyebrow was split and with the tossing and turning in the bed the bleeding had started after the incident. I hadn't picked it up in the middle of the night, because her fringe covered her eyebrows and it was dark.

My main concern was how calm Julia was under all this. I didn't see anything in the middle of the night because it was all dark and I didn't switch on the light. But why did she not freak in the middle of the night? Sure she cried a bit, but went happily to sleep so easily? Was she not feeling any pain? Was she on drugs?

I asked the doctor, who knew a bit about my situation and the divorce. I was careful not to speak to him within earshot of Julia.

"Doc, I don't want to be paranoid or anything, but how would I know if they were drugged in any way by their mom. I mean they're falling out of bed, they complain of dizziness, tripping over their own feet and so on."

"How long have they been back with you?"

"Since yesterday midday."

"Next time when you pick them up, look at their eyes. If the pupils are dilated, come and see me immediately and we'll do some tests."

"Can't we do that now?"

"No we need urine tests. I don't have them here now and the pharmacy is closed. I don't want to subject them to drawing blood now either. Just go home and keep the plaster on her eyebrow for five days. If you want to change the dressing, come back and see me. I won't charge for that. Just relax and try and enjoy what's left of Christmas."

I bought Julia an ice cream for being such a strong and brave girl and we went home. The kids were calm and settled for the rest of the day, but I didn't want to take them anywhere wild that day, so we stayed home.

I immediately sent an email to Jane and copied in the lawyers, psychologists and the family advocate of the happenings that transpired. I had to bite my tongue though and I could not make any accusations for which I had no real proof. I used the opportunity at the same time to respond to her ridiculous email of the day before.

> Further to the above, it is clear you are once again covering your tracks prior to handover to avoid potential consequences. You attempted parental alienation has also come to light again via Sean this time which has already been reported to the children's court.
>
> 1. Yesterday on handover, the children were neglected and arrived filthy dirty, unwashed hair and bodies, both covered in insect bites, stick-on tattoos all over their bodies (from a few days ago) and nail polish on both kids again. The nail polish has also been addressed before specifically for Sean.
>
> 2. Julia complained about dizziness yesterday and this morning (which corresponded with her pale complexion). Again the children suffered from restless sleep and nightmares on their return from you.
>
> 3. In the middle of the night Julia fell out of the bed and this morning she fainted.
>
> 4. She hit her head hard on a box and split her eyebrow open. I immediately took her to the emergency Doctor in the area, (Dr Wilson) who stitched her up.

In discussion with the Doctor, the following came to light:

a) the bites on Julia are flea bites which she picked up at your house.

b) She likely suffered an allergic reaction to these.

c) The cortisone and antihistamine protocol are the correct route to go for the arm in the interim.

d) The swelling is going down, but I have a script for steroids in case it flares up again.

e) Her eyebrow is stitched with 3 stitches which will come out on Thursday.

5. Ensure that the kids have an adequately suitable, clean and safe sleeping/living environment whilst in your care.

6. Please revert via the yet un-appointed case manager which is now way overdue (November) as per court order. This is yet another high court violation on your part.

7. I cannot engage in further communication with you directly with your stalling techniques. Your manipulation, controlling and your neglectful parenting are only hurting the children gravely. I have and will take this up further as a matter of urgency.

As you are aware a warrant of your arrest has been issued a few weeks ago already. I shall be following up on this too.

Within half an hour she responded in her defense.

Mark, no warrant has been issued, please stop abusing the protection order. I speak directly with the investigating officer constantly in his ongoing investigation and am sitting with him and his superior upon his return from leave. As per Johan you owe my attorney a copy of the 'affidavit' I find your claims astounding false and blatant alienation. If need be I shall get 10 affidavits from people who were with the children yesterday. I also find it unacceptable that you failed to inform me of the stitches Julia received while in YOUR care this morning, as does Marianne Bavel. Why is she having nightmares and falling out of bed in your care. Your unprovoked attack seems nothing more than a smoke screen to cover this fact. Glad to hear that the doctor agreed with the treatment that Brad and I had already initiated on Christmas morning when the bites were first noticed.

In her response, which was highly defensive, she used all the techniques a narcissist is likely to use. Specifically projection (i.e. YOU were wrong and it happened under YOUR care), blaming, triangulation (hiding behind her boyfriend), lying (Going to get 10 people's affidavits, which never came forth of course) and grandiosity (i.e. am I not fantastic for diagnosing the right medication).

There was not an ounce of compassion, concern or empathy for her own daughter's wellbeing. Even that night when she phoned during her six pm phone call, she didn't ask Julia once how she was feeling or doing. All mom wanted to know was how her day was.

I had hoped the authorities would step in at this time, but neither the family advocate, nor the psychologists responded or got themselves involved. Everyone was too busy with Christmas and Holidays to really care. The only ones who cared were my own family and those who regularly asked how Julia was doing.

Julia, thankfully, healed quickly and the stitches were out within five days. The cut wasn't huge and Julia's main toddler concern was that she couldn't put her head under the water when we went swimming in the pool.

The rest of the holidays were more peaceful and the 'beast' had retreated somewhat. However by mid-January 2016 when the courts re-opened and the lawyers were back from holidays the onslaught would start all over again.

Fifty-nine

Confucius confused the shrinks

With resistance coming from all angles, Jane was upping her game and driving her smear campaign even harder. Endless emails and correspondence was sent to my lawyer. Her third lawyer had now also officially resigned from the case and Jane had made it clear that she was now going to represent herself because she was financially unable to do otherwise. The state wasn't going to help her with a legal representative either.

She rejected Madelein's report, but wanted to keep some items in terms of the recommendation and she demanded an immediate increase in access to the children (control). However, due to her "financial constraints" she could not attend therapy for herself, but she did think it was important for me and the children to go—at my costs of course. Great, the head case has made up her delusional mind and opinion! The fact that there was a court order out for the last three months stating a case manager had to be employed, didn't feature in her agenda! She avoided that at all cost. She also brought up a phony letter from Marianne Bavel which she had written two month earlier that said:

> This serves to confirm that Mrs de Jager provided me with a copy of Madelein O'Connor's report on the day it was issued.
>
> On the same day she requested that therapy between herself and Julia commence as soon as possible in com-

pliance with the report.

To date Julia's contact with her mother has not increased as suggested in the report. For this reason regular weekly reconstructive therapy between Julia and Mrs de Jager has not been able to commence.

As soon as the contact arrangements are modified, weekly reconstructive therapy between Mrs de Jager and Julia will commence.

That letter was once again a clear fake. This was now from the unilaterally appointed occupational therapist. It reeked of fraud from all sides. A therapist agreeing to take mother AND child? A therapist demanding an increase in access arrangements before therapy would continue? Wow.

Either it was a fake letter or Marianne had other interests and risking her license to be in cahoots with driving this smear campaign. It was obvious she had NOT read the forensic report and the requested therapy she mentions was not requested at all. Marianne was becoming dangerous.

Firstly, she had nothing to do with the court ordered contact arrangements, secondly, she was not complying to the report which stated that Jane had to go for separate therapy, failing which the contact with mom should be reduced as she would escalate with her bizarre behaviour. Thirdly, Marianne was/is a child play therapist, who could not treat an adult with an emotional disorder. Fourthly, Marianne was being unethical and unprofessional for even suggesting she would treat a parent and a child and fifthly, I still had not given my express consent as the primary caregiver of the children for her to undertake therapy with my kids.

Besides that fact, the personal email correspondence on email between her and Jane was in the body of the email. It read:

Dear Jane

Herewith your letter as requested.

Please let me know if you need more detail or modification.

Love

Marianne

That response alone was a clear indication that Jane had written the letter for her or drove the process at least and that Marianne was writing letters under instruction. What a silly woman! She could lose her practice over this. Not only that, but the relationship with her client was clearly not very professional, signing off with 'love'.

When it became clear later in February, that the kids were going to therapy again without notifying me, I contacted Marianne. First I left a couple of voice messages which went unanswered. Two days later I send an SMS.

> Hi Marianne, I left various voice messages for you yesterday and the day before. Let me know when you're able to talk. Despite Jane's re-assurance that you have an open door policy and I can talk to you at any time, I am not getting feedback at all from you. This is unprofessional and unethical conduct, as you are treating my children without my consent. I have no other option but to resort to the legal route and report you accordingly.

She responded within an hour.

> I assume this is Mark. This number does not register on my phone under your name. I have NOT listened to voice m3ssages (*sic*) in 2 days as my father-in-law is VERY ill in hospital. How can I help you?

What a childish way of responding. Sorry to hear of your personal dilemmas but my God, what kind of professionalism is that? I responded very matter of factly:

> I am sorry to hear that. I am getting conflicting messages from Jane about treatment. I need to establish the following:
>
> Who is currently being treated by you? Julia? Sean? Jane?
>
> Why are you sending me Linked in Contact requests? If that was even you. (She did so a week earlier.)

Did you write a letter of treatment in November stating you will treat Jane?

What is your email address, just to confirm.

Her response was now even more pathetic.

Mark, I am not at home now. My email address is marianne@gigimail. Could I please answer all these questions by tonight or tomorrow am at the latest?

I answered back

I don't understand the difficulty in answering simple questions which could be done via SMS.

Are Sean, Julia and Jane currently your patients?

Did you send me a Linked in Friendship request? (I got a Linked in request from her a week earlier.)

Did you write a letter for treatment of Jane in November?

Yes/No answers will suffice. I am tired of being excluded out of the 'process' especially in the light that your name is being mentioned and used by Jane in nearly all legal correspondence. Your avoidance towards me as the primary caregiver of the minor children is unprofessional to say the least. Sorry to be so harsh, but that is the reality.

She responded. The pressure was obviously too much and I think she must have been worried.

I saw them for the first time in a long time on Wednesday. They will all be starting relationship building therapy next week. The Linked in was an accident. Yes I said I would be able to do the therapy with Jules and Jane as recommended by Madelein O'Connor.

Thank you. That was all I needed. Not only is my divorcing ex cooked in the head, clearly the occupational therapist, who, in her own three page credentials boasts about her specialty in handling acrimonious divorce cases, is cooked in the head too.

She just put herself deeply entrenched in my divorce by being biased, using favoritism, being unprofessional, noncommunicative and putting her ability to practice gravely under scrutiny. I needed to report her to the Health Professionals Council, which I did, but this was never followed up by the Council. Welcome to South Africa's efficient systems!

Sixty

Life as we know it

Jane's self-driven legal campaign continued. The litigation by paper between her and Johan was insane. Her allegations, insinuations and accusations were getting more bizarre by the day and I started to call her the 'drive by lawyer'. Johan in the meantime, was getting sick and tired of her as she was trying to 'prove' that I was alienating the kids from her. He received numerous emails per day, about the most absurd things. If I was five minutes late for drop offs she'd instantly send messages to the lawyers, Marianne and the Family advocate (audience) stating that I was denying access, despite my notification to her that I would be five minutes delayed.

I became so sucked in and so used to these allegations that I just didn't react any more. I needed to focus on the main prize which was, at all costs, protecting the kids and avoiding having them too exposed to her mental instability. The kids were being brainwashed, manipulated and programmed not to speak to me about their weekends and time spent with mom. If I questioned them (excitedly) with a 'how was your weekend?' their heads would drop down or they'd just ignore me and stare out of the car window.

Financially I wasn't coping very well and I started relying more and more on handouts from my sisters and parents. I hated being in this space. The drama had gotten to me. I failed to make enough money, justice was extremely slow and the system was not

331

protecting the kids adequately. I had fought so hard up until now. I had huge debt with my lawyers and started to feel like a failure. Raising kids on a full time basis was already a full job in itself and Jane was certainly not contributing anything towards their school, medical expenses, household expenses or general wellbeing. I was fighting a continuous uphill battle.

I had to focus on what was important. I had to pick my battles carefully, which was hard as I was constantly defending my position to the authorities. She still hadn't been arrested for her violation of the protection order. I tried to contact the investigating officer on a weekly basis, but my calls and SMS's were ignored. They probably thought that my issue as a male against a female was trivial. The other alternatives were that she was bribing them or the Police were just plain incompetent.

How is it possible that the authorities took no action while one head-case like this was eroding me at the core, financially, emotionally and physically? And not only me. It affected the kids, her ex-husband and others too. But I was the main target and bore the brunt of her smear campaign.

Johan was brilliant though. He could see my suffering and assisted me greatly by forging ahead. We had become somewhat 'friends' through the years, which wasn't surprising with all the information he knew about me. But I was frustrated and got upset with him over the lack of results.

"I can't deal with this bitch any more, you need to sort her out for once and for all."

I was angry and his response was just as angry back. For the first time ever he raised his voice at me:

"Well for your information, I wasn't the one who stuck my dick in a psycho and married her."

Wide eyed silence followed. He never used words like that, but at the same time, it was the harsh reality. He had spoken the truth and all I could do is burst out laughing.

"Yea, you're right. I have to take responsibility for that. Guilty as charged!" I said to him.

The email correspondence between him and Jane continued on a daily basis. She didn't communicate with me anymore as per my request, so he got the brunt of her. Due to the sheer volume of email and nonsense, he put her on terms that she was only allowed to send him emails once a month and he'll respond with one letter back. This was also to alleviate any further costs to me, as each letter read and responded to, was billed to me with an hourly rate. She knew that it would cost me so that instruction fell on deaf ears. The beast was relentless.

My car had broken down. Just what I needed! I was now super dependent on family and borrowed cars, as I just did not have the means to repair my twelve year old 4x4 with a blown head gasket. That car had also been nothing but drama for me over the years and it was really time for a replacement. But with what? I was stuck between a rock and a hard place.

In the meantime the designated handover point was still sixty five kilometres away and that never changed. I had to drive to Johannesburg twice a week. Fuel, mileage and time were all for my account and I had to stick to this regime until we could change the court order. She refused to pick up the kids from where we were living now.

To me it was a simple solution: If you don't pick up, you forfeit your access time with the kids. That didn't fly as the court order stipulated otherwise.

Johan told me not to take that approach. I had to keep clean hands for the divorce case which he had now enrolled for November that year. Despite my income being erratic, my car broken and my mood heavy I kept on focusing on the kids. They needed the best possible support under the circumstances and I made sure we had access to the basics and kept the problems out of our home.

Thankfully the kids were doing very well at school. We engaged in a lot of social activities and mingled with friends and family. I also made sure we could do fun activities and the area we lived in had loads of those. We went horse riding, swimming, canoeing, cycling and a host of other things without spending a lot at all. With my previous company doing tours and trips, I had access to game farms, elephants, lions and all sorts of wildlife. We had some amazing experiences together and the kids loved being outdoors surrounded by wildlife. Mother Nature was truly becoming the kind of mother they missed. Looking at my Facebook pictures it was almost like we were living a millionaire's lifestyle. But the reality was far from that.

I bought milk from a local farmer fresh from the cows. Not

only is that healthier, but it was a third of the price of store bought milk. I often baked my own bread at home, because driving ten km to the nearest shop for just a loaf of bread was too costly, and homemade tasted much better as well. I made soups and broths from bones and kept the kids well fed and as healthy as possible with the least amount of expense incurred. The belt was tight, but we ate well. With all the cooking and experimenting at home the kids were involved with the activities. They helped me cook and clean. Clearly cleaning up was not part of their favorite activities, but it taught them some important lessons in life.

I got a lot of hand-me-down toys and clothes from my sisters who had kids slightly older than them. It was a tremendous help, and we weren't really short of anything, but I wanted to provide my kids with more. I had to pull my finger out of my butt and make some serious cash, but my sanity was compromised. When the kids were at school, I tried to get business in, but I was exhausted by lunchtime. I had to make a plan with getting my own car and not rely on borrowing my mom's, my dad's or my neighbour's. Everything became a mission. Everything became irritating. Everything became old and outdated. My laptop was becoming corrupted, pixilated and slow. My internet connection outside of town was erratic. My fridge started to become temperamental and my washing machine's onboard PC board wasn't functioning properly. I hadn't bought new clothes for myself in years. I hadn't gone on holidays for years or taken the kids on a weekend away. My savings were gone, my pension was gone, everything was gone. I had nothing left besides myself and my kids.

There were days when I had no money in my pocket even. I panicked from time to time, but reminded myself that things would come right. I started looking for jobs, but as a fortyfive year old male that had been out of corporate now for two years, in an economically challenged country with a thirty five percent unemployment rate, not many options were available. Let alone securing an interview. Explaining the situation to recruitment agents didn't help either. I didn't want to be a whiner and didn't want to become a victim of my own demise either. I had no choice but to push on with my own business and any odd jobs I could find.

I realised that the long term smear campaign and effective on-slaught of my life in conjunction with the character assassination, had taken its toll on me. I realised I was now finally depressed. Keeping a brave face didn't help. I needed to be strong for the court case and the kids, but I started wondering. Am I the best father the kids could wish for? Am I doing everything I possibly can? The answer to that was yes! A resounding yes even, I had no doubt and my surroundings and people in my environment resonated that as well.

I, myself, however, realised that I needed help. I needed to look after myself, live healthier, stop worrying, start having fun, real fun, getting laid, going out, meeting new people, have a party, get some self-esteem back, fall in love. This whole psychopathic divorce situation had become too obsessive. I realised I was fo-cused too much on the fight. I focused too much on the kids. I focused too much on everything else, but myself. I was an empath and in this drawn out process I was becoming a martyr.

I had no money for therapy. On recommendation of Johan I started writing. He told me to write a book about all this. When I told him I'm not a writer, he said:

"Then you just do it for yourself."

That's how this book came about. Writing this book helped tremendously. Writing songs and expressing myself helped me, but I needed more help and to break the shackles I was so bound into.

I started by not allowing her onslaught of accusations to get to me. It was all crap in any case and (hopefully) the authorities would see it that way as well.

I let all the bullshit flow over my head. I focused on me once the kids were in bed after eight pm. After washing up and putting a load of washing in the machine, I'd meditate, contemplate and try to get the narcissistic worms out of my head. I focused on my priorities. I'd ask myself: What was still hanging over me from the various cases? What was important to resolve? I had to categorize and prioritize. It would be a long journey of recovery for myself.

Jane sent an email to Madelein, four months after the forensic report was issued. Of course and again, it was done behind every-one's back. She wanted another evaluation done on everyone, because she 'had been working on herself' and according to her, her relationship with Julia had improved drastically and she herself thought (pretended) that she as much better. I couldn't help but wonder if she was really aware of her behaviour and destruction. Did she have the capacity to self-reflect?

Madelein was aware that Jane had not been in agreement with her initial report and also that she had not stuck to the court order, for her to appoint a case manager.

Madelein responded that she'll do a supplementary report if all parties are in agreement with this, however she questioned the necessity of this. Now that all parties were copied into the email correspondence again, Jane quickly backtracked and claimed she wanted another report on just on herself and for herself 'in light of the developments that had been happening and because she did so much work on herself in the last three months.'

Madelein put her in her place, but in a very professional manner:

> Hi Jane,
>
> It would seem that what you require is an assessment of yourself and of your and Julia's relationship and not a full supplementary forensic report. Such an assessment would fall under the role of a case manager. I must reiterate, as per my recommendations, that it would be advisable to appoint a case manager who can assist you in this regard I refer you to pg 102–113 of my report, in which I outline the function of a case manager:
>
> *It is at the case manager's discretion to include further parenting training, therapy or further drug testing. Furthermore, it is the role of the case manager to manage scheduling of any change of contact, specifically in the event a crisis emerges that needs immediate attention. The case manager should also attend to any changes on a six monthly basis to accommodate Julia and Sean's maturation needs. Further to the aforementioned, the case manager will be responsible:*

To ensure Julia and Sean's best interests
To monitor their progress
To have contact with their teachers if necessary
To recommend therapy for Julia and Sean if indicated
and to have contact with this therapist
To monitor the parents' continued healthy parenting
To mediate between the parents when necessary
To guide the parents
To refer either parent for any further appropriate
therapeutic, medical, drugs interventions and
parenting skills training if deemed necessary by the
case manager
To refer Julia and Sean for any appropriate medical
interventions and to have contact with any medical
professionals if indicated
To refer the parties to a mediation process in the
event of a deadlock in the case management process
To instruct any further independent investigation/ as-
sessment to establish what would be in Julia and Sean's
on-going best interest.

Many thanks

Madelein

That email was never responded to. It didn't suit Jane to appoint a case manager clearly, as that would mean she'd be more exposed. She didn't want anybody to monitor her behaviour because her façade would crack wide open. She needed to stay covered up in the dark recesses of her delusional mind. She had to devise another plan. Another wicked plan to get at me!

Sixty-one

A 'playroom' for adults

Despite Johan's letters and requests, no answers or compliance in the divorce matter was forthcoming. Jane still wouldn't communicate with me, but she now started blaming me if I was even a few minutes late for handovers. There were big claims that I was frustrating her access. Big claims that I was withholding the kids from her, and although I would have loved to do so for the children's interest, I never did and stayed compliant and reasonable. Johan's words constantly resonated in my mind.

"Face the judge in the divorce trial with clean hands— Don't give her any stick to beat you with."

I didn't, but she was adamant and grasping at whatever straws were available to her. Actually she had no more straws so it was more a case of regurgitating the little soggy pieces that were left in her mouth. Her accusations were starting to sound like a broken record.

So far, so good. Two social workers' reports in my favour. One forensic report in my favour. Teachers, nurses, and caregivers were all behind me. The only two people she had behind her were Marianne and Brad. One was (stupidly) misled and the other one bias. Her actual legal antics and behaviour in the matter wouldn't help her either. At that point she had launched seven civil matters and two criminal matters against me. A judge in high court would surely look at that behaviour too?

Although it all looked good from my perspective, I was still

338

worried. Was all that enough? I didn't want to take the kids away from her because she had been a bitch to me. I wanted to protect the kids from this criminally inclined and insane mind. To make matters worse about her bizarre behaviour, I got a call from the Estate Agent who had my house on the market.

"Hi Chantelle. Tell me you have some good news for me! Do we have an offer?"

"Hi Mark, no not yet. We have someone interested, but no firm offers on the table at this point. The market is still weak."

"Okay. No problem. I know it'll take some time."

"Can you come to our office the day after tomorrow? I need to give you that spare set of keys, but I also have something to tell you."

"Okay, fire away!"

"No not on the phone, I'll tell you in person."

She piqued my interest. What was the reason for this mysterious call? I couldn't wait to see her.

I knew Chantelle well. In fact I had bought the house from her some ten years earlier and we had always remained in contact. She had had my house on the market for a few months now. I needed to sell urgently as my tenants were a disaster and I needed the cash from the house liquid to send some money Johan's way for all the legal bills.

I entered her office. Chantelle and her assistant were there.

"I have something to tell you. But it needs to stay confidential." She started.

"Oh yeah? You did mention it. I'm curious now. What's up?"

"Jane and Brad approached us to rent out their house for them."

"Oh?" I said. "Is she moving?"

"Well it would seem so! But that's not the main part."

"What is then?"

"Are you aware of a playroom in their house?"

"No? Jules and Sean never told me that they had a playroom in there."

"No not that kind of playroom. An adult playroom!"

"Whaaaaa? What the heck is that?"

The assistant answered that in a nervous jittery kind of way.

"We went to take some pictures. It's a really creepy place. It's even soundproof apparently—well that's what Brad tells us. He locked me in there to demonstrate how soundproof it was and it really creeped me out. It gave me shivers."

"Hang on, hang on... whoaaaa. You mean they have like an S&M or bondage type of set up in their house? A dungeon type of thing?"

"Well... uhhm... something like that. It has mirrors on the ceiling and black velvet walls, and a bed."

"Shit. You're kidding me right?"

"No, no, no, for real. And Brad thinks that it's a really good selling point to rent their house out."

"Oh my God..."

"We think it's bizarre and have never come across something like this in twenty years of dealing in real estate."

My mind went into a spin again. A frigging soundproof S&M 'playroom'—IN THEIR HOUSE! I had to control myself not to get paranoid. Were they up to strange things with the kids? Were they taking photographs of them in some sort of bizarre manner? Was he a child molester? I felt nauseous from the mental imagery. I wanted to puke. What was worse was Julia's commentary and behaviour the year before and the fact that Sean's nails were painted and that they were always returned totally frazzled. Fuck... Fuck... Fuck. Ironically I had no other words to describe it.

I was flabbergasted! I was totally unsure of what to make of this. But the picture in my mind didn't help. Chantelle continued.

"Look, I needed to tell you this because I know the situation you're in with that woman. I am personally not comfortable with her or Brad for that matter. They're creepy and I'm scared of them. Please don't let this get any further. I'll send you the photos we took."

"Thanks."

I left their offices and I phoned Johan. I told him what had transpired. He responded in a very matter of fact kind of way.

"It's not good enough to use in a court of law. What adults do in the bedroom is their prerogative and you have no proof that they're using the kids."

I wanted to cry and die and disappear into a hole. THEY invest money into an S&M room in their home and I can't do anything about it for the sake of the kids? Someone who invests money into their sex life and on that level in their house must be pretty sexually deviant! This was just getting too sick for words. What happened to law? What happened to protecting innocent little children? The estate agents think it's bizarre enough to call me over this, but I can't bring in an application to the court to protect the kids? What on earth is this world coming to?

I had to let it go. We'd bring it up in the trial of the divorce of course, but for now nothing could be done. I had to sit it out and control my paranoia. Maybe it was just for them. Don't pre-empt anything else. I didn't even know if I should tell my parents. They'd just worry, but I couldn't keep it to myself.

So I told them.

"My God. These people are sick!" my dad exclaimed.

My mom cried for the sake of the children. She made matters worse by fueling the conversations with 'what ifs'.

"What if they're drugging them? I believe they're drugging them. Maybe they take pictures of them naked. Sean has been coming back with nail polish on his hands and feet and we don't know anything about this Brad guy. Maybe . . . Maybe Maybe. . . ."

"Stop it mom. You're making matters worse. We can't prove anything. The courts won't look at it. Let's not sit and get all paranoid over this now. I know it's not normal. It's totally sickening actually, but let's not jump the gun here. We have to come up with concrete stuff and not what ifs and imaginary scenarios."

It took a few days and lot of self-control, but I kept it quiet. I wanted to shout it off the rooftops in the neighbourhood and tell the world how sick these people were, but I controlled myself. Even with Jane. I didn't let her know that I knew about the room.

Well. . . for a while at least.

Johan and I had ceased almost all communication with each other and I didn't engage with her bullshit any more where I could avoid. She was still trying to harass Johan and got hold of his cell phone number. She now started SMS-ing him at all hours of the weekend, nights and whenever she felt it was appropriate. Having no boundaries, she demanded answers immediately and, what should have been managed by a case manager by now, was now imposed on my lawyer. Of course it was all part and parcel of driving up more legal costs for me, so we ignored what we could.

In April, and in order to harass me and the kids even more, she decided that she should call twice a day as she 'needed to build a better contact with the kids' as per Madelein's report. In her own, much loved words, this would be in 'Best interest of the Children'. I straight away told her to take a hike, as the kids never asked for mom nor did they want to talk to her in their daily phone call at night. Her phone number also changed and now started reading 'No caller ID' on my screen.

When she again tried to call a second time that night, I sent her an SMS.

> Please stop harassing me and the children. You've already spoken to them today and the court order states 'reasonable access'. This is not reasonable!

Her response came in immediately.

> The children want to speak to me and you're denying me my rights. This is not in the best interests of the children!

The SMS onslaught went on for a good half an hour, plus attempts to call in between. While this was happening the kids were totally unaware, happily playing games and making puzzles. I shouldn't have responded at all as it just fueled her narcissistic need and fury.

When she hit a dead end with me, she started harassing Johan via SMS's. Johan called me in frustration asking me what the heck was up with that woman. He agreed with me that she shouldn't harass him and she was irritating and trying her luck.

I was annoyed though. Annoyed to the point where I told her via SMS:

> Stop harassing me and go back to your playroom. Go and whip your boyfriend there.

That made her instantly aware of the fact that I knew about their 'playroom'.

This was followed by another barrage of SMS's denying having
a room like that. She was now threatening to sue me and Brad
is going to sue me. She wanted to know how I knew about this.
The SMS's were a confusing mess of denial, blaming, questioning
and admittance. The words she used were even more interesting
and an amazing display of smoke and mirrors:

How do you know about the décor of our family home?

I had to laugh at the pretentiousness of the word décor! That
sentence should have read:

How do you know about the sick S&M dungeon in our
filthy house?!

The next SMS came in.

Did you break into our house?

I let the SMS's wash over me. I switched the phone onto silent
and built puzzles with the kids instead. That night she sent forty
three SMS's with all sorts of accusations. Even Brad jumped
on the bandwagon too sending me messages from his phone too,
threatening to sue me.

I didn't respond, but it was clear from both their reactions,
that they had a lot to hide and didn't enjoy the fact that I knew
about the S&M room.

It went quiet after that. I think I had shocked the narcissist into submission a bit, but as I well knew, that wouldn't last
forever. The silence only lasted about a month.

Sixty-two

A failing legal system

Every time she got quiet, I knew that she planning her next attack. I was waiting in anticipation what her next move was going to be. She got to work behind my back. She was also busy with her ex-husband Michael, who had put her on terms in respect of obtaining his son's passport and for her to allow him to travel overseas. She was in total contravention of the high court order issued some twelve months earlier and he had opened a case against her of contempt of court, which potentially carried a penalty of six months incarceration. He was also in the maintenance court where he had to defend himself for an application she opened. She had unanimously applied for a fifteen thousand Rand per month order to 'support' her son Steven, who wasn't even living with her. Again, and needless to say, the affidavit that was submitted to the magistrate was nothing but fabrication and bullshit and it was clear that she was desperate for money.

The worst was that the magistrate had allowed it to be featured in court without even looking at the paperwork and Michael now had to apply for a rescission of this via the Canadian and South African court system, before this order could be enforced. To everyone it was clear that this should not even be given the time of day, but the relevant magistrate attending to the matter was not on top of his game. Another failure on the part of the family court system.

In the interim I was still sticking nicely to my court order, and had to allow unsupervised access weekly on a Wednesday afternoon and every second weekend. I never deviated from that and did what I was told by my lawyer. Keep your hands clean!

Keeping them clean was not a problem, but Jane viciously turned everything into an allegation or a fault. I couldn't even fart and there'd be a lawyer's letter. It was mostly on the topic alleging that I was denying and frustrating her access. Oh... if only I could!

Unfortunately, for me, most 'professionals' in their field, they somewhat believed her shit. She was cunning and the system was biased. I was often asked if the kids wouldn't be better off with their mom, as that is 'usually' the case— especially in the tender years. This question was asked without them even looking at the matter or the case history that was before them. It was a total bias on the system's behalf and made my legal battle twice as hard only because I happened to be male. Maybe it was because I stopped reacting so much to her crappy, unfounded statements, believing that the professionals would see her devious plan. That, it turned out, was not the case and often they gave her the benefit of the doubt without digging deeper into it. Maybe I didn't voice my complaints enough about her. But if I did, I was branded a drama queen.

By the end of May, I visited the Randburg Police station to find out what had happened to the arrest and case that I opened some six months earlier for her violating my protection order.

The investigating officer, Bobani, had ceased communication with me since January that year and flatly did not answer my calls nor respond to my SMS's. According to other sources, I was supposed to get an update every month or so as to the status of that case. This never happened.

Bobani wasn't in. He was on leave again, this time he was on family responsibility leave, because his mother had died, so I went through the cop shop searching for his superior or someone who could help me. I was sent from office to office for a long time, but I wanted to know what had transpired with the arrest. Eventually a Warrant Officer Crooks assisted me in a very rude and obnoxious manner. He checked on the computer system under the case number and told me that the file had gone to the National Prosecutor and was returned two month earlier to Sergeant Bobani with further instructions to investigate deeper.

"I can't see what those instructions are. I'm assuming Bobani has to investigate more."

"OK," I responded, "but why am I not getting feedback on this?"

"Give that man a fucking break, will you? His mother has just died!"

"Excuse me? I'm sorry for his mother, but I've been following up once a month for over six months now, with numerous SMS's and calls which all go unanswered. Clearly he's either not doing his job, or there is something else going on! There's a warrant of arrest out there for over six months already and you guys have gotten nowhere! What kind of service is this? You are supposed to act in the best interest of the public!"

Crooks was angry. I clearly pissed on his battery, because I had challenged their incompetence. With an arrogant tone he responded.

"You know what? Get out of here and follow up with Bobani when he's back next week. Don't come and bother us here at the station."

OK, I clearly hit a nerve. Did he know more? Was he involved with my arrest initially and made the dockets disappear? Was Jane instrumental in making sure that nothing happened on the system? I didn't know anymore, but it was all dodgy. I started to believe someone was being bribed and manipulated, but if so, how did she know the system? Did she have informers, people higher up? Were there other parties involved in the background?

I left the station and reported it to Johan. He'd look into it and come back to me. It was clear though that it wasn't just me getting sick and tired of this story. Johan, the cops, the psychologists, social workers and everyone was getting tired of this story too. No one had answers or resolution.

But that didn't stop Jane. She was now on top of it all. She was escalating just like Madelein o'Connor predicted in her psychological report. The stories and allegations were getting more and more strange and out there day by day. In June she sent an email to the Family advocate:

I have definitive proof that your client entered our residence in our absence during April 2016. This is trespassing and in light of the protection order, clear abuse. As to why your client felt the need to enter our home, again shall be dealt with in the correct channels.

This was total hogwash of course and she pretended (or alleged) now that she was the one having a protection order! She was completely losing it! Not only that, but she was again in gross violation of the protection order for publishing false information about me. Never mind it being a total lie!

I called Johan immediately and told him:

"Johan, I'm going to the cop shop and lay another charge of violation of the protection order."

"Don't, keep your hands clean."

That response irked me.

"Johan, you didn't hear me. I am going to the cops and I'm going to lay another charge of violation of the Restraining Order. I've had it with this bitch. In fact I should also open a case of defamation of character. I don't have a restraining order for nothing here."

"Let me phone you back."

"OK, but be quick, because I'm on the way to the police station and I will be laying charges."

"I'll talk to you just now. Be patient."

"OK."

Johan was busy in court and obviously didn't expect me to go to the police. I was furious and I did go to the police. Seeing as though the Randburg cop shop was clearly useless and not very amicable in terms of handling restraining order violations, I went to the local police station in Brits.

There was no queue and I was assisted straight away.

"Good morning sir, how can I help you?"

"Hi, I need someone to assist me with a violation of a restraining order."

"OK no problem. If you go back outside and turn left, to the white building, they'll assist you."

"Thank you."

I walked outside and turned left. There is was a prefabricated separate building with a big sign on it:

VICTIM EMPOWERMENT CENTRE.

Oh wow. They have a whole center for this kinda stuff here! They purely deal with battered women, children (and some men). They were especially there to assist in getting arrests, restraining orders, violations, protection orders, harassment orders and where needed, psychology and therapy for victims as well.

I knocked on the door, no answer.

"Hi, were you looking for me?" a friendly voice came from behind. A young lady walked towards me with a cup of coffee in her hand.

"Ehhhm yea maybe. I'm looking for the person that works here."

"That'll be me! My name is Rachel. Nice to meet you!"

"Nice to meet you too."

She unlocked the door and we walked through a children's playroom into her office.

"Sit down" she beckoned.

"How can I help you?"

Wow. I was a bit flummoxed. Rachel's office was organized. Files and folders were neatly arranged and stacked in place, there were children's drawings on her wall and other art. A pot plant decorated her desk. She was friendly and as I was about to find out, she was on the ball as well.

I opened my bag with all my paperwork.

"Well, I suppose you don't see a lot of men coming through here. This is more for women I gather!"

"Not at all!" she responded. "This is for men, women and kids. Anyone going through any form of domestic violence, harassment or abuse. Physically or otherwise."

I explained my story to her. She listened intently and asked me some questions. Half way through she interrupted.

"OK, hold on for me here, I'm going to open a case docket. You have a restraining order and you can't let her get away with this."

She left the office and came back.

"I'm going to let you fill in the affidavit. From what I see and hear, you've been exposed enough to the courts and law to know how to make an affidavit."

"Rachel, after my experiences in over two and half years now, I could do a thesis on law."

She smiled at me empathetically.

"Shame, I can see where you're coming from. Just remember to be accurate and precise in your statement."

"I will, don't worry."

While I was filling in the forms, she got on the phone to Randburg police station. Her conversations were distracting me.

"Where is Bobani? Who is his superior? Why hasn't this woman been arrested yet? I'm from the Brits police station. Yes...yes...no.. I need answers. Tell him to call me back...My number is 012 ...."

She was on the ball and clearly rattling some cages on the other end. I started having a glimmer of hope with the system again.

I finished my affidavit. She read it and made me do the oath. Stamp. Signed. Case number assigned.

"There you go. Done."

She smiled at me and sat back in her chair.

"So. Tell me something. What did you do to this wife of yours?"

"Huh? What do you mean?"

"Something about you must be very good?"

"I don't know. I don't understand what you mean by that!"

"It's easy. She's smitten with you. Obsessed! She can't let you go. I've seen some cases in my life, but I'll be honest with you, it's rare to come across it in this extreme form."

"Well as far as I'm concerned, whatever you call it, she's mad."

She put the papers in a docket and sent it off to the relevant department.

I walked out of the cop shop three hours later. That's how long it took with Rachel.

I felt good about it. Someone believed me. Someone listened to me. Someone cared and didn't think my stories were overblown. Someone finally assisted properly. A day later I got notification that the file was transferred and moved to Randburg. It was standard procedure. The new officer assigned to the case was Warrant Officer Crooks.

Oh my God. Warrant Offices Crooks! That was the same arrogant dude who 'helped' me some three weeks earlier and chased me out of his office. My heart sank when that message came through. The moment the system started giving me hope, I got assigned a rude an obnoxious bad cop to handle my case. I still hadn't heard from the other officer Bobani on my other case either yet, and my overactive mind started creating scenarios. I feared that they were all on Jane's payroll.

The next morning the phone rang.

"Morning Mr Le Foncé. This is Warrant Officer Crooks from Randburg police station. Could you please provide me with Ms de Jager's telephone number, home and work address? We're going out to arrest her."

Wow. That was a bit of a come-back from the last time I spoke to him! I provided him with the details but didn't hear back from him again.

Johan in the meantime heard that I had lodged another complaint, obtained the case number from me and followed up.

I still don't know the details exactly as to what had transpired, but she was arrested and released on bail for a further hearing at a later date.

The following day Johan called me.

"You won't believe what happened!"

"What?"

"She was here in my office now and dropped off an application to have the restraining order set aside."

"What? How can she do that?"

"I don't know, but she did! And it's a monster application too. I'm not joking, it's probably about four hundred pages of nonsense."

"OK send it to me, I'll have a look at this, even though I don't have the time for this crap now."

"No, I'm also sick and tired of it."

"I'll chat to you tomorrow."

It was four hundred pages of absolute nonsense. Picking out parts of reports, bits and pieces, SMS's from three years earlier, phony affidavits from her boyfriend Brad, Googled websites and a host of other crap.

I called Johan again.

"Johan, she's applying under the Harassment Act. Not the Domestic Violence act and she's making out as if she's the one holding a restraining order against me!"

"Yea I saw that too. You're getting clever with law hey?"

"Well clever or not, she's doing it wrong, but more importantly, how can the court clerk set down a date for this?"

"I don't know. The clerk is clearly not with it. It's definitely incompetence on their part for sure, but be that as it may, we have to appear on the date given. It's on the roll now."

The date was set down for ten days later, so technically it was short served in any case. She had no legal representation and I doubted that even based on the sheer volume of documents she submitted to the court, the magistrate would chuck it out without looking at it. The morning of the case, Johan had to attend another matter in another court in Pretoria. He sent Neil, his junior to assist me. Neil was a fresh graduate understudy to Johan. I'd say early to mid-twenties. He was professional in his manneriSMS and dressed to kill. Although he had spent time studying law, he didn't have much practical experience. In the background he'd been working on my various matters drafting documents, pleas and affidavits, so he knew my case backwards. He appeared nervous having to appear on his own.

"We'll be fine." I told him. "The magistrate won't even look at this."

Neil and I met in the court corridors. Jane was there bright and early and on time. She was alone! There was no lawyer nor her boyfriend in tow. The boyfriend probably didn't even know about this matter and the crap she was causing again.

The matter was listed on the roll, but when they called out to see who was present, our names weren't called out. There was no file for court. I looked at Neil.

"Foul play?" I couldn't help but wonder.

"Dunno!"

We went into the clerk's office and wanted to know what was going on. She didn't know either, but was going to look for the file immediately.

"It's easy" I said to her. "Look for the fattest and biggest file you see. It's that one."

She laughed.

They made us wait outside in the corridor and occasionally informed us that they were still looking for the file. Neil and I chatted about law, the case and the various other things that I'd been through in the last three years. The hours ticked by waiting in the corridor.

Jane was busy looking important. She was still 'preparing for her case' paging through various papers and files and making notes. She certainly looked important with her briefcase and her two other humongous bags she loved to carry around. I suppose if you want to defend bullshit, you need to back it up with bags full of bullshit! But it's not easy to keep a lie straight.

In the middle of the morning, Jane approached Neil with an air of importance and pulled him aside out of earshot. She tried to win over his confidence and asked him some questions. I could see him shrugging his shoulders and he walked back to me.

"Man that woman is sick in the head."

"Why?" I asked.

"She asked me if I knew what sort of time frame we're looking at before it goes into court and then has the audacity to ask ME to call her on her phone when we get called in as she has to attend to another so-called urgent matter!"

"What the heck?"

"Yea, she's clearly not well. And the way and mannerism she asks as well. Pretending to be my best friend! She really is something else."

"I know. I know. Just ignore her."

After a long morning waiting, we were called into the Court Clerk's office.

"We've found the file. It was in the prosecutor's office because the matter is in criminal court over a violation. I sent it to the magistrate, who isn't going to look at this matter."

I looked at Neil and remarked.

"I told you!"

The court clerk continued.

"The application was also incorrectly submitted and applied for under the wrong act."

I sniggered.

"I know."

"The applicant, Ms de Jager, had misled me when she applied for this case to be opened."

"Hang on a second there, Elizabeth. Did you just say the applicant mislead you? You? The court clerk? Could you please do a statement to that effect?"

"No I'm not allowed to, but I have informed the magistrate to that effect."

"OK thank you for that, but I could have told you that this application was crap and under the wrong act and so on."

"Why didn't you call me and tell me?" Elizabeth said.

"Because I am not here to do your job!"

"Fair enough. I'm sorry. I really am. I should have looked into this more. You've wasted an entire morning with legal costs. Do you want to proceed with costs charges against her."

"You bet ya!"

Johan had just come from his other case and popped into the court to come and see us. He joined us in the clerk's office and butted in.

"She's probably going to launch another application under the right act. Let's wait and see it out the next couple of days. We can join the two and claim wasted costs on that matter as well in one sitting."

Johan was right.

The very same day of that wasted morning where she was basically chased out of court, she was back at Elizabeth's office applying again for a rescission of the restraining order. This time with the correct paperwork, forms and in the correct manner. She short served us again and the new court date was set for ten days later. The short serving didn't really matter, because we had responded already so the answers to her absurd case were already filed. I couldn't wait to see her in court now.

Sixty-three

Fraudulent forgery and other shenanigans

The whole week was a blur of bizarre events already and very pacey. A few days prior she popped into Julia and Sean's school as well; harassing the teachers while pretending to be a concerned mother. She claimed that Sean needed speech therapy and she as the concerned mother had already incurred all the cost of play therapy with Marianne in Johannesburg. She told the headmistress about some phony disease she clearly Googled on the internet that Sean had, called Auditory Sensory Disorder. This was so called diagnosed by Marianne! A quick Google search indicated that that certainly was not the case, as Sean loves dancing to and making loud music and noises! A load of crap in other words. Concerning for the kids though was, that she would probably make the kids themselves believe they were suffering from syndromes and illnesses that didn't exist, or weren't of any concern. She was now busy making hypochondriacs out of them. I was concerned she herself was developing Munchhausen Syndrome by proxy.

The kids were being negatively affected the last couple of months. Jane was working them emotionally to the maximum and Madelein's reports about the attachment disorder with Julia had made Jane very uncomfortable. She took it upon herself to 'build the relationship' with Julia herself and the damage was clear.

Julia was totally potty trained, night times as well, but in the last two months she started having accidents again. These accidents were always the day she had seen her mom or had visited her over the weekend. I didn't make a fuss over it with Julia and played it down, so as to avoid insecurity issues with her, but in reality this regression gravely concerned me. Every time on pick up or drop offs, the kids were not themselves. They were wild and rude and full of sugar. It was almost like they had to switch personalities when they had to go to mom in order to please her. Even before drop offs they became angry and cranky with each other on the way there. They were tense and couldn't express it in any other way.

Julia loved her horses and about once a month I'd take her on a pony ride on one of the farms around us. Their school had stables next door and regularly we'd go and visit there. She loved all animals, but horses were Julia's favorite animal.

Traditionally Jane would take Julia to therapy on Wednesday's to Marianne, but that stopped all of a sudden. Jane decided that the Julia needed horse riding now. Fine by me, but eeehhhmmm she couldn't afford it really and ignored her court ordered child maintenance payments! There were no contributions for medical expenses, housing, schools or anything, because she pretended to be poor! How could she afford to take the kids out for horse riding lessons every week? Besides, them being a little too young for official lessons, I could smell a rat.

After a couple of weeks, Julia started asking me if she could live at her mom's house. I was surprised by this request, because never in her short little life, did she ever want to go to mom's house. Visitations were resisted and even though she accepted her fate, she was never keen to go to mom or even speak to her on the phone! So I was a bit taken aback by this, but carefully probed with Julia as to why the change in mindset. She told me that mom promised she could go horse riding every day if she came and lived with her! Wow. Now she was using blatant lies and false promises on a four year old who didn't know any better, in order to set her up against me! This was just too sick. Johan also noticed it.

Julia was in a total state of confusion though, because she

didn't really want to leave me, but the promise of horse riding every day appealed to her. The stables where Jane took them horse riding were close to her office where she now worked in Kyalami. I left it because I knew the kids, especially Julia enjoyed it. I did warn her in advance though that mom would and could never take her horse riding every day though.

The reality of that situation kicked in shortly thereafter. One Sunday, I picked up the kids from our usual petrol station (under camera) hand over spot. The kids had spent the weekend with their mom and I was expecting some adjustments to happen in the car. I expected them to be in their usual rowdy and cranky moods, which, I had learned, was best to ignore and not ask questions. That way they wouldn't feel pressured and they would snap out of their moods quite quickly on the way home.

Julia flew into my arms and clamped onto me more than usual. She didn't want to let me go.

"Hey Julie, how's it going?"

No answer.

"Are you OK?"

She seemed upset.

I looked at her. Her eyes were downcast and couldn't look me in the eyes.

"What's up baba?"

I strapped her and Sean into their car seats. Sean seemed OK. I worried about Jules and we drove off. Sean babbled a bit, but Julia was silent and not herself. I adjusted my rear view mirror to see her on the backseat.

"What's up my girl? Do you want to talk about something?"

She caught my eyes in the mirror and pulled her eyes away from mine.

Sean babbled away about face paint and cats. He was chatty and I communicated with him, hoping Julia would come out of her shell soon.

In a moment of silence a few kilometres down the road, Julia spoke.

"Dad?"

"Yeah?"

"I only want to go horse riding with you. Not with mom."

"Oh?" I acted surprised.

"Why?"

"Because."

"Alright." I said. I wanted to know what transpired and what made her say that.

"Did you go horse riding with mom this weekend?"

"No."

"Oh no, that's a shame. Why not? What happened?"

"I don't know."

It clearly was a case of having been disappointed by mom. Mom had promised her horse riding every day on so many occasions, but that was an impossible promise to keep. At the tender age of just five, this was not the first time Julia had been disappointed by her mom over something, but this broken promise was clearly a big issue for her.

I didn't know how to respond properly.

"Shame my girl, we'll have to make a plan for next weekend if we can."

"I only want to go horse riding with you." She re-affirmed.

When in Joburg, I'd mostly meet up with my cousin, Caroline. She was always there for me, my confidante and was very involved with a lot of things in my life. She knew everything and we had daily communication on the progress of the various matters. Although often she got overly involved in my case, it always came from a good heart and out of deep concern for me and the kids. She was emotionally my biggest support throughout the whole process.

After my wasted morning in court with Jane, I met up with Caroline for a quick lunch and coffee. I was in Jo'burg after all and since my move sixty kilometres up north, I'd often meet up with her like that if I had spare time.

The mornings' topics came up and we were debating the various outcomes and options that were on the cards.

My phone rang. It was an unlisted number.

"Hello Mark speaking." I answered.

"Hello. Is this Mr le Foncé?"

"Yes it is."

"Hi there, my name is Brett Mc Donald from CLHA."

Alarm bells went off.

"Sorry Brett. From where?"

"The CLHA."

The Chartwell Lowveld Home Owners Association was where Jane worked. This was her employer! A nervous butterfly feeling in my stomach kicked in and my mind reacted very quickly. This was bound to be an interesting call.

I grabbed Caroline's phone off the table and found the recording app on her phone. I switched my phone on speaker and carried on talking to Brett. Caroline, realizing that something important was happening held her phone near the speaker so it could record properly. I could see the nerves kicking into her as she held her phone up with her hand shaking, listening intently to the conversation.

"Yes Brett, how can I help you?" I responded politely.

"Well, I'm doing an investigation, and your name has come up."

"OK."

"I need to establish from you if you have vetted for a credit and driver's license check to be done."

"Sorry, I'm not getting you. What does vetting mean?"

"Vetting means you are in agreement or you have agreed to have a check done on you."

"Ehhmm no. What kind of check?"

"In your case, one of our employees used our system to check the validity of your driver's license, and she also performed a criminal check, as well as a financial check via our systems."

"Oh my God." I exclaimed."

Brett continued.

"So basically, in terms of the law, the POPI act in particular, when we do a check on someone, the person needs to be in agreement with that."

"Right. I am assuming that your employee you're referring to is Jane de Jager?"

"Yes. Do you know her?"

"Somewhat," I replied sarcastically and continued, "She is my wife."

"What?"

"Yea. You didn't know that?"

"No, she never mentioned you before nor were we aware she was married. We thought she had a boyfriend?"

"Yes she does. A crossdressing one! We are separated and busy divorcing for nearly three years now, but I'm not surprised when you tell me she's never mentioned anything. She tends to be rather sneaky when it comes to divulging information."

"Tell me about it. We are having a hearing on Tuesday next week. She has done checks on you as explained and when we noticed there were no documents on file. She produced via email some scanned documents with false signatures and a wrong contact number. She explained that you were a contractor doing some work for us in our secured estate."

"What? I've never set foot into your estate. Ever."

"Don't worry about that. Let me explain. She used to work for us, and our lawyers are doing a hearing next week with her. It's all a proper legal process. Currently she's suspended, and we might take her on further for committing fraud. She is in contravention of the POPI act after all and we stand to lose out credibility and our license should this come to light. You might have to testify that you never signed any paperwork or agreed to a credit check. We will send you all the documentation paperwork of the hearing after that. You have the right to take her on personally for committing fraud, forgery and identity theft and I recommend you follow that channel with the police. Would you have any objection in testifying against her next week during our hearing to explain you have never agreed to the vetting of the checks to be done on your name?"

I was flabbergasted and Caroline nearly fell off her chair.

"No. Absolutely not... Give me a call any time. Whatever you need from my side. Do you mind if my lawyer contacts you on this? I was in court with her just this morning. I have a restraining order on her too."

"Your lawyer is welcome to call me anytime."

"Thanks."

At the end of the call all I could do was to stare at Caroline with my jaw on the floor. Her response was pretty much the same besides an

"Oh... My... God......! Do you know what this means?"

"I have an idea!" I responded.

It was at that point four months before the divorce date. Here comes, out of the blue, information and an investigation from a third party that wants to take her on for fraud. If this went to court, which I knew it would, she'd be toast!

The act of what she had done, on its own, was enough to put her behind bars for a good couple of years in accordance with common law. Put in context of the divorce, what she had done was going to be even more huge! I couldn't even begin to think about what consequences this would have on the various matters that were now laying ahead of us.

I immediately sent Johan a copy of that voice recording. He called me within an hour. All he could do was laugh and laugh.

"This is brilliant." He exclaimed in between his sniggers.

"I'll call Brett for you and let you know what he says."

The next day Johan had told me he had spoken to Brett.

"This guy is like a parrot. He gave me all the dirt. We need to wait for their report and information and we'll incorporate this into the case and affidavit already next week in court."

The report hadn't arrived yet the week after, but it didn't matter in any case. Jane had managed to get a date in court for the rescission of the restraining order. Although we didn't have her employers' reports yet, we were able to proceed. The trial wouldn't happen in any case that day, and because she had short served, we could still claim an extension for defense.

Neil from Johan's office joined me that morning in court. Jane sat waiting on the same spot in the corridor with her usual three bags of 'evidence'. She was paging through the documents she had with her as if she had to memorize all her stuff. I suppose she had to. It must have been difficult to keep up with all the lies, so she had to rehearse to make sure her stories made sense.

She looked like shit. Unkempt, badly dressed and she wasn't even wearing shoes. She had slippers on. Worn out slippers. The type you wear at home in front of the fire place. God only knows why she looked like that. It was probably to create an impression on the judge that she was poor and couldn't afford shoes. Whatever her reasoning on that, it was bizarre.

The clerk approached us with a file that was probably about fifteen hundred pages thick. It was a monster. I wondered what she submitted to the court behind our back. That file, on its own was about twice as thick as all the other applications heard in court that day combined. The magistrate arrived in court.

"All rise."

The magistrate beckoned for us to sit down. I knew this guy. I'd seen him in court before, but I couldn't remember for which case or if it was one of my previous cases. Jane took her spot in the front in the lawyers' area. Neil took the other spot with Johan next to him. It was to be Neil's first appearance in court. The magistrate spoke.

"I just want to get some clarity first. You are Ms de Jager right? And you are?"

"Neil Swindon from Johan Brooks Attorneys, your worship. On behalf of the respondent."

"And it appears the respondent, Mr Le Foncé is holding the restraining order against you Ms de Jager?"

"That's correct your honour." Jane responded using the incorrect address for a magistrate. It should have been 'your worship' in magistrate's court and not 'your honour'.

"And you want to apply for a rescission on this very same restraining order?"

"Yes your honour."

"OK." He glanced through some papers, looked up at Jane and continued.

"Before I take on this matter, I just want to make sure of a couple of things. Firstly, are you sure that you want to proceed with this matter and apply for the rescission?"

He placed his hands on the humongous pack of paperwork that was filed. It appeared like he was giving her a warning. Johan turned around to face me in the public gallery and winked at me. Warning confirmed.

"Yes your honour, I do want to proceed." She said.

"And I am of the assumption that you want to represent yourself in this matter?"

"Yes your honour. I have lots of..."

The magistrate interrupted her and raised his hand, beckoning for her to keep quiet. In a neutral, but stern tone he addressed her.

"I do need to advise you that you have the right to legal representation. Mr le Foncé has legal representation and you have that same right. If you cannot afford a lawyer, I can appoint a state lawyer for you.

He continued in a soft spoken, almost sarcastic tone.

"Lawyers, in a courtroom, use evidence to prove their case. Lawyers know what kind of evidence can be produced in a court and what cannot be produced. They use legal terminology in a court which they studied for a long time. These are not the kind of words you can throw around in a courtroom haphazardly. Neither can you Google them on a computer and interpret their meaning. What is it going to be Ms de Jager? Would you like to continue to represent yourself, which, I do not recommend, get a lawyer to represent you or do you want to use the state lawyer in this case?"

Jane shrank in her position and replied hesitantly with a slight stutter:

"I-I-I'll appoint a legal representative to assist me in this matter."

Wow, I was surprised. She actually took someone's advice.

"Very well. I will set down the matter for three weeks, for all the parties to get up to speed and respond in writing one more time. Is everyone OK with this date?"

Everyone agreed and the date was set down. The magistrate continued.

"I will not allow any further extensions or delays. There are costs and time involved. I'll examine the evidence, have a hearing and the matter will be closed. I must warn either of you though. If you are not here at the next hearing or try to interfere with the process, it may have some serious consequences."

Ouch. If that wasn't a direct warning, I don't know.

We both shook our heads. This magistrate wasn't up for nonsense.

The magistrate wrote in his file and closed it. He looked up to Johan and Neil. His demeanor changed from the stern magistrate, his face softened and with a witty smile addressed Johan.

"Mr Brooks. I assume this is your junior and you're over here to oversee his appearance in court?"

"That's correct your worship."

"Do you mind if I give him some pointers and words of advice?"

"Not at all your worship."

He turned towards Neil.

"Mr Swindon, may I call you Neil?"

Neil started blushing and nodded yes. He was definitely not comfortable with being addressed so casually and privately like this in a court by a senior magistrate.

"You are clearly an intelligent and strapping young lawyer wanting to make a career in the law profession."

Neil started to beam with this compliment, thinking he was going to get a valuable lesson from the magistrate himself.

"Yes your worship."

"I have a son about the same age as you. I need to know what it is with you young people about trying to look, ehhhm, how do you call it...Hip...yes, hip is the word I'm looking for. I mean look at your hair. You're representing clients here in this courtroom and that kind of style does not really do justice to the law fraternity in general."

Granted, Neil did have a full bush of hair kinda set in a bed-head style with gel. It was quite hipster really. Neil just died on his feet and lost about two inches in size trying to shrink into the courtrooms' lush carpet.

The magistrate smiled.

"Don't take it as criticism. It's just an opinion from my side. My son is very much the same as you. Long hair and all. Sometimes I see lawyers appear in front of the bench with 'funky' outfits, cool sunglasses on top of their heads and even female lawyers with miniskirts on. People that have been practicing for years. A courtroom is not the place to be cool. So please don't take it personally young man. Just a bit of opinionated advice from my side. Oh and just on other thing. Please invest in a razor blade a well. You can buy those at the local supermarket.

By now, Neil had disintegrated into the carpet and woodwork. Whatever was left of his ego, managed to squeak out a slight

"Yes your worship."

"Court is recessed. You may go."

The magistrate smiled, stood up and left. The door automatically closed behind him. Johan looked at Neil and turned to me. His face beaming with a grin from ear to ear. I was sniggering.

"Now there's a chapter for your book, he remarked."

I agreed. Neil managed to pick up some of the broken pieces of his ego off the floor and approached us. We were laughing straight in his face.

"Consider yourself shat out!" I remarked.

"Oh my God... Oh my God... I'm going for a haircut now!" was all that he managed to come up with.

We left the courtroom into the car park. We didn't discuss any topics of the matter at hand walking towards the car. Whatever the magistrate had said was self-explanatory.

Sixty-four

A stoned ex and a fuming magistrate

It was three months before the divorce date. Things were heating up. Tensions mounted and Jane, with her various applications tried everything to get me down. She was now losing her job, her court cases and her mind. I was surprised she hadn't lost her boyfriend yet.

In June 2016, Jane had the kids for half the holidays as per court order. She didn't have them that long, but I was worried for their sake. Jane's mind wasn't stable. I was worried that she might do something stupid with the kids. Something dangerous. I wasn't in a position to make any amendments to the schedule and I had to stick to the court order. Half the holidays were hers with the kids. The access arrangement for this holiday was that she'd have them from the Wednesday twelve noon until the next Sunday at five pm. Four and a half days to be exact.

Reluctantly I took the kids through to the designated petrol station for handover in Johannesburg. They weren't overly excited to go, but I didn't want to make matters worse for them either. I kept my worries to myself. I told them that they'll have a good time at mom's house.

We arrived five minutes early. Jane wasn't there yet. That was odd, I thought to myself, because when it came to pickups she was always obsessively early.

The kids were messing about in the back seat of the car. Occasionally they'd ask.

"Dad? Where is mom?"

I didn't know either.

At five minutes past twelve I took the kids out of the car to get some fresh air and I SMSed Jane.

> Hi Jane. What time do you think you'll be here?

No answer. Very strange! Normally she'd respond in seconds. In fact normally she'd be pre-empting excuses even before she would be late, pretending to be the 'responsible' mother.

I SMSed her again at ten past.

> ????

Again no answer.

The kids were getting bored in the forecourt of the petrol station. We had waited long enough and I wasn't getting answers at all.

I phoned Johan at twenty past twelve.

"Hi Johan."

"Hi Mark, whats up."

"Jane hasn't pitched for the handover yet. I don't know what's going on. I have no communication from her at all. I SMSed her a couple of times already. This is very strange."

"Try and call her and see what she says."

I phoned her. No answer.

I phoned her again a second time. Again it went straight to voice mail.

Stuff this, I thought. She's not here for her holiday access, I'm going home. I put the kids back in the car and tried once more. The phone just rang and went to voice mail. I left a message.

"Hi Jane, it's me. I've been SMSing you and tried to call. You're not here for the handover. I don't know what to do. It's now nearly half past twelve and I can't stay around any longer. I'm going home."

As soon as I put the phone down an SMS came through.

> Wher arew yuo now?

I responded

> At the garage waiting for you! The arrangement was
> for 12 noon!

Her reply:

> On my way. Whe I confirmed with Joahn last week he
> said to met at the oher petrol station!

Bullshit. Another lie covering up something. She would have phoned me a hundred times already if she was there at noon. Her responses were illegible and scrambled. Did I just wake her up? Did she have a heavy night? Was she on drugs? It was past midday already.

I bit my tongue and responded.

> I'll wait at the coffee shop next door with the kids.
> They have a play area there.

Her response came in quick.

> Thanks.

Did she just say thanks? Oh my. I've never ever heard a polite response from her in my life. I was dumbstruck.

I took the kids over to the coffee shop and ordered some drinks. They were playing on the jungle gym and having fun.

Jane arrived more than half an hour later. More than an hour after she was supposed to meet us. Her hair was in a mess, her clothes unmatched and it looked like she'd just stepped out of bed. She was wearing massive dark sunglasses almost covering her entire face. She walked past my table straight up to the kids on the jungle gym, taking no notice of me. The kids shouted "Hi mom!" from the top of a tower, but carried on playing. Jane walked to the play contraption, didn't pick them up or hug them. Instead she gave them a high five. They carried on playing, not giving mom much attention. Jane looked on. She looked around nervously. He jaw was moving from side to side, but she wasn't chewing gum. Her demeanour was jittery and edgy. Was she high? Did I wake her up from a heavy drug fueled night? I wasn't sure.

Julia shouted from the top of the jungle gym pointing at me,

"Look mom, Dad is there!"

Jane mumbled something incomprehensible and went and sat two tables away from me with her back towards me. Bizarre, I thought to myself.

I paid my bill and called the kids over. I gave them big hugs and told them to enjoy their time with mom.

"I'm gonna miss you daddy." They exclaimed.

"I'll miss you too guys."

With big kisses and hugs I left them reluctantly in the care of their mom.

I called Johan the minute I got to the car.

"Johan, she was cooked out of her bracket. Can't we do anything about this?"

"Not without a court order." He told me.

My five days off just became a five day worry session.

I wanted and needed to take a well-deserved break from all the tension and stress of the last few weeks without the kids being around. I needed some me time to heal and have a breather. So with difficulty, I convinced and promised myself that the kids would be OK and I shouldn't worry about them. But matters got worse.

All the dramas, court cases, financial worries and stress now also started affecting my direct family. The situation was out of hand all over. I had a huge fight with my sister later that day over the house in Johannesburg which was starting to get run down. She wanted me to hand over my shares and she'd invest and fix it up. Over my dead body. It was the only investment I had left for my kids and my sister just wanted me to sign it away? The fight became bitter and hard.

The next day my dad got involved. He was calling me names and protecting my sister, but didn't give a rat's arse about me. It got totally out of hand, while my mother put herself in a position of 'neutrality'.

I started ignoring them flatly and needed to stay away from yet another toxic scenario. Were they teaming up against me? Was I being paranoid? Naïve? Stupid? Was I being stubborn? Were they right?

Being on edge and with only weeks to go until the divorce I didn't cope well with this additional drama. I had to keep my cool and not be thrown off course by emotional reactions from anyone else. In the end I reluctantly gave in, as I needed to get the money out the investment which had now become a liability. I sold the house at a bad price and moved away from all the drama. I had no choice but to save myself and the kids.

Losing my last bit of financial security, I sunk into my depression further. I felt it happening to my body. I was well aware of it, and tried to deal with it in a way that I thought was best for me. I increased my vitamin dose and voiced my grievances with the people I trusted most. At that moment in time it felt like it was only my cousin, my lawyer and the kids that gave me the strength, hope and support. It was a dark space to be in, but I remained hopeful, as that and the kids was all that I had left.

I was summonsed to be in court again at the end of the month. Jane wanted that restraining order gone and the case was still ongoing. I also found out that the day before our appearance, she was in the criminal court for violating that very same restraining order. I wasn't notified about that, but I didn't have to sit in those hearings. I wanted to go and attend the criminal proceedings against her, but Johan advised me against it.

"She'll just use that against you. Leave it to the state to deal with. It'll be postponed in any case."

He was right. It was postponed. But we were in court the next day for the rescission application.

"All rise."

The magistrate walked in. He started.

"I see you're still pursuing the case?" He addressed Jane.

"Yes your worship."

She was standing in the spot normally reserved for lawyers and court personell.

"Where is your legal representation?"

The magistrate was visibly irritated.

"Your worship, my lawyer couldn't make it today and ... "

"So you are telling me that you got a lawyer and he doesn't even have the decency to appear or come or send someone else from his office? Madam I am..."

"Your worship, my advocate..."

"DO NOT INTERRUPT ME!"

The magistrate bellowed out. He was now losing his cool.

369

"So you are telling me that you have a legal representative and they don't have the decency to appear on your behalf? I am not inclined to believe you madam. But I will tell you what I will do. You were in court yesterday for a violation of this protection order. The same protection order you now want me to set aside? Is that correct? Were you arrested for a violation of this order?"

"Yes I was."

Jane had no emotions in her voice, but had this smirk on her face. The fact that the magistrate just shat her out didn't faze her in the slightest.

"I am going to set aside this order. You are wasting everyone's time here. Including that of the courts. You are premature in your application. You can wait for the outcome of the criminal case and re-open this matter if need be at a later stage. I am also going to make a provisional order for costs in this case. Mr le Foncé has the right, pending the outcome of the criminal case, to apply with me for a cost order. He is not the one who asked for three wasted appearances in this matter."

Jane stood there grinning and nodding her head as if this was just another day's work.

"Court dismissed."

I walked out with Johan.

"I'm happy with that." He said.

"I'm not. I want her to pay. Now."

"She'll never pay Mark. Get it out of your head. She'll plead poverty for the rest of her life. And she really doesn't have money."

"So you're telling me that I will be paying you off for the rest of my life with that outstanding massive bill of yours?"

I didn't get a response. I was convinced Jane did have money stashed away somewhere. She was that sly.

Sixty-five

The narcissistic mind

Parenting, making money and trying to look after myself proved to be difficult. I had a lot of challenges to deal with emotionally, financially, mentally and legally. There was so much going on that I couldn't hold much of a schedule. I was exhausted and day-to-day living was becoming difficult. I didn't have energy any more. The little time I did have off for myself every second weekend, I used for resting and recovering. I was trying to get some energy back. I tried as much as possible to keep the kids in a sort of routine, as I knew they needed regularity and predictability in their lives.

We were now poor—by my standards at least. We had the basics and food on the table, but things in the house were in need of servicing and repair. With a power-surge my fridge bombed out and wasn't working properly, my washing machine became temperamental and the car needed servicing. I was now almost entirely reliant financially on my parents. I couldn't take the kids to therapy (also because their mother wouldn't sign off the paperwork as a 'coparent'). I couldn't afford extra mural activities for them, yet I did as much as possible for them that didn't cost a lot of money. And time, of course. Spending time with them was crucial.

Two months to go... A mere two months... Johan was pressuring me for money now as well. He also knew it was nearly over and wanted to see some cash on the table for all the hard work he had done. He had been fantastic in this whole journey, but no one knew any more where the money was going to come from. And I owed him hugely on all levels.

Thoughts were pre-occupied now with that crucial divorce date. Knowing what I was dealing with psychologically, I started to wonder if her obsession with breaking me down was ever going to end. That August she had a criminal trial, three civil cases to deal with from me and two cases from her ex-husband in court. Jane still didn't seem bothered in the slightest. At handovers, she was cool and colleced. She didn't show any signs of distress in her life. The demands and requests and emails kept on coming in from her. She just didn't stop harassing me, my lawyer or the kids. She was living in a delusional world. I really wondered how she could cope. If I was in her shoes, I'd either run and hide on an island far far far away. My God, she had resilience and was extremely tough. Unbreakable. The nickname Teflon Queen was very apt for her, as nothing would stick.

I, on the other hand, started becoming fully aware of how her mind worked. I knew I would never completely understand it though and I would certainly never be able to help her or fix it. I also resigned myself to the fact that she was going to be harassing me for a while to come. The more I reacted to her games, the more I'd fuel that narcissistic need of hers. Since earlier that year I had realised that no contact was the best and as much as humanly possible, I stuck to my guns there. It was a necessary evil, although not ideal at all if there was going to be any form of co-parenting going forward. I found the below article online from Greg Zafutto which helped me tremendously in understanding the narcissistic mind:

> A Narcissist is only as strong as the audience that believes his/her lies and inflated world. NO they do not love you or anybody in this world.
>
> The Narcissist's personality is very disorganized BUT compartmentalized and precariously balanced to meet his/her NEEDS! We all have our roles to support their grandiose world of lies AND that is what our worth to them comprises. We are there to 'feed' the Narcissist because they NEED us to regulate their false sense of

self-worth by consuming Narcissistic Supply from us and others. Any threat or interruption to their flow of supply compromises the Narcissists psychological integrity and ability to function. This is perceived by the Narcissist as life threatening. It is what is clinically known as Narcissistic injury. A Narcissist needs supply 24/7 so more than likely you are not the ONLY person having a relationship with them. Narcissists are known to have multiple relationships going on at the same time. They believe they are so good at hiding the truth but they are just too needy and akin to an addict seeking out a new and stronger fix to be as careful as they need to be to keep the façade up.

That grandiose, omnipotent and false self is nothing but a concocted and ever changing role the Narcissist creates so that they fit into our world like puzzle pieces. They create different roles to match the needs of the next AND the next person that they are conning into their world. We are only a reflection in the Narcissist's many mirrors that reflect that grand image back to them and makes them feel real. The Narcissist is incapable of feeling, or experiencing emotions, love, growth or any human dynamic that involves any type of relationship with another. Relationships to them are a means to an end and that is basically extracting supply or conning people into believing they are real participants in a relationship so the Narcissist can extort what they can. The Narcissist has fully mastered the dynamic process of conning the world with the ever changing charades they play with life because the payoff is huge and the only way they can survive in the REAL world. Their image is also important in this process so they APPEAR to be normal, moral and good because they have to keep their personal demons at bay through their projection (the false good, the accurate bad and the real ugly projection that defines them!).

This concept is very hard for 'normal' people to understand because we are wired with empathy, love, trust, acceptance and many other qualities that enable bonding and growth with other human beings. The Narcissist depends upon creating this bond through lies, manipulation and that huge façade to gain our acceptance into their world because they harvest people to supply them with ALL of their needs. As rigid as this definition sounds it is merely the truth that any relationship we have with them is based solely on our interpretation, acceptance and belief in that Narcissist's façade and it is personalized for us. The Narcissist just plays along as a con artist does. The love, dreams, promises, relationship, marriage, biological children, etc., is just part of the fiction as personal and believable as it all was to you! We are just the 'new supply' because this Narcissist is fleeing from their last criminal act of abuse and if you think back they were coming out of a relationship and whose fault was it as far as it concerned that last relationship—their 'ex's' fault! They are ALWAYS the victim—and they are akin to criminals because of the disabling damage they do to escape exposure by destroying their target/victim's integrity. We HAVE to accept the truth and define them in the realistic light of what they are and detach any and all emotional connection. You could get more love from a rock then you could from a Narcissist.

A Narcissist will completely lie to your face, without flinching, and there is absolutely nothing you can do but believe them because you perceive it as a normal conversation and trust that you are talking to a normal and honest person. In fact the Narcissist does not even consider that their lies are lies at all. They ARE the truth to the Narcissist because it is just part of their agenda to con you. It is THEIR 'game' and façade that they need to emulate to seduce you into their disorder and support their agenda. This is just your turn to be used and abused because of your unfortunate connection. You were at the right place at the wrong time—or better yet at the wrong place at the wrong time and you are now the latest target/victim. You believe them, because we generally believe people and many of the Narcissist's lies do not sound or feel like lies because their lies are all encompassing and personal as it concerns seducing us.

There are little lies, bigger lies, hideous lies and everything in between—they are ONE BIG LIE. Unfortunately on this journey the Narcissist will betray, manipulate, prey on your vulnerabilities and make you pay for your involvement with them. Their hate and envy burns inside of them and surfaces as if it is your fault that they are as disordered. They blame and shame you for their indiscretions in life. WHY— because in time you make them face reality and they SEE their REAL reflection in your eyes. They can't accept the truth so they act out and make your amazing love wrong, and disable it as well as you. When you hurt they feel accomplished in the fact that they forced you to feel their pain as retribution for how the world has wronged them. They will never see anything else but fault in people and life. It would be like trying to house train an alligator and inviting it into your home as a beloved pet. It will eat you when it gets the first opportunity because that is what it does and it doesn't feel anything but perhaps full after its meal! It doesn't love or regret its actions, it just feeds off of whatever it can get—so does a Narcissist.

We just don't perceive most things people tell us as out and out lies meant to deceive us into an abusive situation, YET ALONE a person whose entire premise and life is built on one huge series of lies to extort and destroy people. From the very beginning of your relationship you placed your trust and hopes in them, derived your energy, direction, stability, and confidence from your association or relationship with them AND it was real to YOU. They played right along and even encouraged this special relationship with them,

BUT AGAIN this was all fiction and part of their agenda. Unfortunately lying is the Narcissist's 'norm,' so the Narcissist wonders what the problem is because they pretend to be so supportive, pretend to love you, provide you with the benefits of their amazing charm and personality—so they are providing you a service and so what if it comes with a price? The Narcissist believes they are worth it and then some—you got something out of this so what if they disabled your life completely. If goes far beyond the lies because you are dealing with a creature that is completely void of empathy and can rationalize their lies, betrayal, how they extort your life out from underneath you and everything else, right down to the damage they have even imposed on their biological children because they are malevolent, and malignant abusers or a NARCISSIST. They completely walk away from their families without a thought except to blame. They will PRETEND to be a loving parent after the fact but that is just more of their façade to maintain that saintly appearance to the outside world and to avoid exposure. This is their mindset and how they are wired and there is no changing them.

The Narcissist creates a viable support system with their minions or cult members that the Narcissist also lies to and they are none the wiser to this creature's agenda of abuse or that they are participants in shoring up the Narcissist's façade of purity and goodness. The Narcissist creates their own little world of lies and fictitious stories that includes a 'support team' or minions that they charm into their life also. So if you were to question anything about the Narcissist and ask one of their minions, they will support the Narcissist's many lies and say just how amazing they are. That Narcissist is a very shrewd and manipulative creature that controls their complete environment picking and choosing the RIGHT people to support that 'big lie' that is their life. Within the Narcissist's support system, he/she also expects awe, admiration, adulation, and constant attention commensurate with his/her outlandish stories, assertions, and lies. The Narcissist uses their many 'surface' friends to reinterpret reality to fit the Narcissist's fantasies AND lies. With the onslaught of social media you can see just how they network just like a politician to gain support. Simply put the Narcissist easily charms and seduces these minions to carry out his/her claims to be infallible, superior, talented, skillful, omnipotent, and omniscient. If you were to get real with one of these support minions they could not tell you much more about the Narcissist except what has been drilled into their heads (the lies!) The relationships are just surface friends that don't go deep by any means nor will you find any sense of history as it concerns the Narcissist's past because the Narcissist keeps their past away from their present and vice versa. NOW if you were to connect to the very people that the Narcissist had past 'relationships' with (intimate,) you would probably hear the hideous truth about this creature! I sure did—but after the fact unfortunately. Seriously in all of the years I knew my Narcissist I never met ONE friend from the Narcissist's past because there were NONE. There were lots of stories about these amazing friends but none materialized! After all was said and done in my personal adventure with a Narcissist I realised that our role is to babysit these creatures, entertain them, pay their way, and even play 'love' with them until the truth becomes apparent about how dysfunctional and dangerous they are. Unfortunately we pay a huge debt for our connections with them.

A Narcissist is not a normal person acting on normal human premises. Look at the many ways you have been punished throughout your relationship say for instance with the silent treatment. This is to make you out as unworthy of consideration from the Narcissist or like dirt beneath his/her feet. Every action or better yet reaction is there positively or negatively to deflect from the truth of what they are and what they are doing behind your back OR learning the truth of their past discretions. They HAVE to constantly deflect from the truth that is why we are devalued AND finally discarded because the truth becomes so apparent! Lies always fill in the blanks and you ACCEPT what they say at face value or you are severely punished. This is the conditioning a target/victim deals with on a regular basis. Couple this with the managing down constantly to make you feel like you are the disordered one and always overreacting, jealous, and worthless. The Narcissist is again posing in that mirror, with their pretend grandeur with respect to you and your reactions. They do take their part in all of this to the point of even believing because they default to it naturally since they have disassociated from their real self! Their pour themselves into the delusional depiction of whatever saintly character they are imitating because it is a working part of their con and serves their purpose. They have no reality so whatever opportunity arises to create a working personality they just jump into the role and usually it is from them making us believe that they have so much in common with us from learning through observation. We keep believing so that enables the Narcissist.

The Narcissist is also an egomaniac and feels so deserving; this is part of their infliction and what makes them a Narcissist. They are BETTER than everybody and deserving of EVERYTHING they want in life and they take it no matter if they abuse people or break the law to do so. They act out the part of royalty that feel insulted by any unworthy subjects—like you expecting his/her majesty's affirmation or attention. It is all part of the fictional novel going on in the Narcissist's childish mind, that magnanimous work of fiction about themselves in which he/she is the star of a great masterpiece all about themselves. Little children do the same thing in their play fantasies. The Narcissist totally IDENTIFIES with the fictional character that he/she creates in that mirror that is us. You have but a bit part in this show as a character (one of many) that exists to reflect the Narcissist's greatness through your interactions with them period. They will always share how amazing they are and how they have so many friends, how their family and children love them, etc. BUT in reality what they share are usually bits and pieces of small truths that really concern the direct opposite. Their family rejects their hideous actions or perversions that they have inflicted on them but it is always somebody else's fault. Everybody else picks up the slack for these creatures like raising a family, paying the bills and keeping up the real responsibilities in life. The real relationship with them is no give and all take, no love, just nothing but serving the Narcissist— the rest is their fictional story that you believe and locks you into what you believe is a relationship and unfortunately love. In time you realise the truth when their words and actions never back up the façade they personally created for you.

You will fall out of grace when your eyes reflect the disdain of their lies and manipulation and you will enter a battle with them where they will destroy you for making them face the reality of who they really are. They will just run off after they have destroyed your integrity and start up a new life of abuse with someone else. Yet, deep down inside, the Narcissist is aware that their life is a sham, and they are vulnerable as far as being exposed. They are always a step or ten ahead of the game and have gathered up every bit of personal information they can use against you to destroy your integrity so that your voice becomes weak and unheard when you start to speak out. Their out of control life is a constant reminder of how unstable their amazing world is AND how weak and feeble they really are! Clinically this is described as the Narcissist's Grandiosity Gap.

The Narcissist can pretend to know everything, in every field of the human condition and is seamless with all of the knowledge that spills out. Again they are all confabulations and lies that the Narcissist prevaricates to avoid the exposure of their real ignorance. Their knowledge and experience is just copycat information that has no basis of reality or is earned through realistic education, goals, hard work, relationship bonding, real love, or anything else. AGAIN—they have no reality to back it up or empathy to understand life at any level! The Narcissist resorts to numerous prefabricated 'imitations of life' to support their God-like omnipotence. What goes on in the shadows is what really defines them and exists in their REAL world, and that is their vast neediness and out-of-control lifestyle that betrays all of life and love. You can take the power away from the Narcissist by removing yourself from their diabolical and delusional world and stop supplying them with your life. Start with no/minimal contact!

Sixty-six

The self-appointed porn queen

"Can you talk? I need to speak to you urgently."

It was three weeks before the divorce and I was having a productive, feel good day. I was confident with the divorce proceedings, which according to Johan, Jane was now screwing up right royally in the high court without an advocate. All the cards seemed to be stacked in my favour and I couldn't wait much longer any more.

I called Caroline back immediately.

"What's up?" I asked her.

"Check your emails out. I sent your some screenshots. I was checking out Facebook and doing some research on Jane."

"OK and?"

Caroline loved a bit of sensation from time to time and kept me updated on any dirt she could find. And wow, dirt she found.

"Jane is advertising sexual services all over the place."

"No man. What are you talking about?"

I brushed it off because Caroline sometimes had a tendency to become somewhat paranoid about my situation.

"What and how? What kind of services?"

"She and Brad are running a sex site for gay and bisexual men and hosting monthly orgies."

"What? You've got to be shitting me. How do you know?"

"No it's for real! And she's listing these events under her own name, linked with her Facebook profile!"

"Naaah, you've got to be kidding. Gay and bisexual men? That can't be, she's a woman!?" It all sounded a bit too surreal for me.

Caroline became persistent and grew frustrated and agitated with me for brushing her off.

"I'm NOT joking Mark, go and check it out yourself. There's a group and a website called Cocktopia and she's running and hosting these events twice a month. What's more, she's linked to all these swingers groups and BDSM places too."

"Holy crap. I'm flabbergasted. For real?"

"Yea. Absolutely for real. Believe me. Go and check out the web links I sent you on your email."

This was a total mind boggler for me again and I went into denial. I didn't want to believe it. This can't be, I thought to myself. Caroline is talking rubbish.

When I got home, I opened up my laptop as soon as I could.

With trembling hands I clicked on the links she sent me via email.

"Oh My God..."

There is was. It was like looking at a porn site. All sorts of listing, websites, Facebook groups, pages and Tweets about this club called Cocktopia. Each one with her name and contact numbers directly listed. Holy crap. Caroline wasn't wrong.

I couldn't help but think.

"What the fuck is all this about now?"

The pages contained the most graphic pictures of pornography and photos of past events, men dancing naked, club rules and links to other sites, affiliated swingers clubs, cross dressing services and so on. It was disturbing beyond belief—and my estranged wife was the organizer in all this!

I, myself, started Googling other avenues and keywords on her name and the club name. More and more stuff came up. I was not an internet virgin, so to speak, but some of the stuff that was on display there was quite frankly, bizarre, tasteless and scary.

This was the mother of my kids? Holy... holy crap.

I started getting scared and nervous. It turned out that Jane and Brad, who was also involved, had been running these orgies and weird parties for over a year already. It was all listed there.

They had a following of hundreds of depraved freaks and orgy party goers.

She was out partying and orgy-ing every weekend. What kind of a mother does that?! Now I had my fears confirmed that the kids were indeed being left alone on her access weekends. Oh my God. My mind started going straight into paranoia and I had the vilest visual mental imagery of what the kids could have been exposed to.

What kind of people were hanging around their house on her access weekends?

Were they doing orgies at home?

Had the kids seen anything?

Were they being molested?

Were they being groomed?

Clearly, from the historical questions and things they brought up, they had been exposed to much more than they should have been.

I felt sick to my stomach. I felt stupid for not knowing and seeing this earlier. It was advertised all over the place and had been so for over a year! She even managed to keep this away from the forensic psychologist at the time!

I notified Johan of the discoveries. He jumped on the opportunity and co-researched the net for me for proof that very same day. It was indeed all over and there was no ways that she could deny her involvement in it. And she didn't.

Her response on the allegations was that she had to earn an income and that she was 'employed' as an events coordinator doing the internet and communications aspect of the 'businesses'. The internet, however, showed a much different picture. She was the owner—organizer.

Johan wanted this evidence to be brought into the divorce application, while Caroline and I were regularly checking the sites for events and updates.

I wanted to bring an urgent application to the court to have the kids under supervised visitation only, but only the high court could rule on that now under the divorce application itself. The lower courts wouldn't look at this, until the matter was out of the high court. We only had three weeks to go.

Jane, in the interim, had, at the last minute employed yet another lawyer. This time it was a free lawyer from the state. They came on record for a week and then they pulled out again. The entire application was in such a mess, they wouldn't take it on. I started losing track on the amount of lawyers she had been with.

The whole sex industry thing made me worried though. What was she up to with the kids? What was she doing to them? Was she doing anything at all? Was I being paranoid? I had to resign myself to the fact that archaic, slow and corrupt system of the courts were of absolutely no use and any complaint to them would fall on deaf ears. I was angry at the system for not investigating properly. I was angry at the system for allowing this to continue while the kids were being mentally and emotionally manipulated by a psycho and her cross dressing boyfriend. It worried me to the core and every alternate weekend and every Wednesday I had to hand them over to this rot to be exposed to God knows what!

Johan called.

"Mark, I've submitted all the sex paperwork to the advocate and he had a look at it. We can't use it in court."

"Why not?"

What was this all about?

"It's too close to the trial. We're not allowed to bring in further evidence."

"You've got to be joking."

"No I'm not. Court rules."

I was angry at this news. Yes I had interim custody and yes I fought hard to have this. Yes, I was convinced the courts would see it and even award me legal custody or supervised visitations for her at worst. But she was slippery like an eel. It was smoke and mirrors all around. Clever illusions while the kids were being used as pawns and manipulated to the core. My poor babies. Poor me. Smoke and mirrors... smoke and mirrors... smoke and mirrors. Ten days to go.

Sixty-seven

Divorce matters

I had now been waiting for three years to get a divorce. The process killed me emotionally, mentally and financially. But I was still standing. The seventeenth of November couldn't come fast enough in my book. Although it was a messed up file with all Jane's unorthodox and confusing allegations and antics, we were good to go for the courts. We could proceed with the case. Finally! It would be a done and dusted deal. Time to leave the past behind me and move. It had a happy ending kind of feel to it. I could just feel it coming.

When D-Day came I was up early and got dressed in my best suit with power tie. (Oh and red undies for good luck.) I arrived at the high court early with nervous anticipation. Both Johan and the advocate arrived shortly thereafter. My parents were there too, hoping to celebrate a happy outcome in a few hours. The drama would be over soon! Of course Jane arrive with Brad in tow, carrying her 'bags of evidence' for her.

She was unrepresented and only had herself (and her bags of evidence) to rely on.

The austere entrance hallway of the Johannesburg courthouse loomed over us as it was rapidly filling up with black robed and serious looking legal eagles. The feel of the building, and people in it, had a somber effect. Many heavy columns supported the imposing domed roof. For some those pillars were a symbol of strength. For others those pillars would mean absolutely nothing

385

and could come tumbling down on their heads. Some lives would be changed forever by the fall of a hammer and the decision of a judge. I couldn't help but think that decisions would be made by antique judges that day, would have far reaching effect. It would change people's entire lives. Some would get locked up in jail. Some would be declared innocent. Some would be divorced, hopefully, like myself. Some would lose their children, some would be ordered to pay money. How do these judges decide on these sentences? Was it only based on the evidence presented or was there an element of psychology involved as well? Psychology like attraction to a person? Feelings, emotions and empathy for a person. It must be a tough job to play God sometimes.

"Mark. Come, we've been looking for you. We're going in."

My pensive, daydreams were abruptly interrupted by Johan. My gaze left the domed roof columns and arches and I was snapped back to reality.

"Okay, I'm coming."

There was a nervous knot in my stomach and Johan led me through to an enormous court room filled with lawyers and advocates. Jane, Brad and my parents stood out like sore thumbs, being dressed colorfully in the sea of black robes.

The room was jam-packed like sardines in a can. The air was thick and warm with people's second hand breath, halitosis, unbrushed false teeth, body odours and stale garlic smells from the pizza the night before. And someone nearby by let rip an egg-fart, well concealed in the mass of people. The combination of smells reminded me vaguely of the jail I spent some time in and chuckled. Divorce definitely stinks!

"So this is it?" I asked Johan inquisitively, not knowing what was happening.

"No this the roll call."

The whole thing was confusing. It was a very different than the lower courts. A process I had inadvertently gotten so used to by now.

My mom commented on the smell and the fact that it was so packed in there. She waved her hand in front of her face and pinched her nose with her eyes rolling upwards. I knew that look all too well. We giggled.

Jane and Brad were a few rows in front of us. Brad had a staring competition with my mom which made her upset.

"Just ignore him, don't look that way."

"He is staring at me."

"Yes, just leave it be, he's provoking a reaction. He's a sick individual. Just imagine him in a dress and high heels."

The thought made her chuckle.

"Did you see they're wearing wedding bands?"

"No I didn't see that. But it's probably another ploy to get a reaction. They're being childish. Just ignore it."

In the front of the court the Chief Justice mumbled incomprehensible words. Richard, the advocate was in front to listen. The rest of the room was pretty quiet, but we could still not make out what the Judge said. A few minutes later Johan beckoned us to come outside. Richard was there already.

"We're going to have to settle."

"Oh? How come?"

"Because we won't go to trial today. There are a hundred and eighteen cases on the roll and only twenty four judges available today. So I propose that I go and talk to the other party and get a settlement."

What a disappointment. Years and years of nonsense, crap, jailtime, near bankruptcy, emotional dramas and now Richard is proposing a settlement? You got to be kidding.

"No, absolutely not! No!"

I didn't come all this way for a settlement.

"I won't have it Richard. This is not on. We got a damn good case and it's my day in court. No."

I was upset and walked away. It felt like a ton of bricks came down on me. It was a total injustice. Johan came running after me.

"Mark, calm down. Let's go outside and have a smoke."

He managed to pull me outside somehow although I wasn't interested in listening to speeches or lectures. His lecture started regardless:

"Listen to me. As your legal advisor I have to tell you that this is best option we have. If we proceed to trial, we'll be on the waiting list for another eighteen months at least. They will not prioritize divorce matters today."

I puffed away on the cigarette and lit another one. I was absolutely not in the mood for this.

"Believe me, Mark this is for the best. Richard is already talking to them. Let's see what they can come up with. We need to get this divorce over with. You simply cannot afford to carry on with this divorce for another few years. Do you want that? Don't you want to move on with your life?"

I managed to let out a low grunt and walked back into the building.

So this is how they do it. They keep you occupied with paperwork. Leave you hanging for years and years. Litigation by email and affidavits and when it's time for court, the courts simply chucks it out because they actually don't have time for you and they prefer it if you settle. It was a money making racket.

I bitched and moaned to my parents about the news I had just received. They just shrugged their shoulders being confused as well and told me to blindly follow my advocate's advice.

"It'll be for the best. Let's get it over and done with. He's right, you cannot endure another eighteen months of legal bills and emotional drama. They're your legal advisors. They know better."

After ten minutes Richard came back all smiles.

"Good news. She's accepted our proposal."

"Our proposal? Our proposal? Or yours?" I piped up. I hadn't even discussed any form of proposal with him.

"Look at this. You got residential custody of the kids. Full time. She only wants them every second weekend and half the holidays. There's no financial claims against one another either. Take it Mark. Take it. It's the best you can get."

"What about maintenance."

"She doesn't want to pay that."

"I'm not surprised about that. She even defaulted on her previous orders."

"Don't worry." Richard continued.

"I've made provision for that. Look, here it states that either party still has the right to apply for maintenance on the kids at a competent court. Take her to the maintenance court and they'll sort her out. It'll be much quicker in any case."

(Little did I know that that would be another story and years of dramas.)

I wasn't interested anymore. My parents, my lawyer and advocate were all telling me that it was a good deal and that I had to take it. Sign... sign. The pressure was on. My mind was elsewhere and felt that a huge injustice was being done on me and the kids.

They quickly typed up the document at an admin service office and we went back into court. They called out our case.

"Divorce matter three three five of two thousand and thirteen."

I stood before one of the highest judges in the land. So did Jane. The judge appeared fairly casual with us. Richard handed the settlement to him via the court clerk. The judge read it and addressed Jane.

"Madam, you are unrepresented in this court. Are you aware of what you are signing?"

"Yes your honour."

"And you understand the contents of this document?"

"Yes your honour."

"Are you sure you understand what you signed here?"

"Yes your honour."

The judge looked at her and held his gaze with her.

"Madam, I'm going to recess for ten minutes. Please read the document carefully again before I make it an order of the court. We will return in ten minutes. Court dismissed."

I left the dock and approached Johan.

"What was that all about?" I asked him.

"Judge is concerned. She is signing her kids away. It's an unusual settlement. He's just making sure that she fully understands what she is signing. He's giving her a chance."

A chance. She doesn't deserve a chance. All the judge sees is a mother signing away her rights. He hasn't seen or lived what the kids and I have been through.

The ten minutes crawled by slowly. ... Tick-tock... tick-tock ... the waiting game was a suspense movie in the making. What if she had a change of mind? What if she felt like stuffing me around for another couple of years just to piss me off. I mean clearly she had a bone to pick with me and was obsessed. Were we really getting divorced now? We were back in the dock afrter the recess.

"Ms de Jager. I've given you the opportunity to re-read the settlement agreement. Do you wish to go ahead and make it an order of the court?"

"I do your honour."

I could feel the tension slide off my shoulders and neck. She took it.

"Very well, and you Mr le Foncé? Do you understand and are you in agreement with the settlement agreement presented in front of me?"

"Yes your honour."

The judge picked up the stamp and stamped the settlement agreement.

"Mr and Mrs le Foncé, you are now officially divorced. Best of luck to you both. You're dismissed."

Sixty-eight

In the best interest of the children

So. That's how the divorce was done. Just like that, a rubber stamp from a judge. I wasn't entirely happy with the outcome and felt forced into accepting a mediocre settlement from someone that had been obsessed with ruining my life. There was no accountability for her actions, no punishment for what she had done to me, the kids and my surroundings. She single-handedly drove me into a bitter battle for years. All for the sake of getting even with me. Worse, she used the kids. Even worse, the authorities did nothing about it.

I resigned myself to the fact that this was it. I had to be content with the outcome. I could now move on with my life. The long awaited and anticipated divorce day felt bitter sweet. At least I had the kids most of the time. I had the custodial residency and they'd remain living with me. I would do whatever it took to protect their innocent minds from any form of abuse, neglect or harm. I never thought in my wildest nightmares that a mother could have no feelings for her own offspring, but alas, it appeared that the crazy stuff you see in psycho thriller movies is real after all, and it had crossed my path. There were obviously lessons I had to learn from this too.

I said my goodbyes to Johan and Richard and told my folks I'd see them later for dinner that evening with the kids.

"Even though it's not what you'd entirely hoped for, we will still open a bottle of champagne. C'mon, chin up. It's over now. You've been waiting for this for years and it is a good outcome. We'll see you a bit later and discuss it more. But first let's celebrate," my dad said.

I wasn't really in the celebratory mood. It felt more like—and now what happens next? I somehow knew my ex wasn't done yet. There was more to come.

I got in my car and wormed my way through the crowded streets of downtown Johannesburg. People were everywhere: hustlers, beggars, traders, pedestrians and workers. The humdrum of the bustling city was a background noise in my mind. I didn't pay any attention to it. My mind was too pre-occupied with the happenings of the morning and the feelings of injustice.

Beep beep...My phone indicated that another message had come though. Family and friends were curious and wanted to know how it went that morning. My phone hadn't stopped the whole morning. Others who had already found out sent me congratulatory messages. I didn't respond to them. I'd deal with them later. I was still processing my thoughts and feelings through my own mind which was racing at two hundred kilometres per hour.

The knock at my window came abruptly and got a fright. I snapped out of my thoughts. A young girl in traditional Zulu dress in a beaded top and short skirt was dancing and bouncing up and down outside my window. She smiled at me as I took one of the pamphlets from her that she was handing out.

"Have a good day sir, and God bless." as she moved onto the next car.

I looked at what she gave me. The cheaply printed pamphlet was another story all together.

DR JABULANI
TRADITIONAL HEALER
Registered practice
Lost Lover?
Money Trouble?
Get Rich Now
Get Stronger Erections
Need Larger Penis?

Trouble with the law?
CALL DR JABU NOW
All your worries will be gone.
Tel: 006 354 4450

I sniggered at the thought. That was just what I needed. All of the above please!

The robot turned red at the next intersection on Pritchard Street. I stopped in front of the light. I was familiar with that intersection as I had been there before. Twice in fact. The building's entrance was flanked by a sign that said Schreiner Building. It was the building of the Family Advocate. A pull up banner bounced lazily in the breeze near the entrance. The aging banner was faded by the harsh African sun. Smiling multiracial children and parents hugged each other under the banner:

OFFICES OF THE FAMILY ADVOCATE
WORKING IN THE BEST INTEREST
OF THE CHILDREN

Sixty-nine

Epilogue

While I went through my divorce and started experiencing the revenge trip from my ex-wife (frequently referred to as the smear campaign in this book) in the form of court cases, arrests, harassment, stalking and false allegations, I thought I was losing my mind. How could someone that supposedly loved me at one point put me through absolute hell and back without an inkling of remorse.

The absolute worst for me was her playing the kids' minds and trying to set them up against me. Her own flesh and blood were just regarded as tools in her arsenal to get at me without any regard or empathy towards their wellbeing. It baffled me, but then, as I started researching more, I figured out that I was not the only one.

In fact I was not alone at all. Millions of men and women globally suffer similar fates during their divorce proceedings and a pattern started emerging. A pattern driven by unscrupulous lawyers, un-checked in an antiquated legal system. A pattern designed within the architecture of law itself and abused by exes and revengeful parents. This is roughly how it goes—in South Africa at least:

Be prepared to destroy your ex at all cost and use a *good* (aka dirty) lawyer. Do not have any empathy and let hatred stew in your mind. If you have any form of empathy, then this won't work. This is an ideal process for those who are narcissistic. (If you have applied this on your ex in the past, you are most likely suffering from a personality disorder and lack empathy.)

Step one: Serve divorce papers

Step two: Get a protection order under false allegations. (This creates internal and emotional chaos on the innocent party.)

Step three: Boot him out of the house and separate him from the children. (Emotional chaos becomes emotional crisis and has a severe impact on the mental health of the recipient.)

Step four: Get an interim order. These are called a Rule 43 or rule 58 in South Africa. This ensures the emotional abuse can be enforced via the legal channels and cripples him financially on a monthly basis sinking him deeper.

Step five: Alienate him away from the kids as much as possible, even if that means breaking court orders. Should this ever get to court, you may get a slap on the wrist—if at all.

Step six: Now that you have the control of the money, kids and the proceedings, postpone and stretch out the divorce matter for as long as you can. When your soon-to-be-exhubby is totally destroyed and in a financial dilemma, he'll settle for any crumbs that he can get, in order to stop the onslaught. By that stage the kids are alienated and halfway grown up not wanting to do anything with their father.

Step seven: Keep him in line by claiming ridiculous amounts of child support. Keep poisoning the kids against him and use social workers (third party enablers) to enforce your child's so-called 'dislike' for the father in court.

Step eight: Move far away (preferably overseas) These steps ultimately guarantee your control and financial wellbeing, BUT it has severe impact on the receiving party and even more so on the child(ren). This is pure ABUSE BY PROXY and PARENTAL ALIENATION at its finest. And the courts are aiding and abetting these kinds of processes!

A quick internet search on support groups for men almost all lead you to parental alienation groups. A worrying statistic is that domestic violence on men is rapidly on the increase as well. And so is male suicide. It is my opinion that men suffer just as much, if not more, emotional, mental and physical abuse as women do, but men report it infrequently to the authorities. Men are told to toughen up, stop being a cry baby, grow some balls or are told to just get on with it. When they do report it to the authorities, they get laughed at. In the odd case they get lucky and it does become a court 'case' the case just gets thrown out of court, because they don't like to lock women up—as was the case with me!

Men's stories need to be told and heard. Men need to be treated fairly and equally as women do. It is a fallacy that men don't cry. It is a fallacy that men are tough. We are weak and we are getting weaker by the minute if we let abuse like this slip by. This is a societal problem.

We are setting an example for our children. A lot of boys who grow up without their fathers or a male role model in their young lives, are lost and seek out that male bonding. Statistically, when boys have no contact with their dads they tend to seek out male acceptance elsewhere and end up in gangs, on drugs or doing crimes to compensate for their loss of masculine influences earlier on in their lives. They grow up lacking empathy and subsequently treat people and relationships without any too. They become bad partners, abusers and perhaps even criminals and rapists. The narcissistic cycle continues. Why? All because they had mom treating their dad badly in their youth without compassion and sympathy? In the same light, girls grow up to become young women with entitlement, and view their partners or husbands as mere sperm donors and wallet fillers (which is what mom has taught them no?). The narcissistic flow in the next generation continues its onslaught in both sexes. It has to stop now! This is a fight we have to take head on before our next generation of leaders and role models start repeating these cycles. It needs urgent and serious intervention from the courts, the psychologists, trainers, educators and society as a whole.

Education is needed as a matter of urgency. People abusing the court system (specially the DV, divorce and children's courts) should be held accountable in a harsh manner. One should not be allowed to get away with perjury or abuse. No leniency should be given to those who abuse the court system. The damage on the receiving party is too great in its totality to let this 'slip' by.

Luckily for me I grew up with both my parents. But I was always taught that people are good, and have the best intentions out for you. You therefore treat them good as well. I believed that and went into the big wide world only to be disappointed, lied to and hurt.

I don't see myself as a victim. I am not a martyr. I'm not a survivor. I am me, and my experiences have taught me very valuable lessons. Lessons on human behaviour, lessons on hurt, lessons in law, lessons in love and also the lack thereof. Lessons that I pass on and hopefully teach others. Let's start by having some compassion and respect for each other.

My story isn't finished yet. I am working on the next book where I made the same mistake in trusting too early. I met a woman who was keen. Keen to abuse me as well for her own narcissistic gain. She was also a woman who grew up without a dad. She herself was a single mom with a fatherless son—he supposedly disappeared and was 'mental'. (Yet I found out this father was also desperately seeking contact with his son—just like Michael, but the court system failed him and mother 'won'.) She was single mom who needed rescuing from her own dramas. And like a fool, I stepped into the relationship as the stereotypical 'I can do it all' male. She was a woman who claimed that she was raped by three different people over a period of ten years. She never reported these rapes. Why? Because they didn't happen. These were just delusional stories to get my attention and to victimize herself, looking desperately for empathy that was so sorely lacking in her life. And I gave that empathy to her. I gave her lots of empathy, but it wasn't enough and she turned on me when her narcissistic supplies weren't being met and I started seeing her for who she was. Just like my ex-wife, (and also because she read the manuscript of this book which she stole) she went the legal route, reporting me for numerous crimes that didn't happen. She knew about Jane's antics and she tried to copy them.

While this was happening Jane kept the onslaught going on me, opening up numerous cases in the lower courts, who, in turn, due to their sheer incompetence, entertained her dramas at great financial and energetic cost to me. Her BDSM, dominatrix and orgy businesses were booming and she even made it on national TV. Needless to say she never spent a cent on the kids' wellbeing, schooling or medical expenses.

More about that in my sequel you can look forward to.

THE NUTCRACKERS
50 Shades gone bonkers

AT BOOKSTORES NEAR YOU SOON
CONTACT DETAILS
Email: marklefonce@gmail.com
Website: marklefonce.com
Facebook group: HaveYouGotBalls

Acknowledgements

This book would not have been made possible without the people and organizations that supported me. Besides my family members and close friends Id like to give my special thanks to the following people, companies and organizations: Thank you for your support and hard work and keep up the good fight. You're all special people and together we will change the world.

Fathers For Justice
South Africa
Contact: Gary da Silva
email: info@f4j.co.za
web: www.f4j.co.za
whatsapp: chat.whatsapp.com/BclFhQ6ENhkG6GHkvJPEaQ
FATHERS-4-JUSTICE SOUTH AFRICA is a civil rights group campaigning for truth, justice and equality in Family Law for children, their parents and grandparents. Children growing up without fathers, mothers or grandparents is an obscenity and social catastrophe waiting to happen.

Fathers' Rights Movement
South Africa
Contact: Brian Ferreira
email: bferreira@tfrm.us
web: fathersrightsmovement.us

Family Focused Law
South Africa
Contact: Charl Botha / Maree Jagga
email: info@familyfocusedlaw.co.za
web: www.facebook.com/FamilyFocusedLaw/
We are a South African based law and mediation consulting
company based in Johannesburg East and West, and consult
nationally, the directors are extremely passionate about creating
holistic interventions and solutions for parents making the
decision to divorce or separate, in ensuring that their child(ren)
of divorce or separation are able to thrive in healthy separated
family structures.

CHILD MAINTENANCE DIFFICULTIES—SOUTH AFRICA

Contact: Felicity Guest
email: felicity.cmdsa@gmail.com
web: www.facebook.com/groups/1497629187138995
CMDSA supports, empowers and guides parents through the intricacies of navigating the complex legal and social constructs of securing financial support for their children.

GERHARD BOTHA & PARTNERS INCORPORATED
ATTORNEYS & CONVEYANCERS

Gerhard Botha
Attorneys at Law
Tel: 011 789 2922
Fax: 011 268 5789
email: gerhard@gbattorneys.co.za

Father's love their kids 2

CHILDREN NEED BOTH PARENTS

Contact: Orrock Robertsen
email: cnbp4fathers@gmail.com
web: www.facebook.com/childrenneedbothparents/

MATRIX MEN
Contact: Martin Pelders
Tel: 078 457 4911
email: martin@matrixmen.org
web: www.matrixmen.org

Matrix Men was established to support Men that have suffered sexual abuse or rape. We have evolved to support men that have suffered abuse, parental alienation, bad divorce situations and recovery groups for survivors of sexual abuse. Essentially we want to help men that are suffering in any sphere of their lives.

List of names

Mark le Foncé	Jane's husband, Julia and Sean's father
Jane de Jager	Mark's wife
Julia le Foncé	Mark and Jane's daughter
Sean le Foncé	Mark and Jane's son
Steven de Jager	Michael and Jane's Son, Mark's stepson
Captain Mandell	Drug squad commander—SAPS
Capt. Van Tonder	Station commander—Randburg SAPS
Darryl	Mark's best friend
Dr Jacobs	Endocrinologist
Michael de Jager	Jane's ex husband
Diane	Psychologist at FAMSA
Johan Brooks	Mark's divorce lawyer
Jeremy Jones	Mark's acting agent
Richard Lawson	Mark's divorce advocate
Sophie	Mark's Housekeeper
Gogo	Housekeeper/Nanny
Agnes	Crèche teacher
Nelson	HR Director—Bell Inc.
Rachel	HR assistant—Bell Inc.
Alice	Mark's boss—Bell inc.
Mike Vermont	Jane's first lawyer
Estelle van der Merwe	First private social worker
Adv. Michaelson	Family Advocate—Johannesburg
Patel	Social worker from the FA
Dr Silver	General Practitioner
Brad	Jane's boyfriend
Sergeant Shai	Sector policing—SAPS

Jacobus Hardus	Sherriff of the court
James	Mark's friend
Desiree	Nurse from local clinic
MNM Attorneys	Jane's second lawyer
Mrs Labuschagne	Children's Court Magistrate
Bronwyn	MNM lawyer
Marcel	Mark's cousin
Caroline	Mark's cousin
Marianne Bavel	Occupational Therapist
Rossouw	Brad's lawyer—Polokwane
Sanette van Jaarsveld	Magistrate—Polokwane
Madelein O'Connor	Investigative psychologist
Jessica Summers	Jane's third lawyer
Dr Wilson	Family doctor
Chantelle	Estate Agent Johannesburg
Sergant Bobani	Arresting officer on DV violation
W/O Crooks	Police at Randburg
Rachael	Victim Empowerment Centre, Brits
Brett Mc Donald	Jane's manager—CLHA
Neill Swindon	Johan's junior lawyer